Mark + Annemarie,

Merry Christmas 2003!

Love,
Brad

DRAWING LINES IN SAND AND SNOW

DRAWING LINES IN SAND AND SNOW

BORDER SECURITY AND NORTH AMERICAN ECONOMIC INTEGRATION

BRADLY J. CONDON AND **TAPEN SINHA**

M.E.Sharpe
Armonk, New York
London, England

Library of Congress Cataloging-in-Publication Data

Condon, Bradly J.
    Drawing lines in sand and snow : border security and North American economic
integration / Bradly J. Condon.
        p. cm.
    Includes bibliographical references and index.
    ISBN 0-7656-1235-6 (cloth : alk. paper) ISBN 0-7656-1236-4 (pbk. : alk. paper)
        1. North America—Economic integration. 2. Free trade—North America.
3. National security—North America. 4. National security—United States. 5. Illegal
aliens—United States. 6. Border patrols—United States. 7. Capital movements—North
America. 8. North America—Foreign economic relations. I. Sinha, Tapen. II. Title.

    HC95.C64 2003
    337.1′7—dc21   2003042759

Printed in the United States of America

The paper used in this publication meets the minimum requirements of
American National Standard for Information Sciences
Permanence of Paper for Printed Library Materials,
ANSI Z 39.48-1984.

BM (c)   10   9   8   7   6   5   4   3   2   1
BM (p)   10   9   8   7   6   5   4   3   2   1

We dedicate this book to the victims of September 11 and its aftermath.

Contents

Tables and Figures

Tables

Figures

Preface

The terrorist attacks and border closures of September 11, 2001, have vividly demonstrated the importance of borders and security on the North American continent. Canada, Mexico, and the United States may be separated by borders, but these lines in the southern sands and the northern snows are in a state of constant flux. The shared borders both unite and divide the three countries.

On the Canada–United States border, the threat to security and commerce prompted unprecedented cooperation on border and security issues. It also demonstrated that the ties that bind Canadians to their American cousins are far greater than any differences that divide them. On the Mexico–United States border, a democratic change of regime opened the door to a new era for Mexico–United States relations. President Vicente Fox went out on a political limb in an effort to get the United States to look seriously at migration reforms. But President George W. Bush's obsession with far-flung regimes left the important migration issue sitting on the back burner to stew.

The United States is a superpower that dwarfs its partners in the North American Free Trade Agreement (NAFTA) by comparison. This makes it easy to sometimes forget that Canada and Mexico are major players in their own right, both economically and politically (if not militarily). The management of cross-border flows of goods, people, and capital affects the competitiveness of business, the economic prosperity, and security interests of all three countries. Institutional problems, such as internal and cross-border business barriers, interagency coordination, and government corruption, affect the ability of all three to provide a secure and prosperous business environment, both within each country and across the region as a whole.

Security concerns affect every aspect of North American integration and the main topics analyzed in this book. Failed policies on both sides of the border perpetuate the migration of undocumented workers from Mexico to the United States and divert resources that could otherwise address real security threats. In Mexico, police corruption and a lack of personal security transfer security costs from the government to the private sector. Transaction costs for legitimate capital flows increase due to the need to disrupt terrorist financing. Finally, security requires investments in the systems used to move and monitor the cross-border flow of goods. However, these investments will increase the efficiency of cross-border goods transportation at the end of the day.

Balancing economic integration with security not only means examining issues on their own, but also entails an analysis of how various issues relate to one another. Laws and policies must be designed to support each other. For example, U.S. policy regarding immigration not only fails to resolve the problem of illegal immigration, but undermines U.S. labor laws as well. The issuing of student visas to dead hijackers six months after September 11 illustrates the need to coordinate the activities and policies of different government agencies within the United States. The same degree of policy coordination must be achieved among the agencies of the NAFTA countries as well.

All three NAFTA members have good reasons to create a common security perimeter to lower border transaction costs and tighten security. With almost 90 percent of Canada and Mexico's exports destined for the U.S. market, they are hardest hit by border costs. However, in terms of security, the United States stands to gain the most from a common perimeter.

Canada and the United States have a much longer history of cooperation on security issues than either of them has with Mexico. Including Mexico in a North American security perimeter will involve overcoming institutional, legal, and political barriers. But Mexico is a necessary element in any security strategy. The United States cannot set up an impenetrable fence along its southern border. Ignoring Mexico leaves a large hole in the U.S. security perimeter. The United States needs Mexico to be a part of its security strategy.

Compared with the United States and Mexico, Canada emerges from our study smelling like a rose. This reflects the reality that Canada has to do better than its neighbors in order to compete with them, given its relatively small market compared to the United States and its small population compared to both of its NAFTA partners. Canada also gets favorable reviews simply because its policies and actions have been well managed in all of the areas we studied.

Mexico still has a lot of work to do. The general lack of security in Mexico remains a problem that affects the movement of goods, people, and capital. Nevertheless, several factors favor Mexico's future. Mexico's growing network of free trade agreements, its large and growing internal market, and its political and economic stability compared to other major Latin American countries all bode well for its economic future. However, Mexico needs to continue to work on the issue of corruption, which affects its ability to advance in all of the areas addressed in our study. The government must work hard to solidify the democratic functioning of its institutions, continue efforts to alter public attitudes, and continue to enhance transparency in order to root out corruption and firmly entrench the rule of law.

The United States earns good grades for working hard to ensure that increased border security would not unduly impede the cross-border movement of goods in the region. The United States moved quickly to enhance and expand border and security cooperation with Canada and Mexico through "Smart Border" plans. However, it must guard against the overzealous application of its laws in freezing assets and prosecuting suspected terrorists, particularly the citizens of its allies. Moreover, the United States gets a failing grade for its policies that affect illegal migration from Mexico. Resolving the problem of illegal immigration would free up resources to focus on people who represent genuine security threats.

To manage North American integration and security in an intelligent fashion, government policies need to be coordinated across internal agencies and international borders. This is no small challenge. Overcoming political obstacles to sensible policies requires leadership. But these challenges need to be met to get to where we want to go—a secure, prosperous, and economically integrated North America.

Acknowledgments

The terrorist attacks of September 11 sent shock waves around the world. In North America, the closing of the borders had a particularly strong psychological (and economic) impact on businesspeople and immediately focused the attention of governments in all three NAFTA countries on border management. Ensuring the smooth flow of goods, people, and capital across NAFTA borders is of special importance to Canada and Mexico, though it is also of great importance to many U.S. businesses.

Similarly, while the security of those borders is of utmost importance to Americans, securing the borders of the *region* matters to all three countries. With border issues now more prominent than ever before in the minds of policy makers and businesspeople in Canada, Mexico, and the United States, we decided that it is an opportune moment to set about addressing some of the key problems that need to be resolved and to offer some suggestions to both government and business.

In this book, we bring a multitude of perspectives to this task. With backgrounds in business, economics, and law, we examine the issues from an interdisciplinary perspective. Since one of us is a Canadian and the other an Indian-Australian, both living in Mexico, our vision of the issues is from the outside looking in. We believe that this places us in a different position from those who see these issues from the inside out.

Bradly Condon would like to acknowledge the help and support of many friends and colleagues. As in all my endeavors, my parents, Kip and Cathy Condon, have offered constant encouragement. Alice DuBose has provided invaluable feedback. María de la Luz S. de Uriarte has provided constant *apoyo*.

Tapen Sinha had help from Dipendra Sinha by sounding out some of the issues discussed here. Discussion with Gaylyn Humphrey was very useful. Support from Rebecca Benedict, as always, was unfailing.

We thank the Instituto Tecnológico Autónomo de México and the

Asociación Mexican de Cultura AC for their generous support of our research. Carlos Alcérreca, Ross Buckley, Edward J. Chambers, Noel Maurer, Brad McBride, Wistano Sáez, Robert Simpson, Rosalie Tung, and Sidney Weintraub provided helpful comments at various stages of the book. We are grateful to our publisher, M.E. Sharpe, for seeing the value in this topic. We deeply appreciate the diligent work of the editors at M.E. Sharpe. In particular, help from Lynn Taylor and Esther Clark is greatly appreciated, as well as Laurie Lieb's meticulous editing of the manuscript.

This project grew out of several articles and conference papers in which we developed some of our early thoughts. We wish to thank the coauthors, journal editors, and conference participants for helping us to develop our ideas. Of course, all responsibility for errors and omissions rests solely with us.

Chapter 1 grew out of the following: Tapen Sinha and Bradly Condon, "Three's Company: U.S. Borders After September 11," *Texas Business Review* 1–6 (February 2002); Tapen Sinha and Bradly Condon, "The Warmth of the North and the Chill of the South: American Borders After September 11," paper presented at Free Trade in the Western Hemisphere: The Challenges and the Future, Center for the Study of Western Hemispheric Trade, Texas A&M International University, Laredo, Texas, April 2002.

Chapter 2 grew out of the following: Bradly Condon, "The Twin Security Challenges of AIDS and Terrorism: Implications for Flows of Trade, Capital, People and Knowledge," in Ross Buckley, ed., *The Changing Face of World Trade: The WTO and the Doha Round*; Bradly Condon, "The Implications for Global Business of Terrorism and AIDS," paper presented at The Changing Face of World Trade: A Colloquium on the Future of the Global Trading System, Bond University, Gold Coast, Australia, August 2002.

Chapter 3 grew out of the following: Bradly Condon and Brad McBride, "Do You Know the Way to San José? Resolving the Problem of Illegal Mexican Migration to the United States," *Georgetown Immigration Law Journal* (forthcoming, 2003); Bradly Condon, "A Study in Contrasts: Professional Visas under NAFTA," *Texas Business Review* (October 2002); Bradly Condon, "Labor and Professional Mobility in the NAFTA Region," paper presented at North American Higher Education Collaboration: The Next Decade, Calgary, Canada, October 2002; Bradly Condon and Brad McBride, "Mexican Migration Trends in the NAFTA Region: Implications for North American Business and Society," paper presented at International Applied Business Research Conference, Puerto Vallarta, March 2002; Bradly Condon, "The Baby Boom, the Baby Bust and Free Movement of Labor in the NAFTA Region: Implications for Mexican Business Strategy," paper presented at Management in the New Millenium: Iberoamerica Looks at the Future, Mexico City, December 2001.

Abbreviations

ABA	American Bar Association
AIA	American Insurance Association
BSA	U.S. Bank Secrecy Act
CITES	Convention on International Trade in Endangered Species
CTPAT	U.S. Customs Trade Partnerships Against Terrorism
CUSP	Canada–United States Partnership
DEA	U.S. Drug Enforcement Agency
DOT	U.S. Department of Transportation
FTA	Canada–United States Free Trade Agreement
FATF	Financial Action Task Force on Money Laundering
FBI	U.S. Federal Bureau of Investigation
FinCEN	U.S. Financial Crimes Enforcement Network
GATT	General Agreement on Tariffs and Trade
GDP	gross domestic product
ICAO	International Civil Aviation Organization
ICC	U.S. Interstate Commerce Commission
IMO	United Nations International Maritime Organization
INS	U.S. Immigration and Naturalization Service
IRCA	U.S. Immigration Reform Control Act
MOU	memorandum of understanding
MP	member of Parliament (Canada)
NAFTA	North American Free Trade Agreement
NBFI	nonbank financial institution
NEXUS	Canada–U.S. Frequent Crosser Border Pass Program
NLRB	U.S. National Labor Relations Board
OECD	Organization for Economic Cooperation and Development
PAN	Partido de Acción Nacional (National Action Party)
PGR	Procurador General de la República (federal attorney general)

PRI   Partido Revolucionario Institucional (Institutional Revolutionary Party)

RCMP   Royal Canadian Mounted Police

RICO   U.S. Racketeer Influenced and Corrupt Organizations Act

WCO   World Customs Organization

WTO   World Trade Organization

DRAWING LINES IN SAND AND SNOW

1

Bordering on the USA

The Political Economy
of North American Integration

"I don't even know what street Canada is on."
—*Al Capone*

"Good fences don't make good neighbors. Good neighbors
make good neighbors."
—*William Graham*

"It is better to die on your feet than to live on your knees!"
—*Emiliano Zapata*

The terrorist attacks on the World Trade Center and the Pentagon on September 11, 2001, brought the issue of trilateral cooperation to the forefront in the countries of the North American Free Trade Agreement (NAFTA). In the weeks following the attacks, heightened security caused serious delays on the southern and northern borders of the United States, with longer delays on the southern end. Delays in the movement of goods created a serious disruption of auto production in the region. The industry depends on just-in-time delivery. Delays in the movement of people disrupted border economies and the travel and tourism industries. While perhaps only a blip on the economic integration radar screen, the delays made addressing the economic impact of borders a priority issue in all three countries.

The lack of any clear sense on how to coordinate policy responses has underlined the need for a road map as to which issues should be resolved by which players, unilaterally, bilaterally, trilaterally, and multilaterally. The only clear point that has emerged is that resources will have to be deployed in a way that minimizes the economic costs of doing business across the borders of an increasingly integrated North American economy. NAFTA has created a trilateral economic structure, but it sits on top of two very different bilateral relationships whose only fundamental connection is the United States.

This chapter examines these relationships against the backdrop of history, geography, economic power, and security interests. The dominant position of the United States in the world—in terms of its military might, the size of its economy, and its political influence—is magnified on the North American continent. Not surprisingly, this results in many parallels in the two bilateral relationships, despite the marked differences between Canada and Mexico.

Karma Company: The NAFTA Region in a Historical Context

In the nineteenth century, America's territorial ambitions produced parallel policies vis-à-vis its two neighbors, but with different degrees of success. In that era, the United States posed the biggest security threat to both Canada and Mexico, sowing seeds of distrust that would linger long after in both countries. The turn of the century witnessed both countries pursuing closer economic ties with their common neighbor. However, the economic benefits of closer ties were overwhelmed by the distrust that had continued to fester in the minds of both populations. It would be several decades before the attraction of trade relations would overpower doubts about American intentions and trustworthiness on both sides of the growing behemoth.

The Nasty Neighbor: A Common Enemy Emerges

It is useful to recall that deep mistrust existed between Canada and the United States for a very long time. For example, Lipset (1991, 42) wrote, "Americans do not know, but Canadians cannot forget that two nations, not one, came out of the American Revolution." In the War of 1812 between Britain and the United States, Americans thought that taking Canada would be simple. In President Thomas Jefferson's words, "The acquisition of Canada this year [1812] as far as the neighbourhood of Quebec, will be a mere matter of marching, and will give us experience for the attack on Halifax next, and the final expulsion of England from the American continent" (Fulford 1998).

During the American Civil War (1861–65), a faction in the United States again wanted to invade and annex British North America as a way of punishing Britain for its sympathy with the South. (The South supplied necessary cotton to the textile factories of Britain.) Such an adventure was preempted by Canada becoming the "self-governing Dominion of Canada" just in the nick of time in 1867. All British troops left Canada by 1871.

If Canada had strong reservations about the United States, Mexico had stronger reservations. It all started with the settling of English-speaking Americans in Texas after Moses Austin received a colonization grant from the Mexican government in 1821. To discourage American settlers in Texas, Mexico abolished slavery in 1828. In 1835, the settlers sought independence from Mexico. In 1836, they revolted against Mexican rule and declared Texas independent. In the process, they defeated the army of General Antonio Santa Anna.

In 1845, the United States annexed Texas after it failed to persuade Santa Anna, then Mexico's president, to sell Upper California, New Mexico, and Arizona. Mexico considered the annexation an act of war. In March 1846, General Zachary Taylor occupied Point Isabel on the Rio Grande (the same river is called Rio Bravo in Mexico). Mexico considered this action an invasion. The Mexican army crossed the Rio Grande and shelled Fort Brown. This shelling was interpreted as an act of aggression by U.S. president James Polk. (The same U.S. president negotiated the 49th parallel with the British, a settlement grudgingly accepted by the Canadians).

President Polk declared war against Mexico. The U.S. Army eventually came to conquer Mexico City's seat of power—the Fort of Chapultepec. The soldiers stayed there from September 1845 to February 1846 until the signing of the Treaty of Guadalupe Hidalgo. The treaty, in which Mexico lost two-fifths of its territory to the United States (but received an indemnity of U.S.$15 million), was viewed as a great humiliation in Mexico.

This event has left a deep scar on the Mexican social and political psyche. For example, every year on September 13 each school in Mexico commemorates the day Mexican cadets—the Niños Heroes (Child Heroes)—died defending their military college. On that day, when the Mexican flag is raised, a roll call is taken with all the names of these young soldiers. Students play the role of the cadets, who wrapped themselves in the Mexican flag and leaped to their deaths rather than surrender to the invaders.

There were attempts to whip up Mexican hatred toward the Americans from within and from without. Mexican politicians from the *Partido Revolucionario Institucional* (PRI) invoked it many times during the twentieth century. Germany tried to cash in on it by provoking Mexico to enter World War I. The famous Zimmermann Telegram was sent by German foreign minister Dr. Arthur von Zimmermann to Germany's ambassador in Mexico, von Eckhardt, on January 19, 1917, in code (curiously, using the American telegram company Western Union). The message, relayed to the Mexican president, Venustiano Carranza, urged him to join Germany in declaring war on the United States. Mexico, in turn, would be rewarded with the territories it lost in the nineteenth century (after the defeat of the United States). President Carranza did not want to risk the wrath of the United States, so he never took up the offer. British intelligence intercepted the telegraph, decoded it, and informed U.S. president Woodrow Wilson of its content. This was a decisive factor for the United States to declare war on Germany.

The Alluring Temptress: The Winds of Economic Integration Blow Hot and Cold

At the turn of the century, both Canadians and Mexicans first pursued, then rejected, closer economic ties with the United States. Canada's rejection came in the form of a democratic vote. Mexico's rejection took shape as a violent revolution.

Under President Porfirio Diaz, from the 1880s to 1910 Mexico opened up to foreign investment and deepened its economic ties with the United States. However, the presidency of Diaz—and his policy of closer economic ties—ended with the revolution of 1910. After the revolution, under the PRI, suspicion of foreign interests was a hallmark of Mexico's economic policy for decades. Economic nationalism with respect to foreign investors hit high points in 1938, with the nationalization of the oil industry, and 1982, with the nationalization of the banks. More generally, Mexico's foreign investment law discouraged foreign investment.

Entering the twentieth century, Canada's threat of "annexation" came in the form of free trade. In 1911 the United States and Canada negotiated a free trade agreement. The Liberal federal government of Canada under Sir Wilfrid Laurier, the first French–Canadian prime minister (1896–1911), championed the agreement in a federal election. The Liberals lost the election to the Conservatives and the free trade agreement was never implemented. Curiously, in 1891, the Liberals and the Conservatives had taken exactly the opposite positions on free trade.

For the most part of the twentieth century, Canada has followed a different course of national policies compared to the United States, creating a national health care system and government-owned broadcasting, railroad lines, and airlines, among other industries. Canada believed that if such institutions were left to the private sector, they would be overwhelmed by larger private counterparts from the south. Thus, Canada's ever present fear of cultural, social, and economic invasion—if not outright military invasion—also resulted in foreign investment restrictions and government ownership of industry. Canada complemented its foreign investment restrictions with trade policies designed to create manufacturing jobs in the country, leading American firms to establish "branch plants" in Canada to gain market access.

After World War II, a less fearsome option to a bilateral trade agreement presented itself. In 1947, Canada, the United States, and twenty other countries signed a "provisional" agreement to reduce tariffs on goods and to begin eliminating other barriers to trade in goods. However, the General Agreement on Tariffs and Trade (GATT) became the primary vehicle for global trade liberalization when negotiations to create a permanent International Trade Organization (ITO) failed. The ITO was to have been one of the three pillars of postwar peace and prosperity, together with the International Monetary Fund (IMF) and the World Bank.

After World War II, policy makers realized that protectionism, in the form of increasingly higher tariffs and other trade barriers, had contributed to the severity of the global depression. The depression, in turn, had contributed to the rise of fascism and the war. They reasoned that countries that were prosperous and linked by international trade would be less likely to engage in war. The goal of the three institutions was to raise living standards and form stronger links between their member economies.

Over the years, GATT significantly reduced barriers to trade in goods between Canada and the United States, as well as other members. (Mexico did not join the GATT until 1986.) However, GATT was not reducing trade barriers quickly enough for the auto industry, so Canada and the United States negotiated the "Autopact" of 1965, creating free trade in this sector. This led to an increasingly integrated auto industry straddling the two sides of the border.

Like Canada, for most of the twentieth century Mexico resisted greater economic integration with the United States. Mexico adopted a trade policy based on import substitution. The aim of this policy was to further the industrialization of Mexico through barriers to imports and foreign investment. The policy worked well initially and Mexico experienced sustained economic growth. However, over time Mexico's protected industry became highly inefficient, producing inferior quality goods and falling behind technologically. In 1965, the same year of the Canada–United States Autopact, Mexico started the maquiladora program. Foreign companies established assembly plants along the northern border that used Mexican labor to assemble imported components that were then exported as finished goods. In the 1980s, the Mexican government realized that its policy of economic self-sufficiency was no longer working and began to open up its economy, first under President Miguel de la Madrid (under whom Mexico joined the GATT in 1986).

If You Can't Beat 'em...: A Century Comes Full Circle

In the 1980s, almost a century after the idea of free trade was rejected, Canada gave free trade with the United States another try. This time the Conservatives championed the negotiation of a bilateral free trade agreement between

Canada and the United States. The government of Canada sought the negotiations in response to rising protectionist pressures in the U.S. Congress. For many years, the Canadian government, led by Liberal prime minister Pierre Trudeau, had tried to lessen Canada's economic dependence on the United States through efforts to diversify Canada's trade relations. In the 1980s, the government of Conservative prime minister Brian Mulroney recognized that geography was working against those efforts and decided that secure access to the U.S. market was an essential element of Canada's trade policy.

The proposed free trade agreement generated heated political debate in Canada and became the central issue in the national election of 1988. The incumbent Conservative government negotiated the agreement, while the opposition Liberal and New Democratic parties were vehemently opposed. The opposition parties split the anti-free-trade vote between them, allowing the Conservatives to win reelection and proceed with the implementation of the Canada–United States Free Trade Agreement (FTA), which came into effect January 1, 1989.

Opponents argued that the FTA would cause job losses and depress wages in Canada. Proponents argued this might happen in noncompetitive sectors, but the net effect on the economy would be positive. The evolution of the economy would cause job displacement in any event, and in the long run Canada would benefit from the elimination of noncompetitive industries. Moreover, the national government could ease the pain of the transition with social programs for those who lost out.

Opponents argued that the FTA would degrade Canada's social programs. In order to compete with the United States, Canada would have to reduce the generous social safety net to bring it down to the level of the United States. Proponents argued that wealth creation must precede redistribution, and the FTA would create the wealth needed to sustain Canada's social security system. Moreover, trade liberalization is not inconsistent with redistributional social policies, in the form of government spending on education, health, and welfare. In the end, decades of poor financial management on the part of Canadian governments created huge government deficits and a large debt that left less to spend on social programs.

Another great fear of the opponents was that the FTA would lead to cultural homogenization, causing Canada to lose its cultural identity. The fear highlighted the cultural insecurity of English Canadians, most of whom had an unclear vision of what made Canadians different from Americans. They feared that the FTA would force Canada to abandon state-sponsored cultural programs and allow the country to be taken over by the commercialized culture of the United States. Proponents argued that interaction between cultures leads to new perspectives that strengthen a nation's culture, and that cultural isolation had become almost impossible with the advent of modern communications and transportation. Moreover, they argued, cultural isolationism leads to intolerance, arrested development, and censorship, none of which are desirable.

The rallying cry of the FTA opponents was that free trade would lead to the loss of Canada's sovereignty. The country would lose its independence and be forced to adopt a wide range of policies that mirrored those of the United States. Nothing less than the country's existence was at stake. Proponents argued that the economic benefits would outweigh the cost of constraints on domestic policy options. They argued further that a trade-dependent nation such as Canada was better off with a rules-based system of dispute resolution than with a power-based system that would leave the country vulnerable to economic blackmail by its much larger neighbor. Finally, many of the rules in the FTA mirrored those of GATT, which had already dramatically reduced trade barriers between the two countries. However, the FTA extended those rules into new areas, such as services, intellectual property law, investment, and energy trade, reflecting some of the directions in which the GATT Uruguay Round negotiations were headed.

This time, the economic arguments won out. Better access to the U.S. market would permit expanded production that would allow Canadian industry to achieve greater economies of scale. Greater competition would enhance productivity and efficiency, making Canadian business more competitive worldwide. The costs of adjustment to greater competition, such as job losses in noncompetitive industries, would be compensated by job creation in competitive industries. The Canadian economy would become more competitive as a whole in the long run. While greater dependence on the U.S. market might make Canada more vulnerable to downturns in the U.S. economy, Canada would benefit when the U.S. economy was doing well. The reality was that this was the largest trade relationship in the world and the two countries were each other's number one trade partner. However, Canada was more dependent on the United States than the United States was on Canada. With roughly 80 percent of Canada's exports going to United States, the U.S. market had become more important than the domestic market for many Canadian manufacturers. The trade relationships of the United States were, and still are, more diversified than Canada's.

While the FTA debate made for high drama in Canada, the negotiation and passage of the agreement was barely noticed in the United States. The same cannot be said for the NAFTA debate in the United States, where opponents took up the same arguments the Canadian anti-free-trade forces had used five years earlier. The Canadian fear that lower environmental and labor standards in the United States would lead to a "race to the bottom" and compromise Canada's higher standards became a central issue in the U.S. debate.

However, it was now the higher standards in the United States that would be threatened by the lower standards of Mexico. The Canadian fear of job losses and wage depression was translated into the same fear in the United States, expressed by Ross Perot as the "giant sucking sound" Americans would hear as manufacturing jobs were moved to lower-wage Mexico. However, being more confident than Canadians, the Americans did not fear a loss of sovereignty or cultural identity under a flood of Mexican cultural influences.

In Canada, as in the United States, the NAFTA debate coincided with an election year. In both countries, NAFTA became an election issue. In both countries, the government that negotiated the agreement lost to the governments that would implement NAFTA. In Mexico, President Carlos Salinas was there for both the negotiations and the implementation of the agreement.

For Canada, the FTA was proof of the special relationship it enjoyed with the United States. The FTA gave Canadian business preferential access to the U.S. market and an advantage over other countries' firms. When Mexico entered free trade negotiations with the United States, Canada was like the wife that has just learned of the mistress.

Canada pushed to be involved in the negotiations and to negotiate a trilateral agreement, rather than two bilateral agreements. As much as possible, Canada wanted to preserve its FTA gains and to make sure that Mexico did not get a better deal than Canada. Moreover, to be able to influence the negotiations, Canada had to be at the table. As almost an afterthought, Canada sought to enhance its access to the Mexican market (the destination of about 1 percent of Canadian exports) and to promote Mexico as the gateway to Latin America for Canadian business.

However, the most important reason Canada had to push for a trilateral agreement was to avoid a hub-and-spoke situation that could have a negative impact on Canada's ability to attract foreign direct investment. With two bilateral agreements, the United States would become the hub and Mexico and Canada the spokes. The United States, as the only one enjoying free trade with everyone involved, would be a more attractive location for foreign direct investment because firms located in the United States would have equal access to the entire market. This would have put Canada, and Mexico, at a disadvantage in attracting foreign direct investment.

In 1988, Carlos Salinas de Gortari had succeeded de la Madrid as president and had begun a radical transformation of Mexico's economy. Perhaps his most radical move was to initiate free trade negotiations with the United States, a move that would have been unthinkable even a few years earlier.

Mexico's motives for seeking a free trade agreement were similar to those that motivated Canada to negotiate the FTA: increased access to U.S. market, more secure access to U.S. market, a larger market that would allow Mexico-based firms to expand production and achieve economies of scale, greater competition to enhance productivity and efficiency, and a trade relationship based on rules, not power.

President Salinas's slogan was that Mexico wanted to export goods, not people. Free trade would promote economic growth, modernize Mexican industry, and attract more foreign direct investment, creating more and higher paying jobs. With better jobs at home, fewer Mexicans would have to risk illegal migration to the United States in search of work. Finally, NAFTA would entrench the series of economic reforms put in place by Salinas, reducing the risk that later governments might roll back the clock on what became known as "Salinastroika."

The immigration issue was also a major motivation for the United States, as was the economic and political stability of its southern neighbor. A prosperous, free-trading Mexico would be less likely to erupt in political violence or suffer economic disintegration, both of which could send a flood of economic and political refugees fleeing north. In terms of its economic interests, the United States wanted to enhance its access to Mexican market, use Mexico as the gateway to Latin America, and protect U.S. foreign direct investment in Mexico.

As members of GATT, all three countries were simultaneously involved in the Uruguay Round negotiations. NAFTA negotiations could move more quickly than GATT negotiations because fewer countries were involved. At the time the NAFTA was negotiated, it was by no means certain that the Uruguay Round would reach a successful conclusion. NAFTA would provide insurance against a failed Uruguay Round, creating a "fortress North America" that could compete against a "fortress Europe."

Howdy, Neighbor! The NAFTA Dynamic

In terms of economic and business trends, NAFTA has led to deeper integration. In terms of political trends, the picture is more mixed. Despite historical parallels in their relationship with the United States, the Canada–Mexico relationship remained remarkably undeveloped before NAFTA. The two countries have pursued closer political ties in the NAFTA era, recognizing the value of teaming up when their interests in relation to the United States coincided. With respect to trade relations with Cuba, their policies have been mirror images that run counter to U.S. policy. More recently, both countries took the position that U.S. policy toward Iraq should toe a UN-sanctioned, multilateral line. It should come as no surprise that both Canada and Mexico coincide in the view that a multilateral approach based on the rules of international law is the course to take. Given the asymmetries of power that exist in the NAFTA region, both countries are better off with a rules-based approach to international relations than one based on the unilateral exercise of power, be it military or economic. Indeed, a central motivation for both countries to sign free trade agreements with the United States was to impose a rules-based regime on the relationship.

However, Canadian and Mexican interests do not always coincide. The reality is that they are competitors in the trilateral arena, both economically and politically. Economically, they compete for foreign investment and trade. Each country sells itself to multinational firms as the better base from which to serve the North American market. Politically, they compete for the attention of the U.S. government on bilateral issues when their interests differ. For example, the issue of cross-border labor movement is a problem for Mexico, not Canada.

Continental Divide: NAFTA in an Economic Context

Despite their position as the two countries in the world that are literally at the doorstep of the United States, Canada and Mexico are very different places. Canada is a largely English-speaking developed country. The United States had a per capita income of U.S.$36,200 (purchasing power parity adjusted) in the year 2000 and Canada had a per capita income of U.S.$24,800 (purchasing power parity adjusted) in the year 2000 (*CIA Factbook*). Mexico is a largely Spanish-speaking developing country with a per capita income of U.S.$9,100 (purchasing power parity adjusted) in the year 2000 (*CIA Factbook*). The three countries are "close" by the tyranny of geography. Although the Mexican and Canadian economies are each no bigger than the economy of Los Angeles, these economies are more important to the United States than the city of Los Angeles.

Figure 1.1 compares the size of Mexico's and Canada's economy to the U.S. economy. The figures are adjusted for purchasing power parity. Thus, they avoid the problem of undervalued or overvalued currencies. In terms of per capita income, Canada is 2.5 times higher than Mexico and the United States is four times higher (once again, adjusted for purchasing power differential).

The governments of the United States, both at the federal and state levels, cannot simply ignore these two neighbors economically or strategically. Economically they are bound simply because Mexico and Canada are the largest trading partners of the United States. Strategically they are bound because of

Figure 1.1   **Relative GDPs of Canada, Mexico, and the United States**

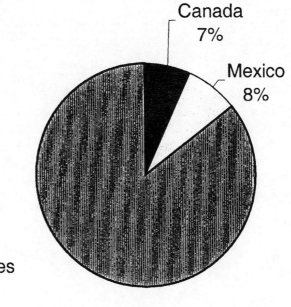

Canada
7%

Mexico
8%

United States
85%

Source: CIA Factbook, internet edition.
Notes: Purchasing power parity adjusted 2000 value. In this picture, we calculated the GDP of each country as a percentage of the total value of all three NAFTA countries together.

their physical proximity. In addition, some 80 percent of the Canadian population lives within fifty miles of the United States.

Some 89 percent of Mexican exports and 73 percent of imports are with the United States. For Canada, 86 percent of exports go to the United States and 76 percent of imports come from the United States. With respect to U.S. exports, Canada is in first place with 23 percent of exports and Mexico is in second place with 14 percent. Of total U.S. imports, Canada has the largest share with 19 percent and Mexico is in second place with 11 percent (*CIA Factbook*).

Figure 1.2 shows purchasing power parity adjusted per capita income in the NAFTA countries over a period of almost two centuries. Several interesting facts emerge from this figure. First, the United States has always stayed ahead of the pack in terms of per capita income. Over time, even though Canada lagged the United States in terms of per capita income, the difference was almost always made up in a decade. The United States and Canada

Figure 1.2   **Real Per Capita GDP in Canada, Mexico, and United States, 1820–1994**

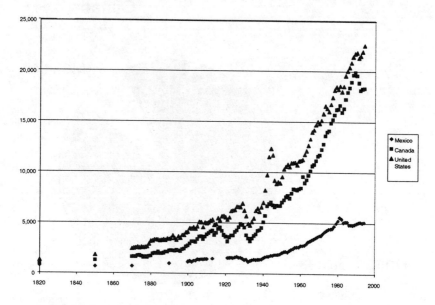

Source: Maddison (2001).
Note: Real per capita GDP is measured after adjusting for purchasing power in each country.

saw a sharp rise in standards of living between 1910 and 1980. Mexico lagged way behind during this period and never caught up. This fact can be seen more clearly in Figure 1.3, where we calculate the per capita income of Canada and Mexico as a percentage of U.S. per capita income. With the exception of 1820, per capita income in Mexico has never exceeded 30 percent of the per capita income of the United States. It declined from 30 percent to 15 percent between 1900 and 1940, then rose back to 30 percent in 1980 only to fall again during the following decade.

NAFTA Geographic: What Do These Neighbors Look Like?

Canada is a country with 3,601,941 square miles (9,220,970 square kilometers) of land. It shares its land boundaries with the United States alone: 5,558 miles (8,893 kilometers), including 1,548 miles (2,477 kilometers) with Alaska. Of the total land, only 5 percent is arable. There are 31.6 million people living in Canada, most close to the border with the United States. Life expectancy in Canada is 79.56 years with an infant mortality rate of 5 out of

Figure 1.3   **Per Capita Income of Canada and Mexico as a Percentage of U.S. Per Capita Income**

Source: Maddison (2001).

1000. Adult infection rate of HIV/AIDS is 0.3 percent. Since only 1.6 children are born per woman in Canada, the population will shrink in the future
unless immigration is increased dramatically (all figures are for the end of
2000). Although English is spoken by the majority, there is a politically strong
presence of French speakers (slightly over 23 percent of the population).
The size of the Canadian economy is U.S.$774 billion adjusted for purchas-
ing power parity.

Mexico has a landmass of 75,119 square miles (1,923,040 square kilometers). Of the border of 2,836 miles (4,538 kilometers), it shares 156 miles
(250 kilometers) with Belize, 601 miles (962 kilometers) with Guatemala,
and 2,079 miles (3,326 kilometers) with the United States. Of the total land,
some 12 percent is arable. The population is 101.8 million. Life expectancy
in Mexico is 71.76 years and the infant mortality rate is 25 per 1000. The
estimated HIV/AIDS prevalence rate among adults is 0.3 percent. The fertility rate is 2.62 per woman. Although Spanish is the official language and
more than 90 percent of the population can speak and understand Spanish,
more than 25 percent of the population speaks some other language at home
(mostly indigenous languages, such as Nahuatl). The size of the Mexican
economy is U.S.$915 billion adjusted for purchasing power parity—larger

Table 1.1

United States Borders in the North and in the South

Northern border (Washington to Maine)	Southern border (Texas to California)
Length: 3,987 miles (6,379 kilometers)	Length: 1,933 miles (3,093 kilometers)
Border patrol agents: 350	Border patrol agents: 9,106
Customs inspectors: 1,165	Customs inspectors: approximately 2,000
INS inspectors: 498	INS inspectors: 1,378
People crossing through U.S. inspection stations in 2001: 100 million	People crossing through U.S. inspection stations in 2001: 314 million
Apprehensions by border patrol: 12,338	Apprehensions by border patrol: 1.2 million

Source: U.S. Dept. of Justice, Immigration and Naturalization Service, U.S. Customs Service, special tabulation for the calendar year 2001.

than the Canadian economy on this measure. (However, Canada still ranks ahead of Mexico when GDP is expressed unadjusted in U.S. dollars, with Canada at U.S.$668 billion, Mexico at U.S.$524 billion, and the United States at U.S.$9,563 billion in 2000, using figures from the World Development Indicators Database, World Bank, April 2002.)

The United States has a landmass of 3,577,719 square miles (9,158,960 square kilometers), thus making it slightly smaller than Canada and four-and-a-half times bigger than present-day Mexico. Given that Mexico lost half of its territory to the United States in the nineteenth century, boundaries have changed radically in the last 160 years on the North American continent. The United States shares borders with the following countries: Canada, 5,558 miles (8,893 kilometers) including 1,548 miles (2,477 kilometers) with Alaska; Cuba, 18 miles (29 kilometers)–U.S. Naval Base at Guantanamo Bay; Mexico, 2,079 miles (3,326 kilometers). Of the total land, some 19 percent is arable. The population of the United States is 278.0 million. Life expectancy is 77.26 years and the infant mortality rate is 7 per 1000. Estimated HIV/AIDS prevalence rate among adults is 0.6 percent. The fertility rate is 2.06 per woman. Although English is the official language, some 15 percent of the population speaks Spanish at home (and more than two-thirds of the Spanish speakers are of Mexican origin). The size of the U.S. economy is U.S.$9,963 billion adjusted for purchasing power parity, thus making it more than ten times bigger than the Mexican or the Canadian economy. In fact, it is the biggest economy on earth. Access to that market is of vital importance to both Canada and Mexico, making effective border management a high priority issue (all figures here are July 2001 estimates).

Figure 1.4a **Gross Product Share of the World, 1998**

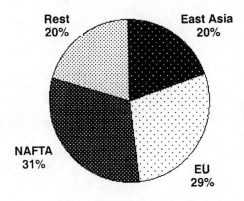

Source: Maddison (2001).

Figure 1.4b **Trade Share of the World, 1998**

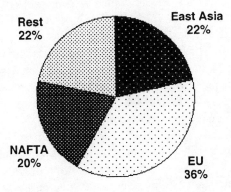

Source: Maddison (2001).

To put NAFTA in the world perspective, we compare NAFTA as a regional bloc with others such as the European Union (EU) and East Asia. We
are not treating these blocs in a formal sense. Figures 1.4a and 1.4b show
that NAFTA and EU are of roughly comparable size at around 30 percent
each of the world output. East Asia and the rest of the world take up around
20 percent each. In trade matters, the EU has a bigger share at 36 percent.
The other three regions take up the rest in approximately equal parts.

On the CUSP of Deeper Integration: Border Talks
before September 11

During his visit to Washington on September 6, 2001 (what a difference a week makes in politics!), Mexican president Vicente Fox raised the issue of legalizing the status of Mexico's illegal migrants in the United States within a year, through some form of guest worker permits. For President Fox, legalization would provide a way to protect citizens making a dangerous migration that killed over 400 in the year 2000 alone (although the numbers have fallen since then). It also would reduce the volume of illegal human trafficking.

For President George W. Bush of the United States, such a policy had its own charm—this policy would appeal to Mexican-American voters. According to the 2000 Census of the United States, 12 percent of Americans are of Hispanic origin and at least 65 percent of them are of Mexican origin. By 2010, the United States will be the second largest Spanish-speaking country in the world. With 43 million native Spanish speakers, it will rank second only to Mexico. In the 2000 presidential election, only 35 percent of Hispanics voted for Bush (and that was the best showing by a Republican among the Hispanic voters since Ronald Reagan in 1984).

In Texas, Bush got 43 percent of the Hispanic vote in 2000. In Florida, where Hispanics include traditionally Republican Cuban-Americans, he received 49 percent. But in California, Bush polled 29 percent. And in New York, where Puerto Ricans are a major component, he got only 18 percent. After September 11, many Bush aides have argued that it is not necessary for him to rely on Hispanic votes, yet for Republican congressmen, these votes still matter. Precisely for that reason, members of Congress jostled to appear pro-Hispanic before the midterm elections.

On October 5, during his first visit after the September 11 attack, President Fox made a very clear statement of his vision of trilateral cooperation. He said, "We have to share information about intelligence, share control of migratory movements, customs issues, information about airports and aircraft in our territories."

Prior to the attacks, the notion of a common security perimeter was widely discussed in Washington and Ottawa, amid security concerns and growing cross-border traffic. In Ottawa, U.S. ambassador to Canada Paul Cellucci suggested a European-style perimeter that would have Canada, the United States, and Mexico jointly manage North America's external border entry points while dismantling internal borders. In Detroit, the Canadian ambassador to the United States, Michael Kergin, pointed out that the average nontariff border cost had reached about 5 percent of the price of products

and 10 to 13 percent in trade-sensitive industries (in 2000). Somewhat pro-
phetically, he asked whether Canadian and U.S. customs and immigrations
rules should be aligned, while improving controls "to keep undesirable
elements away from our common North American space." In none of these
discussions was Mexico ever considered as an integral part of "North
America." It is also interesting that whenever Mexicans talk about
"Norteamericanos" (North Americans), they mean only the people from
the United States, not Canadians.

The Canada–United States Partnership (CUSP), an advisory group created by Prime Minister Jean Chrétien and President Bill Clinton in 1999, has
called for policy harmonization on visa requirements, immigration, and security operations between the two countries. The Canadian cochair of CUSP
warned that businesses are being hurt by the potential for border gridlock.
However, he acknowledged the need to reassure citizens in both countries
that their security would not be compromised.

To be sure, there are conflicting views about the common perimeter idea.
Canada's minister for international trade supported the idea of reducing border frictions, but his comments have focused on the Canada–U.S. border.
The Canadian minister of foreign affairs rejected outright the idea of a common perimeter that would include Mexico, preferring to focus on the Canada–
U.S. border. Canada's minister of immigration objected to the notion of
harmonizing immigration policies, voicing concerns over the independence
of Canadian policy. Similarly, the deputy prime minister of Canada has
challenged the idea of a common perimeter because of the implications for
Canadian sovereignty.

However, free trade with the United States has changed Canadian attitudes toward closer integration. Pollara (a Canadian pollster) conducted a
poll September 27 to October 1, 2002, in which 66 percent of 1,200 Canadians surveyed favored greater economic integration with the United States.
The same number expressed confidence that Canadians can compete in the
U.S. market. In a vote of confidence for globalization, 87 percent believed
that economic survival requires international integration. A majority also
supported stronger cultural ties to the United States (Fife 2002). It thus appears that politicians who resist closer ties are out of touch with the majority
of the Canadian people.

Essentially, a common perimeter between Canada and the United States
would mean that people or goods entering either country from other countries would gain entry to both simultaneously. As one commentator has pointed
out, that would require "a lot of sharing . . . and a lot of trust." Among the
NAFTA countries, the relationship that enjoys the least amount of mutual
trust is that between the United States and Mexico.

"Staunch Ally" versus "Fair Weather Friend": Perceptions after September 11

September 11 brought into sharp focus just how different the northern and southern bilateral relationships really are. The day after the attack, the U.S. ambassador to Canada reiterated his support for a North American perimeter and suggested that Canada and the United States consider harmonizing immigration policies to reduce such threats in the future. In the weeks following the attack, some of the U.S. media advocated reinforced patrols and inspections on the Canadian border, while others supported the views of the ambassador.

The U.S. customs service stationed one hundred extra officers on the Canadian border in order to staff all crossing points twenty-four hours a day following the attack. The United States decided to end the practice of placing orange cones in the middle of the road when some border crossings with Canada were closed at night. For example, on the Canadian border of North Dakota, only three out of seventeen border crossings were manned twenty-four hours a day. They would be on the highest level of alert for the foreseeable future. Initially, wait times to enter the United States increased dramatically. On September 13, the U.S.-bound commercial flow faced line-ups ten miles long at some points and wait times as much as twelve hours. At the Windsor Ambassador Bridge, a major crossing point for North America's integrated automobile industry, backup was so extreme that it was impossible to estimate wait times. Those times were reduced to near normal within one week (in part due to a sharp drop in freight volumes).

On the southern border of the United States, trucks formed long lines on the Mexican side of the border. In some cases, they were delayed by days, upsetting production schedules of U.S. manufacturing companies that depended on intermediate goods for just-in-time production processes. While delays for commercial vehicles were later reduced, delays for passenger vehicles remained longer than on the Canadian border. Figures 1.5a and 1.5b compare delays for commercial vehicles and passenger vehicles at major land crossings on the Canadian and Mexican borders following September 11. These figures have two important characteristics. First, delays for both passenger vehicles and commercial vehicles came down substantially in the months following September 11. There was considerable doubt in the beginning about this happening. Second, the reduction of wait times was much swifter for commercial vehicles.

Table 1.2 reveals an important fact. The top ten land ports account for more than 80 percent of commercial value of all goods for both borders. Thus, the first step toward reducing border delays for commercial traffic

Figure 1.5a **Commercial Delays**

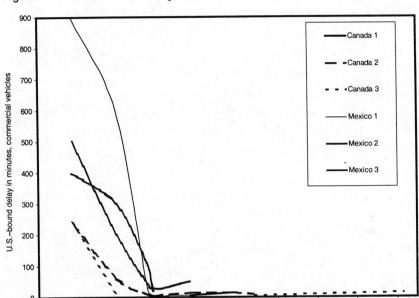

Source: U.S. Customs, Border Wait Times, http://nemo.customs.gov/process/
bordertimes/bordertimes-asp

Notes: Canada 1 refers to Detroit, MI border. Canada 2 refers to Buffalo–Niagara
Falls, NY border. Canada 3 refers to Port Huron, MI border. Mexico 1 refers to
Laredo, TX border. Mexico 2 refers to El Paso, TX border. Mexico 3 refers to Otay
Mesa, CA border.

will involve improved infrastructure for less than one dozen border crossings. Given budgetary resources, this can be achieved in a fairly short
amount of time.

Northern Exposure: From Cold War Allies to
Terror War Allies

When the United States and Britain launched attacks against Afghanistan,
the president of the United States asked Canada to provide military assistance. Canada agreed to send ships, planes, and troops to support the United
States. Canada provided the third largest military contribution, after the United
States and Britain, in the Bush government's operation in Afghanistan.

Canada and the United States have a long history of military and security
cooperation, most recently including World Wars I and II, the Korean War,

Figure 1.5b **Passenger Delays**

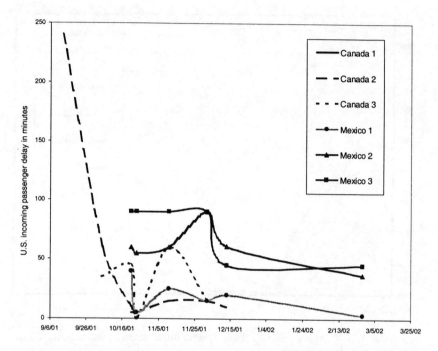

Source: U.S. Customs, Border Wait Times, http://nemo.customs.gov/process/
bordertimes/bordertimes-asp

Notes: Canada 1 refers to Detroit, MI border. Canada 2 refers to Buffalo–Niagara
Falls, NY border. Canada 3 refers to Port Huron, MI border. Mexico 1 refers to
Laredo, TX border. Mexico 2 refers to El Paso, TX border. Mexico 3 refers to Otay
Mesa, CA border.

the Cold War, and the Gulf War. The two continue this tradition through the
North American Aerospace Defense Command (NORAD) and the North
Atlantic Treaty Organization (NATO). The Canada–U.S. Joint Defense Board,
which reports to the prime minister and the president, has existed for over
fifty years. There is a high level of trust between these culturally close countries. Together with the extensive cooperation links that already exist, the
high level of trust makes even greater cooperation likely in the wake of the
September 11 attacks. Indeed, a 2001 survey found that 85 percent of Canadians generally favor making the changes necessary to create a North American security perimeter. Another poll found that 59 percent of Canadians "don't
mind giving up some of our national sovereignty if it increases the overall
security of North America." However, the campaign of the Bush administration to wage war in Iraq soured Canadian views. On February 26, 2003,

Table 1.2

Top Twenty NAFTA Land Ports, 1995 and 2000

2000		Port share (percent)	
Rank	Port	2000	1995
20	Eastport, ID	0	0
19	International Falls, MN	1	1
18	Portal, ND	1	1
17	Eagle Pass, TX	1	1
16	Highgate Springs, VT	1	2
15	Sweet Grass, MT	1	1
14	Calexico, CA	1	1
13	Pembina, ND	2	2
12	Alexandria Bay, NY	2	2
11	Brownsville–Cameron, TX	2	2
10	Blaine, WA	2	3
9	Hidalgo, TX	2	2
8	Nogales, AZ	2	2
7	Champlain–Rouses Pt., NY	3	4
6	Otay Mesa, CA (1)	3	2
5	El Paso, TX	7	6
4	Port Huron, MI	10	8
3	Buffalo–Niagara Falls, NY	12	15
2	Laredo, TX	15	8
1	Detroit, MI	16	22
	All U.S. ports and customs districts	100	100

Source: U.S. Department of Transportation, Bureau of Transportation Statistics, Transborder Surface Freight Data, 1995 and 2000.

Notes: (1) 1995 data for Otay Mesa, CA, include traffic crossing the border at San Ysidro, CA, which has since been closed to truck traffic. Land trade includes truck, rail, pipeline, and miscellaneous and unknown modes. These are calculated in terms of value (and not in terms of volume).

liberal member of Parliament, Carolyn Parrish, was overheard saying, "Damn Americans, I hate those bastards." She later said it was a reference to President George W. Bush's policies on Iraq and apologized to the U.S. ambassador and Parliament for her remark. The *Globe and Mail* later conducted a poll, in which 52 percent of respondents said yes to the question, "Do you agree with Carolyn Parrish's remark that Americans are behaving like 'bastards'?" ("Defying U.S could chill relations," 2003).

Despite the public protests of some politicians, Canada quickly began the process of harmonizing some of its laws with those of the United States after September 11. New legislation on terrorism, border operations, and immigration procedures resembles its equivalents in the United States and Britain. As of December 31, 2003, to reenter Canada, Canadian permanent residents (landed immigrants who are not yet citizens) will be required to use new, tamper-resistant identification cards, with photographs and a magnetic information strip, that are similar to the U.S. green card. In addition, Canada decided to hire 300 new officers to screen refugees and immigrants more rigorously.

The Southern Blues: Hard Cases Need Better Policies

Mexico has had an uneasy relationship with the United States ever since it lost about half of its territory to the Americans some 150 years ago. With a long history of foreign invasions by both the United States and European powers, Mexico adopted a "live and let live" foreign policy. It was formally enshrined with the adoption of the so-called Estrada Doctrine in 1930 (named after the foreign minister of Mexico, Genero Estrada). President Fox is seeking to change this policy and to involve Mexico in world affairs to a greater extent. This stance may be facilitated by Mexico's temporary seat on the United Nations Security Council.

However, the initial reaction of many people in Mexico was not to get involved in the aftermath of the attacks of September 11. Indeed, public opinion in Mexico sent out mixed signals. A national telephone survey by Mitovsky Consultants in Mexico found 76 percent of Mexicans condemned the attacks of September 11. On the other hand, the same survey found that 73 percent of Mexicans were opposed to sending troops to help the Americans. Polls in Mexico by the newspaper *La Reforma* showed that 62 percent of Mexicans think that Mexico should be neutral.

This ambivalence generated doubts in Washington (and elsewhere) about the reliability of Mexico as an ally. The diversity of views makes it difficult to identify any one opinion as "the" Mexican position. Many Mexican intellectuals are left-leaning. Many of them interpreted the events of September 11 as divine justice. Others believed a show of support for the United States would amount to a demonstration of Mexico's submissiveness toward the Americans. Carlos Fuentes, the prominent novelist, summarized this view when he said, "We are business partners with the United States, but in no way are we their lackeys." This viewed was echoed by the interior minister of Mexico, Santiago Creel, who was quoted as saying, "Mexico is not a subordinate of the United States."

With the backdrop of Monroe Doctrine (which stipulated that the United States had the right to intervene anywhere in the Americas if it found itself threatened), the relationship between Mexico and the United States has been fraught with mistrust.

Ironically, Mexico is one of the countries that was hardest hit by the terrorist attacks of September 11, despite the initial reaction of indifference from the Mexican people. Extra security on the border initially slowed the passage of goods and people. The economic impact on the United States economy echoed across the border in Mexico. Almost 90 percent of Mexican exports are destined for the United States and roughly one-third of the Mexican economy depends on NAFTA trade.

Manufacturing in Mexico grew at the rate of 10 percent a year between 1996 and 2000. Much of the manufacturing growth in Mexico came from the export of durable goods. In September 2001, U.S. consumption of durable goods was down by 8 percent, the single biggest monthly drop ever recorded. Although the effect of this drop is not yet available in the form of hard data in Mexico, it is sure to be a big crunch.

The tourism industry suffered, with American tourists reluctant to drive across the border for lineups and fearful of flying. In the first month after the attack, big tourist resorts in Cancun and Acapulco reported a fall in tourist influx of at least 50 percent. Six months later, the numbers were still down by at least 35 percent.

Hundreds of thousands of poor Mexicans cross the border illegally each year in search of jobs in the United States and send money back to their families in Mexico. They now have a harder time going across the border. There is indirect evidence to back up this claim. The number of people deported by U.S. immigration fell by 40 percent during the first month after the attack, which suggests that fewer succeeded in crossing the border during this period. Moreover, efforts by the United States to legalize this flow of Mexican migrants will likely be delayed by the heightened concerns over border security.

Criticism leveled at Mexico for its lukewarm response to the tragedy, together with the realization that the attacks caused economic damage in Mexico, provoked some soul-searching on the Mexican side of the border that may ultimately do much to improve the relationship. Moreover, Mexican authorities cooperated fully with their American counterparts to monitor the flow of people from the United States to Mexico in the days following the attacks. Mexican airlines also cooperated with the Federal Aviation Administration, working with American officials to ensure that they meet U.S. security standards. The two largest Mexican carriers, Mexicana and AeroMexico, have code-sharing agreements with two U.S. carriers, United Airlines and Delta Airlines. Regardless of past difficulties, there really is no choice but to have Mexico work more closely with the United States on security issues.

'Nsync: Bilateral Border Initiatives

Many border issues are handled on a bilateral basis rather than on a trilateral basis, and that trend may continue. For example, Canada and the United

States formalized cooperation under a 1995 bilateral border accord that was further enhanced by several bilateral initiatives prior to September 11. These include CUSP, USINC-CIC Border Vision (a strategic planning initiative of the immigration authorities to deal with illegal immigration), and the Cross-Border Crime Forum (cooperation and information sharing on transnational crime). In November 2001, Canada passed the first antiterrorism law in its history. On December 13, 2001, Canada and the United States signed a new bilateral antiterror action plan to further integrate border security and immigration. That same month, Canada passed a five-year budget plan for border infrastructure and security measures worth $7.7 billion Canadian dollars. The Federal Bureau of Investigation (FBI) gave the Royal Canadian Mounted Police (RCMP) access to its fingerprint database, the first foreign police force to be granted such access. These initiatives are designed to help the two countries improve the passage of commercial traffic on the border while facing the common external threats of international terrorism, transnational crime, and drug and people smuggling.

Mexico does not have the financial resources or institutional structure to match Canada's efforts. The United States will likely have to subsidize Mexican security measures. Bilateral border initiatives will take longer to negotiate given Mexico's division of legislative powers between the president and the congress and the current political climate that makes cooperation difficult to achieve between the two. Nevertheless, many U.S. border initiatives with Mexico mirror those taken with Canada, such as the so-called Smart Border plans. Moreover, most of Mexico's exports to the United States originate with some fifty companies, making preclearance for electronically sealed containers feasible.

A Matter of Opinion: Opinion Polls about NAFTA

By all accounts, NAFTA makes strange bedfellows. The agreement integrates the economies of a middle-income country (Mexico) and a developed country (Canada) with a neighboring economic powerhouse (the United States) that dwarfs both. As we noted above, it was Canada and Mexico that sought this deal.

One important element that shapes the future of NAFTA is what people in each of these three countries think about this arrangement. Economic theories predict that free trade will generate winners and losers. On this basis, support for economic integration will depend on economic interests. However, the persuasive effects of targeted information campaigns can also shape attitudes.

An interesting study by Merolla et al. (2001) takes a close look at opinion polls in Canada, Mexico, and the United States and asks the following questions: (1) How well do standard economic theories predict opinions toward NAFTA in each of the three countries? (2) How did the rhetorical debate over NAFTA shape opinions in each case? (3) Are there rhetoric and cues capable of trumping economic interests? In other words, can they persuade individuals to adopt policy stances that conflict with their objective economic situation? The study found that noneconomic interests can substantially influence opinions toward NAFTA—even to the point of canceling out the effects of economic interests—and that the significance of these factors is driven by the country-specific nature of the information context. Based on various arguments, the researchers formulated a number of hypotheses (see Table 1.3). Based on opinion polls taken in the three countries, they found strong support for almost all the hypotheses.

Conclusion

Despite the baggage of history and politics, the process of economic integration in the NAFTA region has moved forward at an increasingly rapid pace in recent years. Heightened awareness of the need to balance economic integration and security is now sparking even closer cooperation between the three governments. In the following chapters, we consider how to balance security and business concerns in a North American economy that is increasingly integrated.

Chapter 2 focuses on the movement of goods and considers how costs may be minimized in the various modes of transport. Investments in intelligent border systems will cost money. However, they will pay for themselves over the long term by facilitating the integration of production, reducing border delays, and enhancing security. Cross-border integration of production allows firms to lower costs by exploiting location advantages in each country. The key is to ensure the smooth flow of goods across borders, which in turn requires not only quick passage, but also the further integration of the transportation sector. For these reasons, we examine the integration of manufacturing in the region and the bumpy road traveled by the trucking sector as NAFTA implementation moves into the final phase. We note, however, that there are many issues that will have to be addressed even after the obligations contained in NAFTA are fully implemented.

Chapter 3 focuses on the movement of people, particularly the issue of illegal immigration from Mexico. While NAFTA has facilitated the movement of businesspeople in the region, cross-border migration remains far more problematic on the U.S.–Mexico border than on the U.S.–Canada border. We examine demographic and economic trends that will influence the

Table 1.3

Opinions about NAFTA of Different Groups in Canada, Mexico, and the United States

Hypothesis

H1   Low-skilled workers in the United States and Canada should oppose NAFTA while high-skilled workers should support it. In contrast, high-skilled workers in Mexico should oppose NAFTA, while low-skilled workers should support it.

H2   Sectors harmed by NAFTA should oppose the agreement. Support for NAFTA should come from sectors that benefit.

H3   In all three countries, low-skilled workers should oppose NAFTA while high-skilled workers should support it.

H4   Economically insecure individuals in the United States and Canada should oppose NAFTA, while those same individuals in Mexico should support it.

H5   In Mexico, those more likely to receive cues from the president will support NAFTA, while those who resist such cues will oppose it.

H6   In Mexico, union members will support NAFTA.

H7   In the United States, individual stances on policies related to job provision and protection will influence their attitudes toward NAFTA.

H8   In the United States, individuals who are more in favor of the environment will be more opposed to NAFTA.

H9   In the United States, individuals who are concerned about immigrants, or who have negative opinions about immigrants, will be more opposed to NAFTA.

H10   In the United States, nationalism will be related to opposition to NAFTA.

H11   In Canada, individual stances on policies related to job provision and protection will influence their attitudes toward NAFTA.

H12   In Canada, individuals who are more in favor of the welfare state will be more opposed to NAFTA.

H13   In Canada, nationalism will be related to opposition to NAFTA.

Source: Merolla et al. (2001), various pages.

resolution of this issue and the conflicting U.S. labor and immigration policies that hamper efforts to solve the problem. We also examine the progress made in tightening security with respect to people movement.

Chapter 4 focuses on the movement of capital, which is at once the lifeblood of commerce and transnational crime. The increasing integration of the financial services sector facilitates both capital flows and security measures. Moreover, the participation of all three NAFTA countries in multilateral organizations and international conventions provides a solid basis for harmonizing efforts in this area, particularly with respect to money laundering and terrorist financing. With respect to flows of foreign direct investment, Mexico's strategy of pursuing free trade agreements around the world is designed to enhance its attractiveness to multinational investors compared to the other two countries. With a free trade agreement already in place with the EU, and another with Japan in the works, Mexico will be the only NAFTA member with such trade links to all the major economies of the world. We also wade into the common currency debate, but conclude that monetary union in not in the cards.

Chapter 5 looks at corruption in Mexico and how to reconcile the fact of corruption with closer cooperation on security. As the only developing country in NAFTA, corruption in Mexico is a much bigger problem than it is in Canada or the United States. Indeed, in the NAFTA region, the problem gets worse the further south one goes. However, the Mexican government is working on the problem and recent initiatives provide hope for the future. The alternation of political parties in power, the genuine separation of powers between the executive and legislative branches, the enhanced independence of the courts, the implementation of international agreements on corruption, the use of technology to enhance transparency, and public campaigns to change attitudes toward corruption all look promising.

Chapter 6 concludes by comparing obstacles to doing business in each country and assessing the efforts of each to balance security and economic integration.

The themes we explore in this book are all interconnected. Cross-border flows of goods, people, and capital affect the competitiveness of business, the economic prosperity of the region, and regional security. Institutional problems of coordination and corruption affect the ability of governments to provide a secure and prosperous business environment. In addition to these linkages, there are numerous interlocking connections between all of these issues.

Capital flows in the form of foreign direct investment have a major impact on merchandise trade by stimulating intrafirm trade. In the NAFTA region, foreign direct investment in the maquiladoras has stimulated considerable growth in cross-border flows of goods across the Mexico–U.S. border. Similarly, the regional integration of the automotive sector has sparked considerable foreign direct investment and merchandise trade between the NAFTA countries. In turn, flows of goods and capital require more cross-border flows of people to conduct trade and investment activities and to provide services (such as transportation and financial transactions) that accompany international trade and investment.

International trade and investment also affect people movement less directly. Foreign direct investment creates jobs that attract workers. With greater foreign direct investment in Mexico's manufacturing sector, there are more jobs to keep Mexican workers at home. Export-led growth has the potential to reduce the wage gap between Mexico and the United States, further reducing incentives for Mexicans to seek work in the northern neighbor. Corruption, however, has the opposite effect. Corruption and other barriers to business make it more difficult to achieve the economic growth needed to close wage gaps and enhance the attractiveness of Mexico for foreign direct investment. Corruption also increases the need to scrutinize cross-border capital movements.

Security is an issue that weaves itself into every aspect of North American integration and the central topics analyzed in this book. The migration of undocumented workers from Mexico to the United States—and the wrongheaded policies that perpetuate the problem—divert resources that otherwise might address the movement of people that do pose a security threat. The lack of personal security in Mexico—an issue closely linked to corruption in the police force—makes Mexico a less attractive destination for foreign direct investment by transferring security costs from the government to the private sector. It also complicates the recruitment of expatriate managers that forms an integral part of international investment strategies. The need to stem the international capital flows associated with terrorist financing can increase the transaction costs for legitimate capital flows. Finally, security requires investments in the systems used to move and monitor the cross-border flow of goods (though such investments may in the end increase the efficiency of cross-border goods transportation).

Deeper integration between the NAFTA countries is necessary to strike the right balance between economic and security needs. Much work remains to be done to reduce barriers to business, to enhance security, and to reduce economic disparity in the region. NAFTA is not enough.

2

Get Me to the Plant on Time

Delivering the Goods in an Integrated Economy

"If you don't know where you are going,
any road will take you there."
—Anonymous

"I took the one less traveled by,
And that has made all the difference."
—Robert Frost

"No nation was ever ruined by trade."
—Benjamin Franklin

Despite the political complications that arise, free trade has progressed because of the economic benefits it brings. In this chapter we begin with a brief look at economic theories that explain why countries trade. We then examine trends in NAFTA trade, which show that trade with each other is now more important than it used to be for the three countries and is likely to become even more so in the future. We then look at how increasing trade has resulted in increasing cross-border integration of manufacturing in the region.

The economic importance of NAFTA trade and the regional integration of production chains, together with increased concern over border security, have made border and transportation systems of the utmost importance. We estimate the cost of borders and security measures. We consider how differences between the northern and southern borders may affect the cost and nature of security measures. We examine the principal transportation modes for goods. In this context, we present the case of the U.S.–Mexico dispute over trucking, which demonstrates how security and economic issues can be hijacked by the political process. We look at the implications for business of security measures and how border costs may be reduced. The economic benefits of trade and efficient transport of goods make investments in border and transportation systems a good bet. Moreover, improvements in these systems that incorporate security measures free up resources that can then be dedicated to concentrating on genuine security risks.

What's In It for Me: Why Countries Trade

Economists have posited models to answer the question of why countries trade. The first classic answer came from David Ricardo in 1821. His explanation was based on comparative advantage. A country with comparative advantage in producing wine would export wine. This does not sound like a profound idea until one considers the essence of comparative advantage. One key insight of Ricardo was that a country may have absolute advantage in producing everything, but it cannot have *comparative* advantage in producing everything. Thus, it is logically impossible for a country to be importing everything.

A different model was proposed by Heckscher (1919) and Ohlin (1928). In the absence of trade barriers and without any cost of transportation, a country would export only those goods that use its more abundant factors of production. A logical extension is "factor price equalization." Under the conditions of Heckscher and Ohlin, if all markets are perfectly competitive, the price of each factor of production will be equalized across countries. Free trade will equalize not only commodity prices but also factor prices, so that all workers earn the *same wage rate* and all units of capital will earn the *same rental return* in all countries regardless of the factor supplies or the demand patterns in the countries.

Early tests of the Heckscher–Ohlin model showed that the model, in its simplest form, failed. Wassily Leontief provided one test (later to be called the Leontief paradox) and found that the United States was importing capital-intensive goods from other countries when it appeared that the United States should be exporting those goods because of its own high capital intensity in production of goods. More recently, a suitably amended Heckscher–Ohlin model stands up reasonably well when confronted with data (Davis et al. 1997).

One interesting application of the Heckscher–Ohlin model comes in the form of the Stolper–Samuelson theorem, which predicts that trade will increase the real income of the owners of the relatively abundant factors and decrease the real income of the relatively scarce factors. We can use this theorem to study which political groups are expected to support and which political groups are expected to oppose free trade between countries.

Summarizing two centuries of economic studies of trade in two sentences always risks oversimplification. But if we were forced to do that, we would conclude the following. Trade between developed and developing countries arises due to traditional comparative advantage, largely determined by differences in endowment patterns. Trade between developed countries, much of it intraindustry trade, is based on economies of scale and product differentiation. These two general observations explain the trade pattern between the United States and Canada (a case of trade between developed countries) and the trade pattern between the United States and Mexico (a case of trade between a developed and a developing country) fairly well.

Naked Facts: Intraregional Trade in NAFTA

Merchandise trade between the NAFTA countries has grown significantly in recent years, along with global trade flows. In addition, the percentage of total imports and exports within the region has increased significantly compared to trade outside the region. In 1990, intraregional exports represented 42.6 percent of total exports, compared to 56 percent of a total of $1,224 billion worth of exports in 2000. Similarly, in 1990, intraregional imports represented 34.4 percent of total imports, compared to 40.3 percent of a total of $1,672 billion worth of imports in 2000. Thus, intraregional trade has grown both in volume and in importance, as shown in the value of NAFTA merchandise trade in Table 2.1. As a sign of future trends, imports into the United States from Canada and Mexico are outpacing exports to those countries.

Trade volumes between the United States and its two NAFTA partners have grown enormously. For 2000, U.S.–Mexico trade reached $248 billion, while U.S.–Canada trade amounted to $408 billion, with around $20 billion between Mexico and Canada. The growth in NAFTA trade is especially impressive if one considers that in 1993, the year before NAFTA was implemented, U.S.–Mexico trade stood at just $81 billion, while trade with Canada was valued at $211 billion. Thus, the trade between Mexico and the United States has more than trebled and the trade between the United States and Canada has roughly doubled over a period of seven years, maintaining Canada as the number one trading partner of the United States and propelling Mexico to the number two spot.

The value of trade as a percentage of gross domestic product (GDP) has also increased, particularly in Canada and Mexico. In the case of these two NAFTA members, the vast majority of that trade takes place with the United States. The United States is comparatively less dependent on trade with its NAFTA partners both in terms of its total trade and in terms of the percentage of U.S. GDP attributable to trade. Thus, while the facilitation of trade flows

Table 2.1

Value of U.S. Merchandise Trade with Canada and Mexico, 1994–2000
(in billions of current dollars)

	Imports from Canada	Exports to Canada	Imports from Mexico	Exports to Mexico	Total trade with Canada	Total trade with Mexico
1994	128	114	49	51	243	100
1995	144	127	62	46	272	108
1996	156	134	74	57	290	131
1997	168	150	86	71	318	157
1998	175	154	95	79	329	174
1999	198	164	110	87	362	197
2000	229	176	136	112	406	248

Sources: U.S. Department of Transportation, Bureau of Transportation Statistics, special tabulation, April 2001; based on: total trade, air and water data—U.S. Department of Commerce, U.S. Census Bureau, Foreign Trade Division, FT920 U.S. Merchandise Trade (Washington, DC: various years); all land modes—U.S. Department of Transportation, Bureau of Transportation Statistics, Transborder Surface Freight Data.

in the region is in the economic interests of all three members, its economic impact is felt more acutely in Canada and Mexico, as evidenced in Table 2.2. It shows trade (that is, imports plus exports) as a percentage of GDP. This number is around 66 percent for Canada in 2000, 38 percent for Mexico, and 20 percent for the United States. Thus, trade is far more important for Canada and Mexico than for the U.S. economy.

The importance of NAFTA countries for the United States shows up in another measure—the *mode* of transport for imports and exports of the United States. Table 2.3 shows that in 1965, about 70 percent of U.S. imports (in terms of value) came by ships. By 2000, this proportion has fallen dramatically to around 46 percent. The decrease in the percentage of goods transported by ships, in turn, is taken up by air freight and, to a lesser extent, transport by trucks. Exports from the United States by land have gone up tremendously. Land transportation is now the main mode of transport for exports. Clearly, for this mode, there can be just two possible destinations—Canada and Mexico.

The NAFTA countries have made some progress toward liberalizing investment and services trade in the transportation sector. But, as the politics of trucking (see below) shows, much remains to be done.

Tables 2.4 and 2.5 shows the trade relations among the NAFTA countries in terms of various modes of transportation (along with the explosive growth from 1997 to 2000).

Table 2.2

Trade and GDP of NAFTA Countries in 2000

	GDP	Export	Import	Trade/GDP
Canada	775	272	238	66
Mexico	915	168	176	38
United States	9,963	776	1,223	20

Source: Data taken from the CIA *Factbook,* September 30, 2002.
Note: Trade/GDP is the value of total exports plus total imports as a percentage of GDP. Millions of current U.S. dollars.

Table 2.3

U.S. Trade by Transport Mode (percent of value)

	Imports			Exports		
Year	Ocean	Air	Land	Ocean	Air	Land
1965	69.9	6.2	23.9	61.6	8.3	30.1
1970	62.0	8.6	29.4	57.0	13.8	29.2
1975	65.5	9.2	25.3	58.9	14.1	27.0
1980	68.6	11.6	19.8	54.8	20.9	24.3
1985	60.4	14.9	24.8	43.0	24.5	32.4
1990	57.2	18.4	24.4	38.4	28.1	33.5
1995	51.2	21.6	27.3	34.7	29.3	36.0
2000	45.5	24.7	29.7	32.2	29.9	37.9

Source: Statistical Abstract of the United States, 2001.

The growing importance of NAFTA trade and regional production chains has placed transport issues on the front burner. The border closures of September 2001 and the West Coast port closure of October 2002 underlined the economic importance of international transportation systems to the economies of the NAFTA region and the rest of the world. Appendix 2.1 (p. 61) discusses the West Coast port lockout.

Zooming In: Convergence in Manufacturing

The three NAFTA economies are converging. This can clearly be seen in the context of specific examples. We cite two: first, the tariff reduction by three partners over time; second, the movement of manufacturing activities in the new millennium.

Cross-border transportation of merchandise is of vital importance to all three economies. In order of importance, goods are transported primarily by land, rail, air, and water. Tariffs pose a clear barrier to trade. All three NAFTA

Table 2.4

U.S. Merchandise Trade with Canada and Mexico by Mode, 2000

Mode	Value (percent)	Weight (percent)
NAFTA trade, total	100.0	100.0
Truck	65.6	35.1
Rail	14.4	17.4
Pipeline	3.6	14.8
Air	6.9	0.2
Water	5.0	32.4
Other and unknown	4.5	0.1
U.S.–NAFTA imports, total	100.0	100.0
Truck	59.3	25.7
Rail	19.4	19.8
Pipeline	6.3	20.5
Air	4.9	0.1
Water	6.4	33.9
Other and unknown	3.7	0.1
U.S.–NAFTA exports, total	100.0	100.0
Truck	73.6	55.7
Rail	8.1	12.3
Pipeline	0.2	2.3
Air	9.3	0.4
Water	3.2	29.2
Other and unknown	5.5	0.2

Sources: U.S. Department of Transportation, Bureau of Transportation Statistics, June 2001; based on: total, water, and air data—U.S. Department of Commerce, U.S. Census Bureau, Foreign Trade Division, U.S. Exports of Merchandise CD and U.S. Imports of Merchandise CD, December 2000; truck, rail, pipeline, other and unknown data—U.S. Department of Transportation, Bureau of Transportation Statistics, Transborder Surface Freight Data, 2000; and special tabulations.

countries have taken steps to reduce this type of trade barrier. However, in recent years the reduction in Mexican tariffs has been more dramatic than that of its NAFTA partners.

Over time, manufacturing activities among NAFTA partners have moved more and more in sync. In the past, manufacturing growth in Mexico had been very volatile (and it still is more volatile than in the United States or Canada). What is remarkable is the coincidence of the direction of movement of manufacturing in the NAFTA countries in the past two years. In early 2001, both Mexico and the United States experienced negative growth in manufacturing. It accelerated in the middle of the year. All three countries bounced off the negative territory by the beginning of 2002 although growing at different speeds.

The elimination of tariffs and the opening up to foreign investment flows in the NAFTA region, combined with the need for business to constantly

Table 2.5

Value of U.S. Merchandise Trade with NAFTA Partners by Mode, 1997–2000

| Mode | Millions of dollars | | | | Percent change |
	1997	1998	1999	2000	97–00
Truck	323,298	349,979	385,413	428,700	32.6
Rail	69,844	67,872	78,414	94,198	34.9
Air	27,744	30,127	34,380	44,950	62.0
Water	21,661	20,852	23,357	32,607	50.5
Pipeline	14,132	11,289	12,315	23,592	66.9
Other	18,704	22,596	25,107	29,224	56.2
Total trade	475,382	502,715	558,987	653,270	37.4
Subtotal, land	425,977	451,736	501,239	575,713	35.2
Land, percent of total	89.6	89.9	89.7	88.1	

Sources: U.S. Department of Transportation, Bureau of Transportation Statistics, June 2001; based on: total, water, and air data—U.S. Department of Commerce, U.S. Census Bureau, Foreign Trade Division, U.S. Exports of Merchandise CD and U.S. Imports of Merchandise CD, December 2000; truck, rail, pipeline, other and unknown data—U.S. Department of Transportation, Bureau of Transportation Statistics, Transborder Surface Freight Data, 2000; and special tabulations.

Figure 2.1   **Reduction in the Average Tariff Rates on Goods**

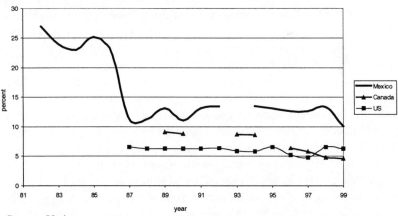

Source: Various.

improve production efficiencies by exploiting location advantages, is integrating the regional economy as never before. At the same time, as one barrier to cross-border business falls, remaining barriers become more noticeable. The constant search for cost savings has thus led to a new focus on efficient cross-border transportation. After September 11, governments became more inclined to heed businesspeople's call for investments in this area.

Figure 2.2   **Movement of Growth Rates in Manufacturing in NAFTA Countries, March 2001–May 2002**

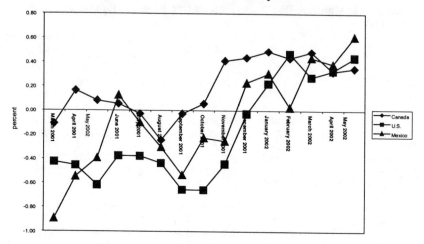

Source: Original data from the INEGI website (www.inegi.gob.mx).

Planes, Trains, and Automobiles: Efficiency in Transportation Systems

Integrated transportation systems provide the vital lubricant for smooth movement of goods across borders. Improved (freight) transportation systems reduce costs for delivery of goods and are essential services; they also support faster, more reliable transportation from one place to another. These systems reduce the costs of collecting inputs and delivering products to markets in four different ways. First, less driver time on the road lowers labor costs. Second, increased trip miles per time period per vehicle means that a smaller vehicle fleet is needed for the same amount of work. Third, the more efficient use of vehicles, together with better infrastructure, lowers overall vehicle repair and operating costs. Fourth, improved transportation reliability reduces costs by reducing delays (ICF Consulting 2002).

A classic example of how efficient transportation can dramatically reduce production costs (by reducing inventory) is just-in-time production. It is a key element in North American auto production, which has integrated production chains across the borders of Canada, Mexico, and the United States. Given the degree of cross-border integration in this industry, it comes as no surprise that the category "motor vehicles parts and accessories" has topped the list of trade between NAFTA partners since 1995 (see Table 2.8).

The economic benefits from improved freight transport systems are both direct and indirect. Direct benefits for the transportation industry come in the form of immediate cost reductions to carriers and shippers, including

Figure 2.3   **Transport, Industrial Production, and the GDP for the United States**

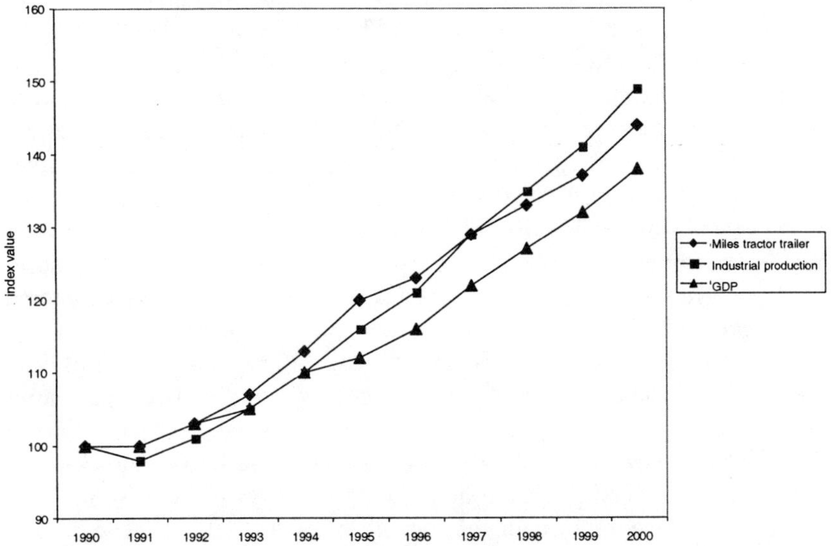

Source: U.S. Department of Transportation website (www.dot.gov).

gains to shippers from reduced transit times and increased reliability. Indirect benefits include improvements in logistics that produce reorganization gains for both the transportation industry and the manufacturing firms that use their services. For manufacturers, improved transportation systems allow the *quantity* of firms' outputs to increase while maintaining the *quality* of their output. In addition, indirect benefits may include additional gains from the reorganization of production chains, such as improved products, new products, or some other change.

One indication of how transport, trade, and GDP grow can be seen in Figure 2.3. It plots indices of transport volume, trade value, and GDP (in real terms) in the United States between 1990 and 2000. They all grow in tandem. However, caution should be used in interpreting correlation with causation. Just because certain indicators move together does not necessarily mean that there is a clear cause-and-effect relationship among them. Nevertheless, the economic benefits of trade and the economic cost of transportation delays suggest that investments in North American transportation and border infrastructure are worthwhile.

Bridge over Troubled Waters: Investing in Borders

The initial border delays that occurred in the immediate aftermath of September 11 produced frantic outbursts of speculation on the part of many commentators as to what increased security might do to border crossings over the long term. But how much delay really does occur in practice for trucks crossing the northern and southern borders of the United States?

Higher security efforts certainly have the potential to increase the cost of borders. In theory, they would impose a higher cost of producing goods with production systems spread across the borders. The convergence of manufacturing activity in the NAFTA region is one indicator of the process of integration that is occurring across the three countries.

However, with technology and with large-scale movement of goods, NAFTA countries should be able to exploit economies of scale. The additional long-run marginal cost of border delays may be negligible compared to the economic benefits of cross-border integration. An instructive example can be drawn from the seizure of illegal drugs—a barometer of drug trade between Mexico and the United States. For the first two weeks after the September 11 attacks, the drug seizures across the border were down by half. By early October, the drug seizures were back to preattack level. Thus, the traffickers quickly found alternative ways of keeping up their supply. The same applies for the movement of legal goods. The cost of border delays was high initially, but commercial traffic delays were reduced quickly after September 11.

A study by the U.S. federal highway administration throws some light on the issue of border delays. Seven ports of entry were chosen for the study: (1) the Ambassador Bridge, Detroit, Michigan; (2) Blaine, Washington; (3) Blue Water Bridge, Port Huron, Michigan; (4) Peace Bridge, Buffalo, New York; (5) El Paso, Texas; (6) Laredo, Texas (Bridge 4, a relatively new truck-only crossing, was the site observed at Laredo); and (7) Otay Mesa, California. These seven points account for more than 60 percent of all the road traffic between the United States and its NAFTA partners.

The measurement chosen to monitor commercial vehicle activity on-site was "travel delay per truck trip." This documents the time taken by the individual commercial vehicle from the initial queuing point in the exporting country, through the exporting country's final checkpoint, and up to and through the first inspection point in the importing country. Travel in both directions was assessed (that is, truck travel into and out of the United States).

The on-site reviews found three important characteristics of border delays. First, the time needed for processing commercial vehicles entering the United States (inbound clearances) is *significantly longer* than for departing (outbound clearances) at almost every location. Second, the average delay was longer on the southern border than on the northern border. Third, increased traffic volume did not necessarily correlate with a significantly increased delay.

In total, for all seven ports of entry, the average inbound travel time was 26.8 minutes, while the average outbound travel time was 14.2 minutes. For the four northern ports in the survey, the average inbound travel time was 24.1 minutes; the average outbound, 12.6 minutes. For the three southern ports, the average inbound travel time was 33.8 minutes; the average outbound, 17.2 minutes.

Average travel time does not tell the whole story. Many trucks took significantly longer to pass through the seven ports of entry. Hence, a "95th percentile" time measurement was used to provide information about the time that it took 95 percent of the surveyed trucks to travel the study distance. A comparison of average travel time with the 95th percentile time shows that a significant number of truck trips could in fact take far longer than the average. For example, while average travel time for all seven inbound crossings was 26.8 minutes, the 95th percentile time for these was over 70 minutes.

This study also revealed that congestion at these ports of entry cost the transportation industry about 2.6 million hours in delay time per year, at a financial cost of at least $88 million. On top of that, trucks wasted about 2.6 million gallons of fuel annually, with a resulting environmental impact of 23,000 tons of carbon dioxide and more than 300 tons of nitrous oxides. In order to reduce this environmental impact of rapidly increasing trade among the three countries, all three governments need to dedicate adequate resources to infrastructure development and manpower along the U.S. borders with Canada and Mexico.

Tables 2.7 and 2.8 show how concentrated the movements of goods are in terms of their location and the types of goods. A few ports account for the bulk of goods movement. The bulk of the goods are also concentrated in just a few industries. This suggests that inspection of goods at the point of loading trucks is the way to go: inspect at the source, not the border. Special routes to let precleared goods enter the United States through special electronically managed lanes could go a long way toward speeding up the passage of most of this value-added trade between NAFTA countries.

The cost of eliminating delays will be borne by government and industry. For governments, the costs of not having delays include increasing manpower at the border and upgrading border technology and infrastructure. These costs will vary with the geographic conditions on each border. For example, rivers require bridges and mountains may require tunnels. However, these costs should be viewed as investments that will generate savings over the long run.

The cost of eliminating delays will also include the costs to firms of implementing government security guidelines, such as the U.S. Customs Trade

Table 2.6

Comparison of Outbound and Inbound Delay in Minutes

Crossing	Baseline time	Average time	95th Percentile time
All outbound crossings	NA	14.2	37.4
All inbound crossings	NA	26.8	70.1
All northern outbound crossings	NA	12.6	34.3
All northern inbound crossings	NA	24.1	70.3
All southern outbound crossings	NA	17.2	45.2
All southern inbound crossings	NA	33.8	64.9
Canadian end			
Ambassador Bridge outbound	5.7	8.8	13.7
Ambassador Bridge inbound	12.9	20.4	33.9
Blaine outbound	4.8	21.5	35.3
Blaine inbound	8.1	17.3	35.6
Blue Water Bridge outbound	5.0	6.2	9.1
Blue Water Bridge inbound	11.1	34.2	80.3
Peace Bridge outbound	9.0	21.7	38.0
Peace Bridge inbound	8.3	23.3	83.4
Mexican end			
El Paso outbound	9.0	13.2	34.0
El Paso inbound	7.6	37.2	77.4
Laredo outbound	1.8	17.2	45.0
Laredo inbound	12.2	31.2	54.9
Otay Mesa outbound	9.5	19.1	36.9
Otay Mesa inbound	6.4	35.0	64.3

Source: Commercial Vehicle Travel Time and Delay at U.S. Border Crossings, Federal Highway Administration, June 2002.

Notes: Outbound refers to outbound from the United States. Inbound refers to inbound to the United States. Baseline time: time needed to travel through the port-of-entry at low-volume conditions; the lowest hourly travel time in that direction for each day surveyed. This value represents "no delay" travel time. Average time: time (in minutes) needed to travel the study distance (between the starting point in the exporting country and the initial inspection station in the importing country). 95th percentile time: time within which 95 percent of the trucks surveyed traveled the study distance. The time measurements were taken in June and July 2001 in all borders with the exception of Laredo. The measurements in Laredo were taken in October 2001.

Partnerships against Terrorism program (CTPAT). In this program, the owners of the supply chain (brokers, carriers, importers, warehouse operators, and manufacturers) voluntarily comply with security guidelines in order to reduce border inspections and border costs. However, there is a trade-off in terms of the cost to the companies of the added documentation, technology, and personnel requirements involved. Canada has a similar program—Partners in Protection—in which the transportation industry works with the

Table 2.7

Top Twenty NAFTA Border Truck Crossings into the United States, 1997 and 2000

Rank in 2000	Port Name	1997 (thousand)	2000 (thousand)	Crossings per day (2000)	1997 (percent)	2000 (percent)	Percent change, 1997–2000
1	Detroit, MI	1,420	1,769	4,848	15.4	15.3	24.6
2	Laredo, TX	1,251	1,493	4,091	13.6	12.9	19.3
3	Buffalo–Niagara, NY	1,054	1,198	3,282	11.4	10.4	13.7
4	Port Huron, MI	679	839	2,299	7.4	7.3	23.5
5	El Paso, TX	583	720	1,974	6.3	6.2	23.6
6	Otay Mesa/San Ysidro, CA	568	688	1,886	6.2	5.9	21.2
7	Blaine, WA	463	517	1,416	5.0	4.5	11.6
8	Champlain, NY	299	391	1,071	3.2	3.4	30.7
9	Hidalgo, TX	235	374	1,025	2.5	3.2	59.3
10	Brownsville, TX	248	299	820	2.7	2.6	20.9
11	Calexico, CA	U	279	764	U	2.4	U
12	Alexandria Bay, NY	220	278	763	2.4	2.4	26.5
13	Nogales, AZ	243	255	698	2.6	2.2	4.9
14	Pembina, ND	152	214	587	1.7	1.9	40.9
15	Calais, ME	126	154	422	1.4	1.3	22.5
16	Sweetgrass, MT	112	146	400	1.2	1.3	30.5
17	Derby Line, VT	101	139	380	1.1	1.2	37.6
18	Houlton, ME	103	133	364	1.1	1.1	28.8
19	Highgate Springs, VT	99	133	364	1.1	1.1	33.9
20	Jackman, ME	87	128	350	0.9	1.1	47.1
	Total, top 20 ports	8,041	10,148	27,802	87.3	87.7	26.2
	Total, all ports	9,215	11,574	31,709	100.0	100.0	25.6

Sources: U.S. Department of Transportation, Bureau of Transportation Statistics, special tabulations, May 2001; based on data from U.S. Department of Treasury, U.S. Customs Service, Mission Support Services, Office of Field Operations.

Note: Data represent the number of truck crossings, not the number of unique vehicles, and include both loaded and unloaded trucks. Data for the port of Calexico is typically reported as a combined total with Calexico East.

Key: U = data are unavailable.

Table 2.8

Top Ten Commodities by Value in U.S. Merchandise Trade with NAFTA Partners for All Land Modes, 1995 and 2000 (current U.S. dollars)

Rank in 2000	Commodity description	Value ($billions)	Percent	Rank in 1995	Commodity description	Value ($billions)	Percent
1	Motor vehicles, parts, and accessories	125	21.7	1	Motor vehicles, parts, and accessories	82	22.1
2	Electrical machinery and equipment and parts	89	15.5	2	Nuclear reactors, machinery, and mechanical appliances	48	13.1
3	Nuclear reactors, machinery, and mechanical appliances	75	13.0	3	Electrical machinery and equipment and parts	48	13.1
4	Mineral fuels, mineral oils and products	31	5.3	4	Mineral fuels, mineral oils and products	14	3.7
5	Plastics and related products	22	3.8	5	Special classification provisions	13	3.5
6	Special classification provisions	21	3.6	6	Paper, paperboard, and paper products	13	3.4
7	Paper, paperboard, and paper products	16	2.8	7	Plastics and related products	12	3.3
8	Wood and articles of wood; wood charcoal	13	2.3	8	Aircraft, spacecraft, and parts thereof	12	3.2
9	Furniture, furnishings, lighting products	13	2.3	9	Wood and articles of wood; wood charcoal	9	2.4
10	Optical, photographic, and precision	13	2.3	10	Optical, photographic, and precision	8	2.1
	Total, top 10 commodities	418	72.6		Total, top 10 commodities	259	69.9
	Total, all commodities	576	100.0		Total, all commodities	370	100.0

Source: U.S. Department of Transportaion, Bureau of Transportation Statistics, Transborder Surface Freight Data, 1995 and 2000.
Note: Land trade includes truck, rail, pipeline, and miscellaneous and unknown modes.

government to identify high-risk shipments and travelers in order to speed the passage of low-risk shipments and travelers. In essence, such programs off-load a portion of the cost of security to the government onto the private sector.

The World Customs Organization (WCO) is working on guidelines for new laws and cooperative arrangements between member governments and private industry to improve supply chain security while facilitating international trade flows. However, with 161 members, it will take longer to make progress than it will take to develop such arrangements between the NAFTA countries. Moreover, the WCO program implies a cost to rich country members who are being asked to contribute money and expertise to assist members who lack the resources to introduce new technology and risk management techniques and whose personnel have an "integrity" problem (a euphemism for corruption) (WCO 2002).

In the NAFTA context, there will likely be an additional cost to the U.S. government of subsidizing Mexican security measures. The cost of securing land borders is higher than the cost of securing ports, since the latter can be monitored by satellite, while the former cannot. A common security perimeter could reduce the cost of monitoring land borders within the NAFTA region. Indeed, reducing the cost of customs paperwork and compliance with security measures will be difficult to achieve in the region without a common security perimeter that includes Mexico.

From Just-in-Time to Just-in-Case: The Cost of Security

Before September 11, 2001, a substantial portion of trade between the United States and its NAFTA partners took place in the form of integrated production. Some parts of a car would be produced in Mexico, while other parts of it would be produced in Canada. But the final assembly would be done in the United States. Cheap labor ensured that labor-intensive parts were made in Mexico. The location of raw materials (such as steel) made it cheaper to produce other parts in Canada. Thus, the NAFTA trio became a model of just-in-time production spread across national boundaries.

The events of September 11 changed the equation. Now, the NAFTA countries have to add a cost to their production—the cost of security. How should the additional cost be treated? Should it be like adding a tax to doing business in the form of an additional cost? Although additional security measures do have some characteristics of additional cost, it is not an entirely appropriate analogy. The reason is simple. This additional cost adds up to a (somewhat nebulous) benefit—a lower risk of terrorist attacks. Thus, a more appropriate analogy would be the purchase of a *mandatory* pollution abatement device by a company. The cost of just-in-case therefore has a benefit.

The important question is how much additional cost would this nebulous reduction of risk entail? Would it add significantly to the cost of production and produce a subsequent rise in the price of imported goods? Theoretically, there are two effects on the price of the product in a partial equilibrium model. A rise in cost will induce a shift in the supply of goods. If the demand for the good in question is totally nonresponsive to price (that is, the demand curve is perfectly inelastic), the cost will be transferred fully to the buyer. If the demand for the good is extremely responsive to changes in price (that is, the demand curve is perfectly elastic), the producers will have to absorb the entire cost burden. In a model of markets where all markets are linked through forward and backward linkages (in economic jargon, what is called a *general equilibrium* model), effects of and effects to other markets have to be explored to understand the net effects of an increase in the cost of security measures. Initial comments by experts put the rise in cost at around 3 percent of the cost of production (see, for example, Leonard 2001).

There were additional accompanying events that masked the economic impact of terrorism-related issues. First, a recession was already under way in the United States and Mexico even before the attacks. This created an excess capacity in the transport market that made it impossible to pass the cost to the consumers. Second, there was a fall in the price of oil in the world market that compensated for the rise in the cost of insurance and security-related measures.

To see the impact of falling demand in the market before the events of September 11, we plotted month by month trade statistics of other NAFTA members with the United States (see Figure 2.4). It compares 2001 figures with 2000 figures. There is a clear seasonal pattern. For example, July is a slow month. It is clear from Figure 2.4 that trade between the NAFTA countries had already slowed in June, July, and August 2001 before the events of September 2001. Thus, we see evidence of an economic slowdown before the attack. Following the attack, trade remained at a lower level than in the previous year. Obviously, some of the slowdown is due to the recession. However, we cannot disentangle these two events (recession effect and terrorism effect) from the data.

There were visible effects of rising costs in different modes of transportation. Air security was tightened with more staff, air marshals, secure cockpit doors, and more careful checking of passengers and their luggage. For air freight, there was more rigorous use of xray and gamma-ray machines. Content match shipping labels were used. Insurers and re-insurers revised their "war and allied perils" clause. In general, they simultaneously reduced

Figure 2.4   **Monthly Trade Statistics for the United States with NAFTA Partners, 2000, 2001**

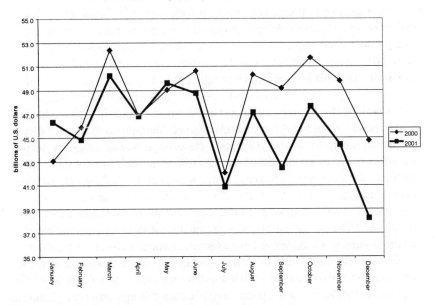

Source: Original data from the INEGI website (www.inegi.gob.mx).

coverage and increased premiums. Similarly, for maritime cargo, a "war risk surcharge" was added. Security was beefed up in ports. In many places, such as the Suez Canal, which is far away from the events of September 11, surcharges went up so much that they added 50 percent to the cost of shipping insurance. Similar rises in road and rail shipping insurance rates came to pass.

How significant are transport and insurance costs? For goods arriving in the United States in 2000, transport and insurance costs amounted to 3.4 percent of the total customs value (OECD 2002). However, such costs are not equally spread across all goods. For goods like pharmaceuticals, the cost is about 1 percent. For big volume goods like fertilizer, the cost is something like 23 percent.

A study by Peter Walkenhorst and Nora Dihel (2002) provides the first empirical evaluation of the economic impacts of the September 11 attacks using a general equilibrium analysis. After extensive analysis of the nature of rising costs, they conclude that an upper bound of the cost will be equivalent to a 1 percent ad valorem tax in the short run. In the long run, the efficiency gain from additional measures (such as streamlined shipping or passage of vehicles) will offset the increase in cost. A 1 percent increase in ad valorem tax leads to a loss of about 0.2 percent in the United States in terms of welfare. In more trade-dependent countries, the loss can be as high as 0.5 percent. Specifically, the welfare loss in the United States and Canada would be around U.S.$13 billion, and in Latin America, it will amount to about U.S.$3 billion. Thus, even the upper limit of such a rise in cost in the short run would be minimal.

Trojan Boxes: Shipping Containers and Security

In October 2001, police in an Italian port found an Al Qaeda suspect inside a Canada-bound shipping container from Egypt. He had a laptop computer, a cell phone, a bed, food, and water, as well as airport plans, security passes, and a mechanic's certificate. About 18 million such containers arrived in American ports in 2001. Customs officers inspect about 2 percent of them ("The Trojan Box").

Containers are "intermodal." They travel by ship, truck, and rail. During their journey, they fall under state, national, and international jurisdiction and are regulated by different laws and government agencies depending on the mode of transport being used at the moment. In international waters they fall under the jurisdiction of the United Nations International Maritime Organization (IMO), but in seaports they are under the jurisdiction of federal governments in different countries. As many as twenty-five different parties may be involved in an international business transaction that involves a sale of goods, transportation, financing, documentation, and inspections ("When trade and security clash"). All of this makes the coordination of security measures very complex.

The efficiency of shipping goods by container allows manufacturers to reduce inventories by just-in-time delivery. Between 1980 and 2000, the ratio of inventory to GDP in the United States declined from 25 percent to 15 percent. A 5 percent increase in inventory would cost American companies an estimated $20 billion more than the $1 trillion now spent on logistics ("When trade and security clash"). The 2002 strike at seaports on the U.S. West Coast demonstrated vividly the economic importance of these trade gateways not only for the United States, but for Canada, Mexico, and Asia as well (see Appendix 2.1, p. 61).

President Clinton established the Graham Commission on Seaport Crime and Security in 1999 to address the lack of security at U.S. seaports. The seaports handle 95 percent of U.S. trade with noncontiguous countries. Commercial port activities in 1996 provided employment for 1.4 million Americans, contributed $74.8 billion to U.S. GDP, and provided personal income of $52.7 billion. The United States has over 100 seaports.

Compared to airports, seaports lack adequate federal administration and security measures. There is no federal agency with control over seaports that equates to Federal Aviation Authority control over airports. For example, the Federal Maritime Commission had only one employee in Florida in 1999, where four of the twenty busiest ports are located. While airports have strict access requirements, seaports do not have identification control, even though the cruise passenger industry moved 10 million passengers in 1999. There is also inadequate screening of workers in ports. Surveys in the 1990s showed that up to 50 percent of dock workers at the port of Miami have prior felony criminal records, many for drug trafficking.

The United States government is examining several ways to enhance security at seaports. One proposal is to have the 162 member nations of the IMO implement a plan to conduct background checks on crew members of every major cargo vessel, create a reliable system to identify the contents of containers, station security officers on all ships, electronically seal cargo containers, and increase budgets for port security. Another proposal is to have U.S. customs inspect containers at the foreign ports of origin, beginning with the top ten sources of U.S.-destined container traffic (including the Chinese ports of Hong Kong and Shanghai). Yet another proposal would require companies to securely seal containers at the factory of origin in return for faster processing through customs.

With respect to stationing U.S. customs agents in foreign ports, discussions with Canada have gone the furthest. There is the precedent of 130 U.S. customs inspectors in Canadian airports, who screen airline passengers headed for the United States. The concept of expanding this to ports was approved by John Manley, the deputy prime minister, and Tom Ridge, the U.S. homeland security director, in their thirty-point Smart Border Declaration, signed in 2001. The United States would like its agents to have the power to open and inspect cargo containers in Canadian ports. However, current talks envisage U.S. agents in Canada and Canadian agents in the United States only being able to flag suspicious cargo for further inspection when they cross the border.

Passengers arriving in the United States can clear U.S. customs and immigration requirements right on Canadian soil. This is possible in all major airports: Vancouver, Toronto, Ottawa, and Montreal. The procedure of being inspected by U.S. immigration agents prior to departure from a foreign state is commonly referred to as "preinspection" or "preclearance." This facility is available for all U.S.-bound passengers (regardless of country of origin of the passengers) in Canada, Ireland, Bermuda, and Aruba. Ireland is the only European country where such a preclearance is allowed. Curiously, preclearance works only one way. For example, it is not possible to get preclearance on U.S. soil for passengers bound for Canada. Mexico is also absent from the preinspection regime. Given that so many Mexicans illegally cross the border with the United States, having U.S. customs and immigration officers posted on Mexican soil is a very sensitive political issue in Mexico.

Once they reach their seaport of destination, shipping containers travel to their final destination via rail or truck. By April 2002, some eighteen Mexican trucking companies had obtained the necessary paperwork for exporting goods to the United States. By the end of 2002, some 500 Mexican trucking companies had precertification paperwork done. This would imply that 90 percent of all goods bound for the United States would have precertification (www.usmcoc.org/pdf/CEGSA percent20250402.pdf, p. 24). The tale of the missing Mexican truck demonstrates the importance of progress in this area (see Appendix 2.2, p. 63).

Keep On Trucking: Mexican Access to U.S. Highways

In February 2001, a NAFTA panel ruled that it was against NAFTA rules for the United States to maintain a moratorium on free movement of trucks between the United States and Mexico. Later, President Bush announced that he would let Mexican trucks in without delay. The ruling and the presidential comment generated a flurry of lobbying by a number of interest groups in Washington.

The dramatic culmination of this dispute came on June 26, 2001, when by a 285–143 roll call, the U.S. House of Representatives voted to block the Department of Transportation (DOT) from issuing permits that would let Mexican trucks operate throughout the United States. This vote was the result of opposition from both the Democrats and the Republicans. The Democrats were pushed hard by the domestic trucking lobby and the Republicans by the insurance lobby in Washington.

Then came September 11. It complicated the dynamics of the debate. On one hand, letting the Mexican trucks in might mean more security hazards. This was the line that the Teamsters union (which has most truckers in the United States in its fold) took. On the other, the September 11 attacks strengthened the position of Bush government with respect to securing funding from Congress. An additional budget was allocated for dealing with trucking. Hence, the high burden of inspectors could be solved—at least in the long run.

In November 2001, both houses of Congress approved measures that would let Mexican trucks in once they have met strict safety and inspection rules. Many of these rules do not apply to domestic truckers and could thus run afoul of NAFTA rules prohibiting discrimination. Moreover, Mexican truckers would be kept out until the U.S. inspector general and secretary of transportation certified that the U.S. government is capable of enforcing the new standards.

A new twist to the story unfolded on December 11, 2001. Mexican truckers filed a class action lawsuit in Brownsville, Texas, accusing the DOT of racial discrimination for denying Mexican trucking companies access to the U.S. market over the past six years, contrary to NAFTA requirements. Filed in U.S. district court, the suit asked for $4 billion in lost revenue for nearly 200 Mexican nationals who have applied for permits in the past six years to drive their trucks into the United States or to operate U.S.-based trucking companies. It argued that since Canadian truckers are allowed into the United States, Mexicans should have been allowed as well under NAFTA.

Teaming Up: The Teamsters and Other Unions

The U.S. trucking unions opposed the entry of Mexican truckers into the United States to transport goods on the grounds that the Mexican truckers will not meet U.S. safety standards. Underlying this opposition is the reality that U.S. truckers are likely to lose a lot of business. Each year, about 5 million crossings are made, hauling about three-fourths of the $250 billion in United States–Mexico trade. Under a NAFTA panel ruling, instead of Mexican trucks transferring their loads to U.S. truckers at the border, the Mexican truckers will be able to carry the load to its final destination in the United States. Moreover, transportation of goods by Mexican truckers would cost less, as the wages earned by the Mexican drivers are a fraction of what the unionized U.S. truckers charge for their services. Between 1990 and 2000, the hourly wage rate of U.S. truckers went from U.S.$11.86 to U.S.$14.52. Although no reliable estimate of hourly wage rate of Mexican truckers is available, it is unlikely that they earned more than U.S.$8.00 per hour in 2000 (www.sddialogue.org/Report/Aug01/pg5.html "guesstimate" of earnings by Mexican drivers). Thus, the economic value of the threat to the U.S. truckers is quite substantial.

A Blast from the Past: A Short History of Highway Access

Prior to 1980, the United States granted operating authority to motor carriers for each individual route, requiring economic justification for each proposed service. It did not distinguish between United States, Mexican, or Canadian applicants. However, the Interstate Commerce Commission (ICC) severely restricted new entry into the domestic market. In 1980, the Motor Carrier Act essentially eliminated regulatory barriers to entry, making it easier for motor carriers from all three countries to obtain operating authority. It did not distinguish between nationals and nonnationals. At the time, Canada already allowed reciprocal access for U.S. truckers in its domestic market, but Mexico did not.

The equal treatment of U.S. and foreign applicants ended in 1982. The Bus Regulatory Reform Act imposed an initial two-year moratorium on the issuance of new motor carrier operating authority to foreign carriers. A presidential memorandum immediately lifted the moratorium with respect to Canada in response to the Brock-Gotlieb Understanding, which confirmed that U.S. carriers would have continued access to the Canadian market. The same memorandum declined to lift the moratorium with respect to Mexico, citing U.S. truckers' continued lack of access to the Mexican market. The U.S. president repeatedly extended the moratorium against Mexican truckers every two years from 1984 to 1995. The purpose of the moratorium was to encourage Mexico to lift its restrictions on market access for U.S. firms.

However, there were some exceptions allowed to facilitate cross-border trade. The commercial zone of border towns exemption has permitted Mexican carriers to operate in the commercial zones associated with municipalities along the border since before 1982, provided they obtained a certificate of registration from the Federal Motor Carrier Safety Administration. Under this procedure, applicants certify that they have access to and will comply with federal motor carrier safety regulations. Applicants are not required to submit proof of insurance, but inside the commercial zones must carry proof of insurance on board. In 1999, 8,400 Mexican firms had authority to operate in the commercial zones.

A second exception relates to Mexican operators that transit through the United States to Canada. They are not affected by the moratorium. Congress has not granted the DOT the authority to require trucks transiting from Mexico to Canada to seek operating authority, so it is not required. These Mexican trucks need only comply with U.S. insurance requirements and safety regulations.

Under a third exception, grandfathered Mexican trucking companies that had acquired operating authority prior to 1982, when the moratorium came into effect, are not affected. Five Mexican carriers are entitled to this exemption.

Under a fourth exception, the ICC Termination Act of 1995 exempts U.S.-owned Mexican-domiciled truck companies—approximately 160 companies—from the operation of the moratorium. A fifth exception, which allowed Mexican carriers to lease both trucks and drivers to U.S. carriers, was allowed until January 1, 2000. The Motor Carrier Safety Improvement Act of 1999 ended the leasing exception when the United States realized that this provision could be used to sell U.S. carriers' operating authority to Mexican carriers for operations beyond the border zone.

On March 1, 1994, the transportation ministers of Canada and Mexico signed three memoranda of understanding to permit truckers to operate between Canada and Mexico. The cargo-exchange agreement permits Canadian truckers to enter Mexico to exchange cargoes at contracted Mexican terminals and facilities along the northern border. The commercial driver's license reciprocity agreement lets Canadian and Mexican drivers operate in each other's country with their own licenses. The transportation training agreement allows Canada to train Mexican personnel in the areas of maritime and port management and truck-driving simulation.

Under a memorandum of understanding (MOU) between the United States, Mexico and Canada, U.S. truck carriers are able to carry freight from Canada to 12 miles (20 kilometers) inside Mexico in a nearly barrier-free environment. Despite the MOU, the governments of the United States and Mexico have been at an impasse over permitting full access to each other's markets since 1995.

Under NAFTA, the United States agreed to give access to Mexican trucks in 1995, but President Bill Clinton, under heavy pressure from religious, labor, environmental, and other interest groups, kept the provision from taking effect, saying Mexico had to do more to address safety problems first. That year, the Mexican government, invoking NAFTA provisions, asked that a five-member panel be set up to determine whether Washington was violating the agreement. In its decision, the panel—two Americans, two Mexicans, and a British chairman—unanimously ruled that the United States would be in violation if it did not begin considering applications from Mexican trucking companies. At the time, more than 160 applications were pending.

Operating authority from the ICC was required to provide interstate or cross-border truck services in the United States. Under NAFTA, a moratorium remained in place on new grants of operating authority for persons from Mexico. However, the United States agreed to phase out the moratorium so that Mexicans would be permitted to obtain operating authority to provide cross-border truck services to or from border states (California, Arizona, New Mexico, and Texas) as of December 16, 1995. Cross-border truck services to the remainder of the United States were to start as of January 1, 2000. In addition, Mexicans were to be permitted to establish an enterprise in the United States to provide truck services for the transportation of international cargo between points in the United States as of December 17, 1995. The moratorium remains in place on grants of authority for the provision of truck services by Mexicans between points in the United States for the transportation of goods other than international cargo.

Deeper Thought: The NAFTA Panel Ruling

The decision of the NAFTA panel requires the DOT to consider applications on individual merit and not to refuse authority across the board to all Mexican companies. In essence, the United States had argued that it could deny access to all Mexican trucking firms on a blanket basis, regardless of the individual qualifications of particular members of the Mexican industry, unless and until Mexico's domestic regulatory system meets U.S. approval. However, the law of the United States considered applications for operating authority from U.S. and Canadian carriers on an individual basis. This differential treatment of Mexicans, on the one hand, and Americans and Canadians, on the other, violated NAFTA nondiscrimination Articles 1202 (national treatment) and 1203 (most-favored-nation treatment).

The United States argued that the continuation of the moratorium was nevertheless justified under the general exception of Article 2101, which provides that "nothing . . . in Chapter 12 (Cross-border Trade in Services) . . . shall be construed to prevent the adoption or enforcement by any party of measures necessary to secure compliance with laws or regulations . . . relating to health and safety and consumer protection." The panel, however, ruled that the United States had to use the least-trade-restrictive means available to address its safety concerns. The numerous exceptions the United States applied to the moratorium proved that there were less restrictive means available to achieve its safety goals with respect to Mexican truckers. Thus, the blanket ban could not be justified under Article 2101.

The NAFTA panel made clear that the United States is entitled under NAFTA to set its own safety standards and to ensure that Mexican trucking companies meet them. Moreover, the United States is not required to treat applications from Mexican truckers in exactly the same manner as applications from U.S. or Canadian firms, as long as they are reviewed on a case-by-case basis and comply with the NAFTA, and as long as decisions are made in good faith with respect to a legitimate safety concern.

Following the panel decision, the Bush administration announced that it would reverse the Clinton administration policy and begin allowing Mexican trucks to haul goods throughout the United States.

Strange Bedfellows: The Economics of Opposition

It is unreasonable to assume that Mexicans will try to send less reliable trucks across the border. Why? Many of these trucks are carrying agricultural products that would be lost if the trucks break down and the products do not reach the final destination on time. The producers on the Mexican side will make sure that only the best trucks are used in such cases. The other trucks that carry intermediate products for just-in-time production will also be reliable for the same reason—any delay would lead to losses for the companies.

Curiously, U.S. truckers are not the only industry opposing the Mexican truckers. U.S. insurance companies are also up in arms. Why? They sell insurance to the U.S. truckers—not only vehicle and liability insurance, but insurance on the goods being transported. A reduction in the market share of the U.S. truckers will also reduce the market share of the U.S. companies that insure them. The Mexican truckers will buy insurance from insurance companies in Mexico. Of course, the U.S. insurance companies may be concerned that Mexican truckers will cause more accidents than U.S. truckers, thereby increasing pay-outs by insurance companies. But if the Mexican truckers are insured by Mexican insurance companies, those payments would not come out of the pockets of the U.S. insurance companies.

The American Insurance Association (AIA) argues that Mexican trucks should only be allowed to operate in the border states until three programs are implemented. First, the AIA wants safety standards among the three NAFTA countries harmonized. Second, adequate enforcement of those standards must be implemented. Third, an adequate database of Mexican truck safety must be developed. The AIA proposal appears reasonable on the surface, but is in fact designed to delay the entry of Mexican truckers beyond the border states for many years. Under NAFTA, there is no requirement to harmonize safety standards, and it may be difficult to get the countries to negotiate such an agreement. Even if such an agreement were reached, corruption in Mexico means that adequate enforcement in Mexico could not be achieved for many years. Finally, the creation of a database on Mexican truck safety would be costly and time-consuming and would likely serve as further ammunition in the effort to keep Mexican trucks out of the U.S. market.

Nevertheless, some progress has been made by the NAFTA land transportation standards subcommittee, which is charged with the task of implementing a work program to make standards for bus and truck operations compatible. In 1991, Mexico became a member of the Commercial Vehicles Safety Alliance, together with the United States and Canada. The same year, Mexico and the United States adopted uniform guidelines for roadside inspections and uniform standards for commercial drivers' licenses and criteria such as knowledge and skills testing, disqualification, and physical requirements for drivers.

Up Close and Personal: A Look at the DOT Report

In 1998, the U.S. DOT produced a report that sealed the fate of the Mexican truckers in the United States. The report claimed that Mexican trucks do not meet U.S. safety standards. The DOT reported that in 1997 44 percent of Mexican trucks inspected did not meet the safety standards. Insurance industry trade groups argue that the U.S. government will have to spend $4 to $7 million a year to increase the number of safety inspectors at the border. Mexican trucks have been allowed to cross the border twenty miles into the United States to transfer cargo to U.S. trucks.

A closer inspection of the report produces a different picture. A much less quoted figure of the report says that although 44 percent of the Mexican trucks inspected did not meet the safety standards, 27 percent of the U.S. trucks (and a much lower 17 percent of the Canadian trucks) did not meet the safety standards either. On the face of it, it still seems that Mexican trucks have a significantly higher failure rate in meeting the safety standards. Such a presumption is false. Why?

When we examine the disaggregated data by state—California (failure rate of 28 percent), Arizona (42 percent), New Mexico (37 percent), and Texas (50 percent)—we find vastly different failure rates. The DOT report also quotes more recent figures (that is, for 1998) showing that the overall failure rate for Mexican trucks decreased to 42 percent rather than the 44 percent quoted for 1997. Thus, it is not the same problem across different states. There should be no presumption that Mexico only sends "better trucks" across to California and "worse trucks" across to Texas!

The problem lies with the process of inspection. The DOT report acknowledges that the process is not random checking (p. 32). If a truck "looks bad" then it is inspected more minutely. Therefore, it seems that the inspection process varies substantially across states, making the overall number of "44 percent bad trucks" completely useless.

Size Matters: Dimensions of the Problem

How large is the problem? How many trucks cross the border to enter into the United States? In many press reports, the presumed number of truck crossings cited is in the region of 4.5 million trucks. Thus, it is argued, allowing Mexicans to enter the U.S. roads will pose a very large problem. For example, the Public Citizen Organization (a lobby group) declared in a highly charged article called "The Coming NAFTA Crash" that if Mexican trucks are allowed into the United States, to have a simple inspection, the DOT would require at least 32,000 more inspectors. This will overwhelm the DOT's border inspection system. It turns out that the number of trucks actually crossing the border (in 1999) was 63,000. How did the 4.5 million come about? There seems to be some confusion about the number of crossings and the number of trucks. It is true that there were 4.5 million crossings made by trucks, but the same trucks crossed the border time and again. Hence the presumed problem turns out to be a storm in a teacup!

Different Strokes for Different Folks: Highway Standards

It is possible to drive along freeways from Mexico City to Winnipeg. An excellent road, Highway 85, runs from Mexico City to Laredo. From Laredo to Kansas City, one takes Interstate 35, then Interstate 29 up to the Canadian border, and then Highway 75 to Winnipeg. This route is sometime called the "NAFTA superhighway." Another such route runs from Mexico City to Edmonton in Canada. It may seem that the only element lacking for such truck routes is smooth passage through the border. But there are many complications.

First, vehicle weight limits are not the same throughout North America. On Highway 75 in Manitoba, Canada, the limit for tractor semitrailers is 100,232 pounds (45,560 kilos) and 137,500 pounds (62,500 kilos) for double trailers. The weight limit in North and South Dakota along I-29 is 79,831 pounds (36,287 kilos) for tractor semitrailers. To make matters worse, for double trailers, North Dakota has a limit of 105,281 pounds (47,855 kilos) and South Dakota has a limit of 124,740 pounds (56,700 kilos). In Kansas, along I-35, weight limits for both tractor semitrailers are the same at 85,323 pounds (38,783 kilos). Along the same highway I-35, in Oklahoma, the limit rises to 89,813 pounds (40,824 kilos) for both types only to fall to 79,831 pounds (36,287 kilos) in Texas. It rises again in Mexico, to 106,700 pounds (48,500 kilos) for tractor semitrailers and 146,300 pounds (66,500 kilos) for double trailers (Prentice and Ojah 2001).

Second, differences in diesel standards can play havoc on the engines. Mexican diesel fuel generally has a higher sulfur content than the corresponding American diesel. Thus, driving the same truck coming from Texas all the way through Mexico City is impractical.

Third, there are also differences in trucking laws between the United States and Mexico. The United States requires front-wheel brakes, whereas Mexico does not. The United States requires drivers to meet licensing standards that include limits on the length of their driving shifts and drug testing, while Mexico does not. The United States requires the maintenance of driving logs or other types of data that would be needed for enforcement, while Mexico does not.

Fourth, there are differences in customs procedures between Mexico and the United States. Mexico is concerned to prevent illegal arms and goods without duty paid from entering Mexico. The main concern for U.S. customs is drugs. Mexican customs requirements are far more stringent than those of the United States. All paperwork has to match the load exactly.

However, differences between Mexico and the United States in these areas would not prevent Mexican truckers from ensuring they meet U.S. standards. Indeed, trucking companies that seek to operate across the border would be wise to impose the necessary standards in-house. In fact, Mexican truck companies that have applied for operation in the United States have pledged that they will send only the trucks that comply with "normal" U.S. standards.

Never Ending Story: The Highway Story Keeps Going

On November 27, 2002, President Bush modified the moratorium on granting operating authority to Mexican motor carriers. As a practical matter, this service would have begun only after the federal government reviewed Mexican carrier applications and granted provisional operating authority to qualified Mexican truck and bus companies. Transportation secretary Norman Y. Mineta directed the U.S. Department of Transportations Federal Motor Carrier Safety Administration (FMCSA) to act on the 130 applications received from Mexico-domiciled truck and bus companies. The truck companies want to transport international cargo to and from the United States and the bus companies want to provide regular route service between Mexico and the United States.

On December 3, 2002, a coalition of environmental, labor and trucking industry groups asked a judge for an emergency stay of President Bush's decision to open U.S. highways to trucks from Mexico. The groups claimed that the federal government did not adequately review the impact the trucks would have on air quality in the United States. So now border air quality is the issue, rather than security or highway safety. This legal action was taken despite a study undertaken by DOT showing that the entry of Mexican trucks would have no significant impact on the environment. Al Meyerhoff, an attorney for the plaintiffs, said more than half the trucks in the Mexican fleet date from before 1994, when there were fewer regulations on their emissions. The U.S. environmental protection agency has adopted even stricter requirements, to be phased in over the next couple of years for new trucks. Meyerhoff said his clients believe that the Mexican trucks are not being held to those standards.

On February 9, 2003, the U.S. court of appeals for the ninth circuit (of San Francisco) ruled that in the case of *Public Citizen* v. *U.S. Department of Transportation*, DOT cannot forsake state emission limits for pollutants under the Clean Air Act and National Environmental Policy Act (NEPA).

The decision requires DOT to prepare full environmental impact statements under NEPA before approving the operation of Mexican motorcarriers in the United States. President Bush ordered the transportation secretary to lift the moratorium on the entry of Mexican trucks before an environmental impact study (EIS) was conducted.

The court ruled that NEPA requires an EIS for all "major federal actions significantly affecting the human environment." In addition, the court ruled that the uncertainty of the level of pollutants from Mexican trucks requires an EIS, particularly since NAFTA creates an increase in cross-border trucking and directly affects the level of emissions in local environments.

Highway Robbery: Hijacking the National Security Debate

In the wake of September 11, the United States could argue that restrictions on Mexican truckers are justifiable under the national security exception of NAFTA. However, the same reasoning the panel applied to the safety exception would apply to the security exception—the numerous exceptions to the moratorium demonstrate that there is a less-trade-restrictive means to ensure national security than through a blanket ban. Nevertheless, the United States could take the position that a NAFTA panel has no jurisdiction to rule on national security measures in the first place and could thus preempt the possibility of an adverse ruling. To date, the border security measures have been implemented so as to minimize disruption to trade while maximizing security. However, the national security argument provides a tempting shield behind which to hide restrictions whose true purpose is to keep out foreign competition.

International agreements restrict the options available to the domestic industry in terms of protecting its national market from foreign competition. The trucking case shows how industry trade groups can influence the trade policy of a government by the selective use of information and by pursuing their economic interests in a way that makes it appear they are really seeking what is in the public interest. Most often, however, their goal is to protect their domestic market from foreign competitors.

The Not-So-Great Barrier: Implications for Business

The liberalization of the transportation industry has business implications for both the firms in the transportation industry and for firms who rely on them to transport goods. The current state of trade and investment liberalization under NAFTA reduces competition in these industries, which in turn leads to higher transportation costs for clients and greater variation in costs across the three countries. As a general rule, the restrictions on trade and investment damage Canadian and Mexican firms more than U.S. firms from both perspectives. For example, with respect to the firms that use the transportation services, firms located in Mexico are put at a relative disadvantage due to higher transportation costs. With respect to the transportation industry itself, U.S. restrictions such as cabotage rules favor the U.S. trucking and shipping industries at the expense of Canadian and Mexican competitors. (Cabotage rules stipulate that only U.S. carriers may transport goods between points within the United States.)

The security measures applied to the transportation of goods have an impact on both transportation costs and the cost of in-house security measures. To counteract these costs, we propose NAFTA reforms to reduce transportation cost by eliminating air and water transport restrictions, such as cabotage and foreign investment restrictions, in order to allow consolidation of the industry. With respect to trucking, we recommend avoiding the use of the security argument to maintain restrictions on trucking and further liberalization of the industry. Allowing full competition within the region will reduce costs. Allowing consolidation in the transportation industry will also facilitate security measures taken by firms by reducing the number of players involved. However, there are serious political obstacles to the implementation of these recommendations, as demonstrated by the trucking case.

Barriers to trade in goods affect sourcing strategies for importers and for manufacturers. Firms that import goods on a global basis—for example, retailers such as Wal-Mart—generally seek the best product at the lowest price. Barriers may cause the firm to choose one source over another. The same applies to manufacturers who import inputs. The cost and reliability of transportation routes are thus a very important consideration for businesses shopping for goods overseas.

The competitiveness of a firm's product in export markets is affected by the price increases implied in the cost of moving the product across the border. For example, import tariffs are designed to protect the domestic industry from foreign competition on the basis of price. If the exporter chooses to absorb the cost of the tariff by charging a lower price in the export market, the exporter runs the risk of antidumping duties. Like tariffs, cross-border transportation costs can influence whether the firm chooses to compete on price or on other product characteristics, such as the quality or image of the product.

Trade barriers also influence whether a firm chooses to enter a foreign market using an export strategy or a foreign direct investment strategy. Where the trade barriers in the target market make exporting impractical, the firm may have to invest in manufacturing facilities inside the market. Similarly, transportation costs can be a major factor in determining a market entry strategy.

With respect to North American imports, these factors may determine whether some imports come from within the NAFTA region or from outside the region and whether North American and non–North American firms locate manufacturing facilities inside or outside the region. With respect to exports to the United States, the comparative advantages of shipping by land, sea, or air can thus influence the attractiveness of Canada and Mexico, both of which have the advantage of being able to ship goods to the United States by land.

Conclusion

Merchandise trade, transportation systems, border measures, and security programs are intricately linked not only to each other but, increasingly, to the competitiveness of business and economic prosperity in the NAFTA region. The good news is that the benefits of investments in efficient border and transportation systems are likely to exceed their cost. For example, preclearance programs pay off in more ways than one, by both enhancing efficiency and security while freeing up resources to dedicate to genuine security threats. Increasing economic integration in the region only serves to augment the benefits of these investments.

The closure of U.S. borders following the September 11 attacks and the closure of West Coast ports in the fall of 2002 (see Appendix 2.1, p. 61) both demonstrate how unpleasant (and inefficient) the alternative to the smooth cross-border movement of goods is. At the same time, the case of the missing Mexican truck (see Appendix 2.2, p. 63) demonstrates the potentially severe consequences of failure to coordinate the actions of NAFTA governments in the area of secure movement of goods. As the Mexico–United States trucking dispute shows, securing a prosperous future in the region will entail overcoming the efforts of special interest groups to hijack the political agenda.

Appendix 2.1
Ports in a Storm: Plugged Passageways
on the West Coast

The twenty-nine seaports on the West Coast of the United States process about $300 billion in cargo a year. On September 29, 2002, in response to a job slowdown, the port operators locked out 10,500 longshoremen and shut the ports. Robert Parry, president of the Federal Reserve Board of San Francisco, calculated that the port closures would cost the U.S. economy $2 billion per day (Greenhouse 2002c). Others estimated that a five-day shutdown could cost the U.S. economy almost $5 billion, while a ten-day closure could cost up to $20 billion as the effects spread throughout the economy (Greenhouse 2002a).

The shutdown came after a temporary, thirty-six-hour lockout. The dispute centered on a plan to introduce new cargo-handling technology (Greenhouse 2002c). Optical scanners would process cargo trucks more quickly and global positioning satellites would track cargo during its journey (Greenhouse 2002a). The union refused to accept the new technology unless the new jobs were unionized (Greenhouse 2002c). The average salary of full-time West Coast union members that load and unload ships is about U.S.$100,000 a year. Clerks who track cargo movements make an average of U.S.$120,000 a year. The value of benefits averages U.S.$42,000 a year (Greenhouse 2002b).

With these salaries, the longshoremen could afford to engage in a lengthy work stoppage. However, shipping lines cannot divert their cargo to other ports. Mexico's infrastructure is inadequate to process the cargo. Nevertheless, between September 27 and October 7, over 10,000 U.S.-bound containers were unloaded at eight Mexican ports. However, this represented only a fraction of the backed-up cargo sitting on ships. Canadian longshoremen supported their U.S. colleagues by refusing to unload the diverted ships. The Panama Canal is too small to divert most of the Pacific ships to East Coast ports due to their size. Moreover, the time-sensitive nature of much of the cargo gave the workers added bargaining power (Greenhouse 2002b).

President Bush initially urged the parties to use a federal mediator to resolve the labor dispute, hoping to avoid antagonizing labor unions just before congressional elections in November (Greenhouse 2002a). The unions opposed the president's invoking the Taft-Hartley Act (Greenhouse 2002c).

On October 8, the White House announced that President Bush would invoke the Taft-Hartley Act to seek a court injunction to reopen West Coast ports for an eighty-day cooling-off period. The decision came after a White House board of inquiry concluded that the dispute had no chance of ending soon. The decision to invoke the act represented a trade-off between risking greater turnout of Democrat voters and negating the growing perception among voters that Bush was neglecting the economy with his focus on Iraq. The eighty-day period would get imports flowing to retailers during the Christmas shopping season ("Bush to Seek Court Order . . ." 2002). In addition, the president was concerned about the movement of military supplies from West Coast ports if fighting erupted in Iraq or elsewhere in the Middle East. These supplies are often transported on commercial shipping lines (Sanger and Greenhouse 2002). On October 9, the federal district court in San Francisco issued a temporary injunction ordering the immediate reopening of the ports, the first such order since President Richard Nixon had invoked the Taft-Hartley Act to stop a longshoremen's strike in 1971 (Sanger and Greenhouse 2002). About 225 vessels were backed up during the lockout (Murphy 2002).

The National Association of Manufacturers and retailers supported Bush's decision, while the AFL-CIO denounced the move. The 1947 Taft-Hartley Act authorizes the president to seek injunctions against strikes and lockouts that "imperil the national health or safety." During a sixty-day cooling-off period, mediators continue to work with the parties. The National Labor Relations Board then has fifteen days to conduct a poll in which employees decide on management's final proposal and a further five days to count the votes. If the workers reject the proposal, they can strike at the end of this eighty-day period (Sanger and Greenhouse 2002).

The shutdown did not appear to have caused serious damage to big exporters like

China, Japan, and Taiwan. Many East Asian companies took precautions in anticipation of the port closings. For example, Taiwan-based Giant Manufacturing Company, which is one of the world's largest bicycle manufacturers, sent huge extra shipments to American warehouses over the summer to avoid a disruption of supply. Some high-technology companies booked extra shipments in advance on special air freight services. Nevertheless, shipping containers began to pile up at Hong Kong container ports, prompting the Hong Kong government to set up a task force to manage the distribution of scarce empty containers to exporters in southern China. Moreover, clothing companies accumulated large inventories of unshipped merchandise because buyers were not willing to pay for air freight. Most affected were businesses supplying parts to manufacturers in the United States that use just-in-time delivery. Toyota increased air shipments of auto parts to the United States while waiting for ports to reopen and backlogs to clear (Bradsher 2002). Honda plants in Alabama, Ohio, and Ontario were closed for several days due to a parts shortage caused by the port closure and the subsequent backlog, which continued to cause problems even after the longshoremen went back to work ("Honda's Ontario Plant…" 2002; Brieger 2002). Toyota and Nissan calculated that the port closure would reduce October vehicle sales by 10 percent ("Automakers Forecast" 2002).

However, the port closure was not all bad news. It was good for air freight companies. China Airlines, the world's eighth largest hauler of air cargo, scheduled eight extra flights of Boeing 747–400 freighters to Los Angeles and Chicago, increasing its cargo capacity on these routes by 15 percent. To free pilots for the extra trips, the airline canceled several passenger flights (Bradsher 2002). Moreover, the impact the closure had on just-in-time manufacturers could make them think twice about the advantages of locating more production in Canada and Mexico, countries that do not rely on seaports to enter the United States.

Appendix 2.2
Cyanara Security: The Terrifying Tale
of the Missing Mexican Truck

On May 13, 2002, a truck went missing in the state of Hidalgo along Highway 85, north of Mexico City. This is not an uncommon event on the highways of Mexico. What forced the FBI to fly down to Mexico to investigate this particular incident was that the tractor-trailer was hauling some ten tons of sodium cyanide in ninety-six drums. Sodium cyanide, while not as lethal as its cousin potassium cyanide, can still kill people with a dose of 100 milligrams (which is as small as a pill). The chemical is routinely used in the silver extraction process. Since Mexico is the largest silver producer in the world, large quantities of sodium cyanide are routinely transported hundreds of miles, from production plants to silver mines located in northern Mexico.

Three days after it went missing, the truck was found. But only thirteen of the ninety-six drums were still in the truck. The missing drums set off alarm bells all along the southern border of the United States. What if some terrorists had taken the cargo and were trying to smuggle it across the border? Following the September 11 attacks on New York and Washington, there had been reports from New Zealand and Italy of cyanide threats against U.S. embassies. With the Memorial Day weekend approaching and with vague threats of a possible terrorist attack occurring over that weekend, the possibility seemed real enough. After all, the amount of cargo that passes between the United States and Mexico by road now exceeds millions of crossings per year (although the *number* of trucks is nowhere near that). Many people were already thinking aloud about the worst possible scenario. For example, Landstar Safety's Steve Gullekson told a local television station in Dallas, "They could transfer it to another truck, mark it as something else, and, unless they look suspicious, nobody's gonna look at it."

Would such a thing happen? Could such a thing happen? Well, it didn't! On May 29, seventy drums were found abandoned near the city of Puebla, in the Mexican state of Puebla. This still left another thirteen drums unaccounted for. Two days later, the remaining drums were also found.

What lessons does this episode hold for the management of security issues between Mexico and the United States, whose complicated relationship has already generated so much heat between the two countries?

One lesson relates to the bilateral coordination of cargo transportation. This episode illustrated how inefficient the "hunt and peck" method of cooperation truly is. This case was specifically taken up by the FBI only after it learned the nature of the cargo. If U.S. and Mexican security forces were to automatically share this type of information, dealing with such incidents could become a routine matter.

With better coordination, trucks that have preclearance would not have to go through the regular inspection process. They would simply bypass the regular checkpoints at the border after being inspected and sealed by U.S. agents at their point of origin. This would be easy to do with the Mexican government's cooperation. It would also solve border bottlenecks for 90 percent of all goods that cross the border. Only a small number of companies account for the bulk of the trade between the United States and Mexico.

Another lesson has to do with the coordination of the cross-border movement of people. The type of preclearance alluded to above can also be applied to people. Any person flying from Canada to the United States clears U.S. immigration procedures on Canadian soil (with U.S. officials stationed at Canadian airports). Frequent border crossers use a special pass when crossing by land (see Chapter 3).

Close cooperation between the authorities in all three NAFTA countries, combined with preclearance programs for goods and people, would not only enhance border security, but free up resources to address genuine threats and enhance the efficiency of business and border systems in the region. Thus, while incidents such as the missing Mexican truck can strike fear into the hearts of Americans, they serve to spark the kind of actions needed to simultaneously improve security, enhance business, and further economic efficiency in an integrated North American economy.

3

Do You Know the Way to San Jose?

Integrating Labor Markets and Securing Borders

> "Tough times never last, tough people do."
> —*Fred Akers*

> "There can be no privileged U.S.–Mexico relationship without
> actual progress on substantive issues. And there will be no
> substantive progress without comprehensively addressing the
> issue of migration."
> —*Vicente Fox*

The exact implications of September 11 for the movement of people in the
NAFTA region remain unclear. Both the northern and southern borders need
to be secured in a way that does not impede the flows of people that form an
integral part of economic activity in the region. However, there is no one-
size-fits-all approach that will work. People movement issues on the two
borders are very different. For this reason, we examine the two borders separately in this chapter.

With Mexico, the central issue is how to resolve the problem of undocumented workers migrating to the United States. These workers do not represent a threat to national security, but they divert resources that could be devoted
to security threats and create a demand for illegal people smuggling and
fraudulent documents.

With Canada, illegal immigration of Canadians is not a big problem. Rather,
the issue is how to structure cross-border cooperation to minimize threats
while maintaining a degree of independence with respect to immigration
policies. In this regard, Canada–United States cooperation sets precedents
for similar arrangements with Mexico and other countries.

Table 3.1

Top Ten U.S.–Canada Border Crossings for Incoming Passengers and Personal Vehicles, 2000

Rank	U.S. customs port/crossing	Passengers in personal vehicles per day	Personal vehicles per day	Daily port share of personal vehicles crossing U.S.– Canada border (percent)
1	Detroit, MI	59,518	22,905	22.6
2	Buffalo–Niagara, NY	45,269	20,980	20.7
3	Blaine, WA	22,560	9,129	9.0
4	Port Huron, MI	18,810	6,390	6.3
5	Calais, ME	8,525	3,875	3.8
6	Sault Ste. Marie, MI	10,634	3,498	3.5
7	Massena, NY	8,340	2,987	3.0
8	Champlain–Rouse Point, NY	7,526	2,685	2.7
9	Sumas, WA	5,583	2,243	2.2
10	Derby Line, VT	4,144	2,190	2.2
	Total, top 10 ports	190,909	76,882	76.0
	Total, all U.S.–Canada border crossings	246,704	101,137	100.0

Sources: U.S. Department of Transportation, Bureau of Transportation Statistics, special tabulation, June 2001; based on U.S. Department of Treasury, U.S. Customs Service, Mission Support Services, Office of Field Operations, Operations Management Database CD.

Note: Rank is based on the number of personal vehicle crossings per day.

Crossing the Line: People Flows

On the northern border, roughly 5 million Canadians and 6 million Americans cross the border each month. An estimated 25 million people cross the southern border each month (see Table 1.1). NAFTA has made it easier for traders, investors, and professionals to cross the border and many border merchants depend on cross-border traffic. As seen in Tables 3.1 and 3.2, the busiest crossings process tens of thousands of passengers per day.

The majority of trips to the United States from Canada and Mexico consist of same-day travel. In terms of overnight visits, Canadian and Mexican residents rank first and second (with Japan a distant third), respectively, as shown in Table 3.3.

The number of legal crossings on the southern border is an astonishing 314 million a year. The Canadian side gets over 100 million. Sometimes these numbers get distorted in media reports. It is mostly the same people who are crossing and recrossing the border—some people cross several times a day. Thus, the number of people crossing the borders each year could be calculated by reducing the above numbers by a factor of 300.

Table 3.2

Top Ten U.S.–Mexico Border Crossings for Incoming Passengers and Personal Vehicles, 2000

Rank	U.S. Customs port/crossing	Passengers in personal vehicles per day	Personal vehicles per day	Daily port share of personal vehicles crossing U.S.–Mexico border (percent)
1	El Paso, TX	132,658	45,746	18.3
2	San Ysidro, CA	85,001	38,649	15.5
3	Hidalgo, TX	60,131	24,054	9.6
4	Brownsville, TX	53,954	21,582	8.6
5	Laredo, TX	48,980	19,592	7.8
6	Calexico, CA	55,053	18,479	7.4
7	Otay Mesa, CA	29,204	13,275	5.3
8	Nogales, AZ	31,511	12,826	5.1
9	Eagle Pass, TX	23,546	9,199	3.7
10	San Luis, AZ	19,365	7,117	2.8
	Total, top 10 ports	539,403	210,519	84.1
	Total, all U.S.–Mexico border crossings	656,971	249,745	100.0

Sources: U.S. Department of Transportation, Bureau of Transportation Statistics, special tabulation, June 2001; based on U.S. Department of Treasury, U.S. Customs Service, Mission Support Services, Office of Field Operations, Operations Management Database CD.
Note: Rank is based on the number of personal vehicle crossings per day.

The number of illegal entrants caught every year is over a million. Once again, many of the same people are caught many times. Thus, the number of people illegally crossing the borders should be calculated by reducing by a factor of 5 to 10. How do we know that? Estimates of numbers of illegal entrants (as opposed to illegal entries) are available. For example, Warren (1995) estimates that the average number of Mexicans illegally entering the United States was around 164,000 per year between 1982 and 1992. Among the nationalities of estimated illegal aliens residing in the United States, Mexico dwarfs the other three top source countries (El Salvador, Guatemala, and surprisingly, Canada), as shown in Figure 3.1.

The fact that El Salvador and Guatemala rank second and third as sources of illegal aliens points to the importance of securing Mexico's southern border.

On the southern border, the politicians may be ahead of the people in terms of the degree of policy harmonization they would be willing to accept. The United States may encounter more resistance among the Mexican people than among the Canadians to the notion of giving up some national sovereignty in order to ensure the security of the region. However, the Fox administration has improved cooperation on many fronts, including a degree of harmonization of immigration policies, in order to reduce

Table 3.3

Top Fifteen Countries for Overnight Travel to the United States, 2000

Rank	Country	Number (thousands)	Percent
1	Canada	14,594	28.7
2	Mexico	10,322	20.3
3	Japan	5,061	9.9
4	United Kingdom	4,703	9.2
5	Germany	1,786	3.5
6	France	1,087	2.1
7	Brazil	737	1.4
8	South Korea	662	1.3
9	Italy	612	1.2
10	Venezuela	577	1.1
11	Netherlands	553	1.1
12	Australia	540	1.1
13	Argentina	534	1.0
14	Taiwan	457	0.9
15	China	453	0.9
	Total, top 15 countries	42,678	83.7
	Total, all countries	50,891	100.0

Source: U.S. Department of Commerce, International Trade Administration, Office of Tourism Industries, "Arrivals to the U.S. 2000 & 1999," available at http://tinet.ita.doc.gov.

Note: Overnight travel includes trips of at least one night or longer by residents of each country. Data for Canada and Mexico do not include same-day travel, which accounts for the majority of trips by Canadian and Mexican residents to the United States.

the attractiveness of Mexico as a gateway for people smugglers whose destination is the United States.

Immigration to Mexico is a long and complicated process. Most immigrants to Mexico have to demonstrate that they have jobs in Mexico that cannot be filled by Mexicans. Getting residency is a decade-long process. In contrast, securing permanent residency in Canada and the United States happens much more quickly. Illegal immigration to Mexico is more of a problem for the United States than Mexico, since the majority who enter Mexico illegally do so en route to its northern neighbor.

Line in the Snow: The Canada–United States Border

There is some support in Canada for the free movement of people between Canada and the United States, but the issue of open borders remains controversial. English-Canadians worry about maintaining separate cultural identity. Americans worry about Canada as a gateway for illegal drugs and immigrants to the United States. However, existing policies already permit relatively free movement across the Canada–United States border for the

Figure 3.1   **Estimated Illegal Aliens in United States, 1996**

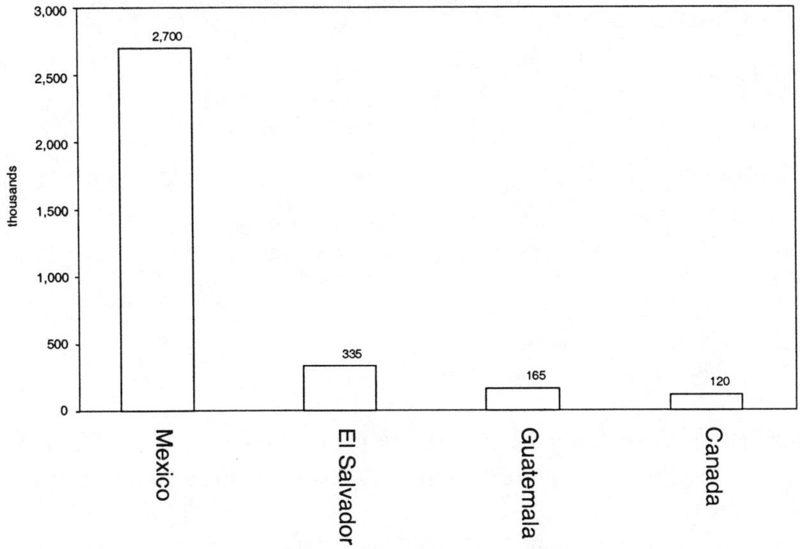

Source: Immigration and Naturalization Service, 2001.

citizens of the two countries. Neither country requires the other's citizens to have entry visas or carry passports. The situation is thus very different than that faced by Mexican citizens, who require visas to enter the United States and who are subject to more scrutiny from U.S. border guards than are Canadians.

Should a more open border between Canada and the United States be accompanied by labor mobility? The short answer is no. To be legally employed, workers require a social security number in the United States and a social insurance number in Canada. Since most of the economic activity in both countries takes place in the formal sector and since the countries have similar employment markets and standards of living, there is not much risk of open borders leading to illegal workers. Indeed, the border is already sufficiently open for that to have occurred, and it has not been a significant problem for either country.

Between Canada and the United States, the major concern is not illegal migration of each other's citizens, but rather the arrival of noncitizens via the other country. On the northern border, the United States has been pursuing the development of a common security perimeter with Canada. Official statements from Canadian leaders suggest that they will resist harmonizing Canada's immigration policies with those of the United States. However, the

Table 3.4

Countries Whose Citizens Require a Visa for United States but Not Canada, September 2002

Antigua and Barbuda	Namibia
Bahamas	Papua New Guinea
Barbados	Saint Kitts and Nevis
Botswana	Saint Lucia
Costa Rica	Saint Vincent and the Grenadines
Cyprus	Samoa
Greece	Solomon Islands
Israel	South Korea
Malta	Swaziland
Mexico	

Sources: U.S. Immigration and Naturalization Service, U.S. State Department, Citizenship and Immigration Canada, United Nations list of member countries.

Canadian people appear to be ahead of the politicians on this issue, and some actions taken by the government appear to contradict the statements of political leaders.

Nevertheless, Canada and the United States have different needs and policies with respect to immigration. The United States follows a "quota by country system" to let immigrants come in. Canada uses a "points system" regardless of the origin of the would-be immigrant. According to recent census data, Canada's population increased by only 4 percent between 1996 and 2001, compared to 5.4 percent population growth in the United States over the same period ("Please Come" 2002). The Canadian government is keener to attract immigrants than is the U.S. government. However, the security screening conducted for immigrants can be further improved without requiring the complete harmonization of immigration policies.

Waive Good-Bye: U.S.–Canada Visa Coordination

As a general rule, citizens of all countries require a visa to enter Canada or the United States. The United States grants visa "waivers." Canada grants visa "exemptions," subject to ongoing reviews. Since December 2001, Canada has eliminated visa exemptions for Dominica, Grenada, Hungary, Kiribati, Malaysia, Nauru, Saudi Arabia, Tuvalu, Vanuatu, and Zimbabwe. These changes were motivated either because a country became a significant source of questionable refugee claimants (for example, Hungary) or because its passports were subject to abuse (for example, Saudi Arabia). However, Canada still exempts nineteen more countries from its visa requirement than does the United States (see Table 3.4).

On May 14, 2002, President Bush signed into law the Enhanced Border Security and Visa Entry Reform Act of 2002 (H.R. 3525). Under section 307, to participate in the visa waiver program, a country must report to the United States the theft of its blank passports in a timely manner. Countries in the visa waiver program must be reviewed by the U.S. Immigration and Naturalization Service (INS) and State Department every two years instead of five years. Under section 302, beginning October 26, 2004, the State Department and the INS must issue only machine-readable, tamper-resistant visas and other travel and entry documents that use biometric identifiers. Likewise, to participate in the visa waiver program, a country must issue its nationals machine-readable, tamper-resistant passports that incorporate biometric and authentication identifiers that satisfy the standards of the International Civil Aviation Organization (ICAO).

Section 401 requires a feasibility study of a program for foreigners traveling to the United States, Canada, or Mexico to voluntarily submit to preclearance procedures. Such a program already exists at Canadian airports, where travelers pass through U.S. customs and immigration before boarding flights to the United States. Section 603 requires the State Department and the INS to study alternatives for encouraging or requiring Canada, Mexico, and countries with visa waivers to develop an intergovernmental network of interconnected electronic data systems that would facilitate access to each country's law enforcement and intelligence information. Canada and the United States have already made some progress in this area since September 11, notably with respect to air passenger lists and access to fingerprint databases.

Section 307 indicates that the United States has decided to use its visa waiver program to promote the harmonization of visa requirements, particularly among the NAFTA countries (Table 3.5 lists countries for which Canada and the United States both waive visa requirements). The United States is likely to pressure Canada to bring its visa waiver policies in line with those of the United States in order to maintain easy access for Canadians entering the United States. Mexico will be under less pressure, since it does not enjoy visa waiver status.

However, Canada still holds some bargaining chips. It is not in the interests of the United States to impose a visa requirement on Canadians. Such a requirement would be opposed by business groups in U.S. states that border Canada and benefit from the money spent by Canadian visitors. It would also be opposed by southern U.S. states that receive large numbers of Canadian "snowbirds"—retired Canadians who spend the winter in the southern United States. The Canadian Snowbird Association and business groups in the southern United States received a positive response to their lobbying efforts regarding an INS proposal to restrict foreign visitors to a maximum

---

Table 3.5

Countries Whose Citizens Do Not Require a Visa for United States or Canada, September 2002

Andorra	Iceland	Norway
Australia	Ireland	Portugal
Austria	Italy	San Marino
Belgium	Japan	Singapore
Brunei	Liechtenstein	Slovenia
Denmark	Luxembourg	Spain
Finland	Monaco	Sweden
France	Netherlands	Switzerland
Germany	New Zealand	United Kingdom

Sources: U.S. Immigration and Naturalization Service, Citizenship and Immigration Canada.

---

thirty-day stay rather than six months. The U.S. director of homeland security, Tom Ridge, expressed confidence that changes to U.S. policy would not impede the travel plans of the more than 100,000 Canadians who live part of the year in the United States (Moore 2002).

To grease the wheels of harmonization, the United States therefore has to provide carrots rather than sticks for Canada and Mexico. In the case of Mexico, that means addressing the issue of illegal immigrants. In the case of Canada, the carrot has taken the form of an agreement on refugees that was long sought by Canada, signed by Tom Ridge and Deputy Prime Minister John Manley June 28, 2002—the "Safe Third Country" agreement.

The majority of people seeking refugee status in Canada arrive via the United States with an American visa. Noting that refugee claimants may arrive from each other's territory where they could have sought asylum, the agreement allows each country to reject refugee claimants arriving at the land border from the other, subject to some exceptions (Article 4). The United States resisted signing this type of agreement because it would thus be responsible for a larger share of refugee claims (Woods 2002). The agreement does not apply to refugee claimants who are citizens or residents of Canada or the United States (Article 2). The agreement is part of Canada's and the United States's strategy to work together to avoid the exploitation of their refugee systems by terrorist groups (see Appendix 3.1, p. 99).

In addition, Canada and the United States are expanding their Frequent Crosser Border Pass Program (NEXUS). NEXUS is a joint Canada–United States border pass program that harmonizes border-crossing procedures for low-risk travelers. Participants complete a single application form to receive a membership card valid for entry to both Canada and the United States. The card entitles them to use dedicated lanes at the border where they are not subject to normal customs and immigration questioning.

Line in the Sand: The Mexico–United States Border

The free trade policy of the Mexican government, as exemplified by NAFTA, provides a means of generating economic growth and greater prosperity for Mexico. However, wages and economic growth rates in Mexico remain insufficient to stem the flow of some 300,000 undocumented workers to the United States each year. Moreover, programs that provide visas for temporary entry by Mexican workers to the United States are underutilized. The events of September 11 have heightened awareness of the need to more closely monitor and to more effectively coordinate immigration to the United States. The terrorist threat has also made closer cooperation on border and security issues between Mexico and the United States essential. In this context, Mexico and the United States have been discussing reforms to current programs governing migrant labor.

Migration Migraine: The Political Economy of People Movement

Rapid change in the patterns of migration (both legal and illegal) has become a matter for major international concern not only for the North American subcontinent, but also for most European and Asian countries. The United States attracts illegal aliens from Mexico. Mexico, in turn, is at the receiving end of illegal immigrants from many Central American countries (mostly en route to the United States). The fact that they enter the United States illegally is a problem. However, many industries (such as agriculture and construction) have come to depend on them. As a result, the number of illegal immigrants apprehended at the Mexico–U.S. border ebbs and flows with the demand in seasonal industries that employ them (see Figure 3.2).

Illegal immigration from Mexico represents both a blessing and a curse for the United States, and the issue needs to be resolved. On the one hand, the U.S. economy benefits from a much-needed supply of labor (especially for the types of jobs no U.S. resident wants). On the other hand, the illegal nature of this flow of people promotes more illegal activities, such as people smuggling and the abuse of undocumented workers' rights. The recent indictment of six executives from the Tyson company shows that illegal activities sometimes involve big business (see Appendix 3.2, p. 103).

Some economists have argued that free entry of migrants could jeopardize the well-being of the host population. It is believed that a country that

Figure 3.2   **Southern Border Apprehension by the Immigration Services in the United States, 1993–2002**

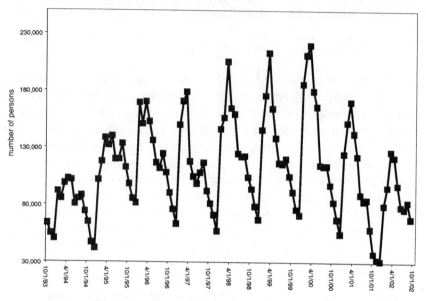

Source: www.ins.gov website.

declares its borders open faces the risk of being overwhelmed by a massive influx of immigrants from poorer countries. If the host country then provides these immigrants with the same benefits it offers to its own citizens, its social and welfare systems could be stretched to the limit. As a result, there is a general tendency in almost all countries to enforce tight controls to prevent illegal migration and to pass more restrictive laws concerning legal admissions.

Ethier (1986) presented an innovative analysis of the effects of increasing resources to immigration controls on the flows of illegal immigration by using a crime-theoretic analysis. In particular he analyzed the effects of border control and domestic enforcement (detecting illegal immigrants while in employment) on domestic policy objectives of reducing the level of illegal immigration and increasing national welfare. He also considered the efficiency of domestic enforcement, where sanctions compel those employers who hire illegal immigrants to verify the immigration status of their employees.

On the demand side, many countries have been trying to control demand by enforcing economic sanctions on employers who hire illegal aliens. On the supply side, the most popular instrument is direct interdiction enforced by border control. However, the implementation and enforcement of instruments and mechanisms to deter illegal migration are costly. It is also difficult to measure to what extent they reduce the illegal entries and enhance welfare.

Recently Hanson and Spilimbergo (1999) studied empirically some of the above questions in the context of the United States and Mexico. They find that border enforcement has no impact on the wages in the U.S. border cities. Thus, the feared negative impact of illegal immigration seems unfounded. On the other side of the border (that is, on the Mexican side), they find a moderate negative impact on the wages in various sectors. Their findings call into question the gut reaction many people have about the effects of illegal immigration.

On February 16, 2001, U.S. president Bush and Mexican president Fox appointed a working group to explore new policies to address illegal immigration from Mexico to the United States and improve protection for Mexican migrants, including proposals to expand guest worker programs in the United States. However, the Mexican government has grown increasingly frustrated by the lack of progress on reforms to U.S. immigration policy as it affects Mexico. A more liberalized movement of labor could be phased in over many years and could be of mutual benefit to the countries involved, given demographic trends. Progress on the migration issue is also necessary to enhance the Mexico–United States relationship and the ability of the two countries to work more closely on other bilateral issues.

Mind the Gap: Long-Run Prognosis

Could the problem sort itself out in the long run? If the gap in income persists for the next three decades, then the flow will continue. An extrapolation model, which simply projects the future based on what has happened in the past, shows that the current migration of 350,000 a year from Mexico to the United States will rise to over 500,000 by the year 2030 (CONAPO 2000). However, such a model misses two fundamental points. First of all, the population is aging in Mexico. It is very clear that only young people undertake such a journey. As the population ages, then the flow will diminish. If demographics were the only source of this migration, the problem would sort itself out as the Mexican population ages. Second, the income gap between the United States and Mexico has been growing. However, the income differential between the United States and Mexico may stay the same in the future. If the income differential stays the same or grows, it will lead to ongoing migration. A study by Gerber (2002) shows that the income differential between border cities such as Tijuana and San Diego has not changed

Figure 3.3   **Fertility Rates of Mexico, Canada, and United States**

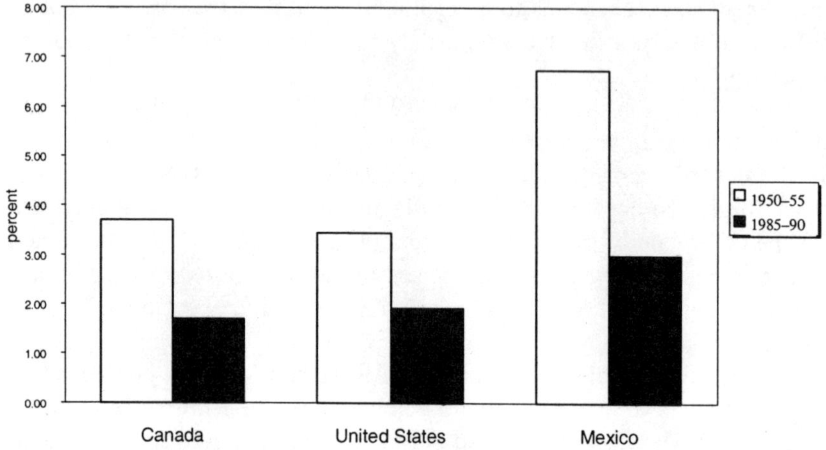

Source: OECD (2002).

at all over a thirty-year period. In 1970, per capita income in Tijuana was U.S.$1,122 dollars while in San Diego it was $5,693. In 1999, per capita income in Tijuana rose to U.S.$6,800 but, at the same time, per capita income in San Diego rose to $35,204. The ratio of income disparity between Tijuana and San Diego has moved during this thirty years from 5.07 to 5.18. If we project this trend into the future, the income disparity will rise. However, the conditions have changed quite dramatically in Mexico during these thirty years. Mexico is a lot more economically open now than it was thirty years ago. It has also forged closer ties with the United States through NAFTA. Thus, it is possible to see Mexico growing more rapidly in the next thirty years than the United States over the same period.

Fertile Grounds: Demographic Trends and Migration

NAFTA fertility rates are declining, as shown in Figure 3.3. Both Canada and the United States have rates below the 2.08 needed to maintain a stable population, although both compensate through immigration. The evolution of the Mexican fertility rate is remarkable. It has dropped from over six in the 1950s to three in 1990. This will rapidly change the population structure in Mexico over the next three decades. As a result, there will be about 30 percent fewer persons in the 15–24 age group (the prime age for illegal migration).

Declining fertility rates in Canada and the United States, combined with aging populations, will increase the likelihood of labor shortages as the baby boomers retire over the next twenty years. At the same time, the declining

Figure 3.4a **Percent of People over Sixty-five**

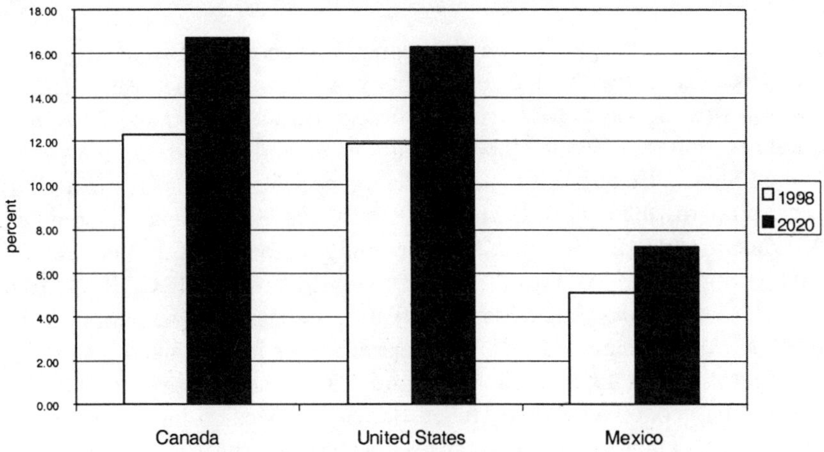

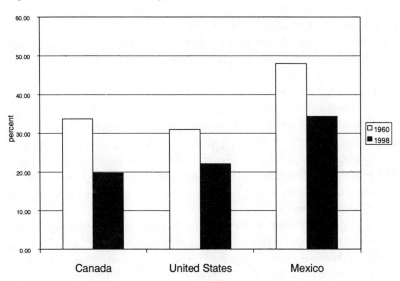

Source: OECD and UN Population Division websites.

Figure 3.4b **Percent of People under Fifteen**

Source: OECD and UN Population Division websites.

fertility rate in Mexico will mean fewer young Mexicans making the journey
north to the United States. Figure 3.4a and Figure 3.4b show the aging of the
United States and Canada and the relative youth of Mexico, respectively.

Catching Up with Old Friends: The Transatlantic Gap

In addition to demographic trends, economic trends in Mexico may raise incomes sufficiently over the next twenty years to reduce the relative attractiveness of U.S. wages for Mexican workers. Between 1970 and 2000, real GDP per capita rose about 60 percent in Mexico and about 87 percent in the United States. There is even greater divergence if one compares real GDP per capita growth between 1981 and 1999—in the United States it increased 48 percent, while in Mexico it increased only 6.8 percent for the entire period (Gruber 2002). As a result, in 2000, Mexico's per capita GDP was 16.6 percent of that of the United States. With the purchasing power parity adjustment, Mexico's wages were 25.7 percent of wages in the United States (using figures from OECD 2002). In Figure 1.3, we see that over a 180-year period, the economies of the United States and Mexico have diverged in terms of per capita income. The gap became particularly acute between 1982 and 1996.

Economic integration under NAFTA should help to narrow the gap in wages between the United States and Mexico, with a reasonable set of economic policies in Mexico. If the difference in economic growth between Mexico and the United States averages 2 percent over a period of thirty years, the average wage rate in Mexico would be roughly 50 percent of that of the United States in terms of purchasing power. This would make the wage gap similar to current differences between northern and southern Europe and reduce migration significantly (as it has in Europe).

The feasibility of a free labor movement regime depends in large part on the wage gaps between participating countries. In 2000, Mexico's per capita GDP was 16.6 percent of that of the United States. By comparison, Greek per capita GDP was 47.3 percent of Germany's. In terms of purchasing power parity, Mexico was 25.7 percent of the United States and Greece was 65 percent of Germany (calculations based on figures from OECD 2002). Mexico thus has a significant distance to go to narrow the gap to European Union levels.

Integrating the Mexican economy with those of the United States and Canada was viewed as a means to create economic growth and jobs in Mexico that would reduce the flow of migrants. However, this was expected to happen only over the long run. In the short run, economic integration would likely increase migration. Historical and empirical evidence (for example, with respect to Italy) suggests that economic integration can produce a "migration hump," by causing migration to increase before it decreases (Martin 2002). In this regard, the experience of the European Union may provide valuable lessons for North America.

The European Union has advanced further in the area of labor mobility than NAFTA. In the decades following World War II, northern Europe experienced labor shortages that led to programs recruiting "guest workers" from southern Europe. Between 1950 and 1973, large numbers of workers from Greece, Italy, Portugal, and Spain migrated to northern Europe as temporary workers, but most later returned to their home countries. Over time, these countries became integrated into the European Union and wage differentials narrowed (Obdeijn 2002). Today, their citizens enjoy the same labor mobility rights within the European Union as the northern Europeans. As North American demographic trends begin to have an impact on the supply of labor in the north, labor shortages may motivate Canada and the United States to adopt similar policies with respect to Mexico.

However, the North American situation is quite different from that of Europe in several important respects. First, a large amount of migration already takes place in North America compared to the situation that existed in Europe after the war. Second, this migration primarily affects only two countries, whereas there were several source and destination countries involved in postwar European migration. Third, the cause of labor shortages was different—namely war, as opposed to more gradual demographic changes. Fourth, the context in which the liberalization of labor migration took place was very different. The history of military conflict in Europe gave greater urgency to the project of economic, political, and social integration that culminated in the formation of the European Union. As a result, European motivations and policy goals differed significantly. Finally, the wage gap between northern and southern Europe has narrowed over time, while the Mexico-United States gap has been increasing.

Another important difference between Europe and North America has to do with agricultural subsidies. In the European Union, agricultural subsidies transfer resources from rich countries to farmers throughout the region. In North America, the opposite occurs. The richest NAFTA country (the United States) subsidizes its own farmers to the detriment of the farmers in the other countries, particularly Mexico. This means more demand for agricultural workers in the United States and less employment for the same workers in Mexico. U.S. policy on agricultural subsidies thus aggravates the problem of Mexican migration to the United States.

The advent of global terrorism provides a new motivation to find ways to balance people movement with security concerns in the context of regional economic integration. In the European Union, seven member states—Belgium, the Netherlands, Luxembourg, France, Germany, Portugal, and Spain—are signatories to the Schengen Agreement. Under this accord, six of these countries removed internal border controls beginning in July 1995. France has maintained passport controls on its borders with Belgium and Luxembourg. Italy (1990), Greece (1992), and Austria (1995) have also signed the agreement, but remain in the process of implementation. Sweden, Finland, and Denmark are expected to negotiate full membership in the agreement as well. The signatories have agreed to harmonize visa arrangements covering 160 countries, as well as other external border security measures, and to allow police from member countries to pursue criminals across jurisdictions (European Union).

Despite the liberalization of labor mobility in Europe, as of 1996 there were only about 5.5 million European Union citizens living in another European Union country, roughly 1.5 percent of the European Union population. The largest numbers were concentrated in Germany (1.7 million), France (1.3 million), and the United Kingdom (0.7 million) (Hémery 1997). In comparison, the United States had some 2.82 million illegal aliens living in the country in 1996 from Mexico (2.7 million) and Canada (120,000) (see Figure 3.1), or roughly 1 percent of the U.S. population. In other words, on a per capita basis there are two-thirds as many illegal aliens residing in the United States from NAFTA countries as there are European Union citizens living legally in other European Union member countries. This suggests that a narrowing of the wage gap to European levels would allow the NAFTA countries to implement a similar labor mobility program without dramatically changing the flows of migrants that already take place.

President Fox has proposed a new guest worker program to allow Mexican laborers to work legally in the United States for short periods. Fox's idea is to follow the precedent set by Europe, whose guest worker programs of the 1980s led to free movement of laborers to the benefit of poorer members like Portugal, Spain, and Greece. President Fox wants to start with a temporary worker program that would allow some 350,000 Mexican laborers a year to work in United States industries experiencing labor shortages. However, the long-term plan is to achieve the integration of the labor markets of all three NAFTA countries.

A Ghost from the Past: The Braceros

The last major guest worker program in the United States, the bracero program, under which up to 500,000 Mexican workers were brought in annually (see Tables 3.6 and 3.7), lasted from 1942 until 1965. The idea was for the guest workers to be "temporary" and go home to Mexico when the work was done, and they did.

Curiously, the unions, the churches, and other groups fought for years to end the bracero program. Why did they want to end it? First, it was very

Table 3.6

Mexican Origin Latino (MOL) Emigration to the United States

Year	Braceros	Deportable total	Deportable Mexico	Undocu-mented MOL	MOL immigrants + undocu-mented	Temp-orary workers
1946	32	100	90	23		
1947	20	194	158	40		
1948	35	193	156	39	42	
1949	107	288	233	58	65	
1950	67	468	379	95	101	
1951	192	509	412	103	109	
1952	197	529	42	11	20	
1953	201	886	676	169	187	
1954	309	1,089	920	230	267	
1955	398	254	221	55	105	
1956	445	88	62	16	71	
1957	436	60	38	10	59	
1958	432	53	32	8	34	
1959	437	45	25	6	29	
1960	315	71	22	6	38	
1961	291	89	23	6	47	
1962	194	93	23	6	61	
1963	186	89	31	8	63	
1964	177	87	35	9	41	
1965	20	110	44	11	48	
1966	8	139	71	18	63	
1967	7	162	86	22	64	
1968	6	212	113	28	71	
1969		159	40	84		
1970		219	55	99		
1971		290	73	123		
1972		355	89	153		
1973		576	144	214		
1974		709	177	248		
1975		614	153	215		
1976		701	175	248		
1977		834	208	252		
1978		846	212	304		
1979		861	215	267		
1980		734	184	240		
1981		797	199	300		
1982		795	199	255		4
1983		1,076	269	328		
1984		1,104	276	333		4
1985		1,218	305	366		5
1986		1,671	418	484		12
1987		1,139	285	357		13
1988		949	237	332		12
1989		865	216	621		22

(continued)

Table 3.6 (continued)

Year	Braceros	Deportable total	Deportable Mexico	Undocu- mented MOL	MOL immigrants + undocu- mented	Temp- orary workers
1990		1,092	273	952		16
1991		1,131	283	1,229		13
1992		1,205	301	514		14
1993		1,269	317	443		16
1994		1,040	260	371		17
1995		1,340	335	424		
1996		1,598	400	563		26
1997		1,478	370	516		
1998		1,614	404	534		51

Source: INS, 2002.

difficult to raise wages under the program and wages stagnated for many years in the 1950s. This had a depressing effect on the larger farm labor market. Second, it was impossible for unions to organize farm workers, because braceros would be brought in to quell organizing drives. Third, the braceros had few rights and complainers were simply sent back to Mexico. As a result, the braceros often endured abysmal living and working conditions, especially in such states as Texas, Florida, and Washington. Finally, the program favored the most productive workers, young single males. Having large numbers of young men alone in a foreign country inevitably leads to social pathologies in the communities where they are housed.

Why did the bracero program actually end? Once again, if we look at data from Table 3.6, we see that the number of "deportables" grew rapidly precisely at the time the bracero program ended. Thus, it is possible that the employers of agricultural workers did not want to continue with the bracero program because they could hire illegal migrants cheaper (and they did not have to provide housing for them either). Perhaps the U.S. government was under increasing pressure from the unions because the program was thought to have depressed wages for union workers. The end of the bracero program coincides with the rise of the United Farm Workers in the United States. (For a detailed account of the bracero program, see Martin 1999.)

Still Waters Run Deep: Efforts to Stem the Flow

In 1954, the Eisenhower administration introduced "Operation Wetback" to raid farms and homes to remove all the illegal Mexicans in the United States. Under the operation, more than a million Mexicans were sent back to Mexico. The administration also passed a law making it illegal to transport or harbor

Table 3.7

Mexican Workers in the United States, 1940–2000

Thousands	1940	1950	1960	1970	1980	1990	2000
(1) Total U.S. population	132,457	151,868	179,979	203,984	227,217	249,666	281,422
(2) Total Mexican population	19,654	25,791	34,923	48,225	66,847	85,782	98,881
(3) Population of Mexican origin in United States	377	450	1,735	4,532	8,740	13,495	20,600
(4) United States labor force	41,870	63,379	71,489	84,889	108,544	126,424	138,386
(5) Mexican labor force	5,858	8,345	10,213	14,489	22,092	31,027	40,666
(6) Annual flow of legal temporary workers	0	150	420	47	20	120	35.9
(7) Cumulative stock of undocumented workers (since 1940)	0	100	200	316	1,095	2,298	5,000
(8) Cumulative stock of legal immigrant workers (since 1940)	0	46	286	673	1,230	2,172	660
(9) Total Mexican workers in U.S. labor force	0	296	906	1,036	2,345	4,590	5,696
(10) Total labor force in United States of Mexican origin	335	571	1,308	2,063	3,498	8,742	14,008
Percent shares	1940	1950	1960	1970	1980	1990	2000
Mexicans working in United States as share of Mexican labor force	0.0	3.6	8.9	7.2	10.6	14.8	14
Mexicans working in United States as share of U.S. labor force	0.0	0.5	1.3	1.2	2.2	3.6	4.1
Total labor force in United States of Mexican origin as share of U.S. labor force	0.8	0.9	1.8	2.4	3.2	6.9	10

Source: "Comprehensive Migration Policy Reform in North America: The Key to Sustainable and Equitable Economic Integration," unpublished working paper by Raul Hinojosa Ojeda, UCLA NAID Center, August 2001.

Notes: U.S. Mexican labor force totals for 1940, 1950, 1970, 1980, and 1990 are from the census data on economically active population (including unemployed). The 1960 census figure was adjusted to correct for over-counting of rural workers. The estimates in row (6) are based on the number of legal temporary workers, including braceros from 1942 to 1964, and data from the INS. Estimates in row (7) are of undocumented workers during the previous five-year period (one quarter of undocumented immigrants deported reduced by one-fourth for non-participants in the work force) and are adjusted by estimates published by the INS. Year 2000 data is based on 1996 numbers. Row (8) is based on the INS *Yearbook of Immigration Statistics*, with demographic growth calculated along with a 0.68 labor force participation rate and a 0.05 attrition rate and is based on 1998 figures. Mexicans in the United States refer to all legal and undocumented immigrants from Mexico who entered this country between 1940 and the present and their progeny, regardless of place of birth. This is clearly not the same as people of Mexican origin as described in the U.S. Census and Current Population Survey. The magnitude of the difference (about half the current total) can be explained as arising from all legal and undocumented immigrants and their descendants who came before 1940.

an illegal alien but not to employ one (Lin 2001). This gap in the law endured for three decades, during which illegal immigration from Mexico continued to grow.

The United States attempted to stem the flow of illegal aliens by enacting the Immigration Reform Control Act (IRCA) of 1986, which introduced laws and penalties against employers for hiring illegal aliens, and by increasing border enforcement. However, enforcement of the IRCA has been largely left to employers, who have tended not to enforce it. Moreover, employers are not required to verify the authenticity of the identification used by the employees, which has led to a booming business in fake identification on the Mexican side of the border (Cornelius 2003). The government's enforcement budget has been focused on the border instead. Between 1978 and 1999, the number of U.S. border patrol agents increased fourfold (Orrenius 2001). Between 1985 and 1999, the time spent patrolling the border increased from 1.9 million hours to 8.6 million (Orrenius 2001). These increased border resources have diverted the crossing of illegal aliens to more remote and inhospitable areas of the border, thereby increasing the number of Mexican migrants who die on the journey, and have created a flourishing people-smuggling industry. However, they have not succeeded in stopping the flow of illegal immigrants from Mexico. Moreover, illegal immigrants represent only about 0.5 percent of total Mexico–U.S. border crossings (Orrenius 2001). In a time when border resources are being reorganized to face the threat of international terrorist attacks, one has to question the deployment of so many agents to catch illegal immigrants, particularly when it coincides with a lack of enforcement in the labor market.

An unintended side effect of U.S. immigration policies vis-à-vis Mexico has been to create a conflict between immigration and labor laws. In *Hoffman Plastic Compounds Inc.* v. *National Labor Relations Board* (535 U.S.S.C. 1 [2002]), the U.S. Supreme Court divided 5 : 4 over the issue of whether the National Labor Relations Board (NLRB) was correct in awarding back pay to José Castro, an illegal immigrant from Mexico who was fired for participating in the organization of a union. Castro violated the IRCA by using false documents to obtain employment with Hoffman. Hoffman violated the National Labor Relations Act by firing Castro and three other employees in order to get rid of known union supporters. The NLRB awarded Castro back pay of $66,951, plus interest, for the three-and-a-half years between the time he was fired and the time Hoffman learned of his undocumented status.

The Supreme Court majority held that the NLRB was wrong to award back pay to an illegal alien because the award ran counter to federal immigration policy, would condone prior violations of immigration laws, and would encourage future violations. The NLRB's order that the employer stop violating the labor law and post a notice detailing employees' rights and its prior unfair practices was sufficient to deter future violations. The minority argued that, on the contrary, the award would deter unlawful activity that both labor laws and immigration laws seek to prevent. Back pay awards not only compensate the victim of a labor violation, but also discourage employers from violating labor laws. In the absence of back pay awards, employers could conclude that they may violate the labor laws at least once with impunity, thereby lowering the cost of an initial labor law violation against illegal aliens. This increases the employer's incentive to find and hire illegal aliens as employees, running counter to the basic objective of the immigration law. The Supreme Court minority noted further that the attorney general, whose department administers the immigration laws, supported the NLRB's order. Moreover, those in Congress who wrote the immigration law stated that the IRCA did not take away any of the NLRB's remedial authority, citing H.R. Rep. No. 99–682 at 58 that the IRCA does not "undermine or diminish in any way labor protections in existing law, or…limit the powers of federal or state labor relations boards…to remedy unfair practices committed against undocumented employees."

In this case, it is understandable that the majority would not want to be seen to be rewarding illegal activity. However, the minority's reasoning is more persuasive, given the impact of the decision on both immigration policy and the enforcement of labor laws. The result of the decision is that the NLRB has been left without an adequate remedy to deter employer violations and undocumented workers are more vulnerable than ever. Congress will now have to amend the legislation granting remedial powers to the NLRB, either to overturn the Supreme Court decision or to add the possibility of employer fines that do not end up in the hands of illegal aliens.

Employers responded rapidly to the ruling. Within a few weeks of the court's decision, there were reports from across the United States of employers relying on the ruling to avoid paying minimum wage and workers' compensation awards and to discourage workers from filing complaints, including sexual harassment complaints. The ruling has led many illegal immigrants to believe that they have lost all protections under federal and state labor laws, which has discouraged them from filing complaints and participating in union activities (Cleeland 2002).

The Law's on My Side: U.S. Nonimmigrant Visas

The immigration laws of the NAFTA countries all have rules in place to allow citizens of any country to become permanent residents and citizens. These laws operate independently from programs for temporary entry for unskilled and highly skilled workers. In general, these immigration laws promote the entry of well-educated people whose skills are in demand and investors who bring capital to the country. They also facilitate immigration on more humanitarian grounds, with classes of immigrants such as refugees or family members. The temporary entry programs for workers supplement the more general immigration programs, where there is demand for specific kinds of workers.

The U.S. H1B visa program is a good example of a temporary entry program. Under this program, the United States issues six-year visas (renewable after three years) to foreign-born workers with college degrees and special skills. H1B classification applies to persons in a specialty occupation, which requires the theoretical and practical application of a body of highly specialized knowledge requiring completion of a specific course of higher education. This classification requires labor certification issued by the secretary of labor (www.applicationsforms.com/temporar.htm). The program is primarily aimed at high-tech workers, but includes other professionals such as architects, engineers, and university professors. Congress passed a bill on October 3, 2000, to increase the number from 115,000 to 195,000 visas per year. Nearly 50 percent of the visas go to workers from India, with China in second place (Alvarez 2000).

As of November 2001, the INS had approved 163,200 H1B guest worker petitions against the fiscal year 2001 limit of 195,000. Approximately 29,000 petitions were still pending, which would bring the total number of requested H1B visas to 192,000. An additional 30,000 H1B visa applications pending from fiscal year 2000 were processed in 2001 under a special exemption. A further 135,000 H1B visas were granted under an open exemption provided to research and academic institutions, bringing the total to over 300,000 (Eye on Washington 2001).

A separate category of nonimmigrant visas is used for unskilled workers. The H2A visa applies to temporary or seasonal agricultural workers and has no numerical limit. The H2A program establishes minimum labor standards, including minimum wage standards, contract terms, and reimbursement for travel expenses. (For details of the H2A program and other United States laws that apply to the workers, see Commission for Labor Cooperation 2000.)

H2B classification applies to temporary or seasonal nonagricultural workers (66,000). This classification requires a temporary labor certification issued by the secretary of labor. In fiscal year 1999, the INS issued only 32,372 H2A visas (26,069 to Mexicans) and 35,815 H2B visas (18,927 to Mexicans), far short of the limits (INS, Table 38, FY 1999). In the year 2000, the United States processed 2,252,594 nonimmigrant visa applications in Mexico, an increase of 37 percent from the year 1999, when 1,635,309 applications were processed (United States Embassy in Mexico). These figures indicate that both illegal migrants from Mexico and their U.S. employers find the legal requirements for these visas too onerous. Another reason they are not used is that many Mexican migrants work in service industries (such as construction) in which they are needed year-round, making seasonal visas inappropriate for these migrants (Cornelius 2003).

In order to be considered as a nonimmigrant, the applicant's prospective employer or agent must file a "Petition for Nonimmigrant Worker" with the INS. Once approved, the employer or agent is sent a notice of approval. The approval of a petition does not guarantee visa issuance to an applicant found to be ineligible under provisions of the U.S. Immigration and Nationality Act. Each applicant for a temporary worker visa must pay a nonrefundable application fee and submit an application form, together with a passport valid for travel to the United States for at least six months beyond the applicant's intended period of stay in the United States, one photograph, and a notice of approval. With the exception of the H1 and L1 visas, applicants may also need to show proof of binding ties to a residence outside the United States that they have no intention of abandoning. The INS determines the period that the holder of a temporary work visa is authorized to remain in the United States. At the port of entry, an INS official validates a "Record of Arrival-Departure" form, which notes the length of stay permitted. Those temporary workers who wish to stay beyond the time indicated on this form must contact the INS to request an "Application to Extend Status" form. The INS then decides whether to grant or deny the request for extension of stay. The spouse and unmarried, minor children of an applicant may also be classified as nonimmigrants in order to accompany or join the principal applicant. A person who has received a visa as the spouse or child of a temporary worker may not accept employment in the United States. The principal applicant must be able to show that he or she will be able to support the family in the United States (www.applicationsforms.com/temporar.htm).

The combined effect of employer demand, lack of enforcement of laws against employers who hire illegal immigrants, and onerous visa requirements is that an estimated 300,000 Mexicans annually enter the United States labor force without visas while quotas for legal entry go unfilled. U.S. agricultural subsidies further exacerbate the problem by increasing demand for workers in the United States and increasing the supply of workers from Mexico.

Security Blankets: Labor Mobility and Social Security

The bracero program has left an unexpected legacy. For every worker, some 10 percent of wages were taken away for social security. What happened to the money? Some of the deductions had been deposited in the San Francisco–based Wells Fargo Bank and then transferred to the Banco Agricola in Mexico. In 1949, the year the deductions ended, the Banco Agricola was reorganized as the Banrural. Banrural officials have denied the braceros and their survivors (about a third have died) access to its archives under the Mexican banking secrecy laws. There are claims that moneys were diverted by the Banco Agricola from individual disbursements into an "agrarian infrastructure fund." A number of bracero workers have sued in the United States in a national class action suit in a federal court.

A class action suit was filed in March 2001 in the San Francisco U.S. district court, seeking repayment of money deducted from the braceros' paychecks. The suit charged the governments of the United States and Mexico, along with Wells Fargo Bank, Mexican Central Bank (Banco de Mexico), and Banrural among others, with breach of contract, breach of trust/fiduciary duty, and unjust enrichment. The lawsuit sought an accounting of the missing funds, repayment of those funds with interest, and attorneys' fees and damages.

On January 15, 2002, the defendants presented motions to dismiss the case. The Mexican government and banks argued that they are immune from suit in the United States because they are a foreign sovereign (in the case of the government) or owned by a foreign sovereign (in the case of the banks). The Mexican defendants also argued that the court did not have jurisdiction over Banrural or the Patronato del Ahorro Nacional (two of the three banks sued) because they do not engage in any business in the United States. In addition, the Mexican defendants argued that the court should not exercise jurisdiction, but rather should defer to the commission created by the Mexican Camara de Diputados (lower house of the federal congress) which is investigating the disposition of the bracero fund. Finally, the Mexican defendants argued that the case was barred by the applicable statute of limitations and that, in any event, the complaint failed to state a valid claim against Mexico or its banks for recovery of funds.

The United States argued that the applicable statute of limitations for claims against the federal government is six years and that this statute started to run in the 1940s because the plaintiffs were aware of the savings fund deductions and the steps necessary to recover those funds. The United States also argued that the only claim to which it is subject is one for a breach of the individual contracts between the United States and the workers, and that there is not recognized legal claim against the United States for breach of trust or fiduciary duty. Like the Mexican defendants, the United States argued that it is immune from suit, but for a different reason. It claimed that compliance with the six-year statute of limitations is a prerequisite to maintaining an action, and that the failure to file a suit within the six years meant that the court had no jurisdiction over the case. Normally, a failure to comply with the statute of limitations is a question of fact. Whether or not the plaintiff did so, or was excused from doing so, does not take jurisdiction away from the court, which can hear and decide the limitations issue along with other issues in the case. Like the other defendants, the United States argued that the complaint failed to state a valid legal claim against it.

Wells Fargo Bank likewise raised the statute of limitations as a defense and argued that none of the claims against it were legally valid. In particular, Wells Fargo emphasized that it did not have a direct relationship with the braceros (even though 10 percent of their salaries were deposited with Wells Fargo, apparently pursuant to some type of trust agreement) and that it therefore could not owe a duty to the braceros.

On August 28, 2002, the federal court in San Francisco sided with the two governments and the banks to dismiss the case. Federal judge Charles Breyer wrote that he did "not doubt that many braceros never received savings fund withholdings to which they were entitled. The court is sympathetic to the braceros' situation." But he concluded that the braceros were not entitled to any relief from the Mexican or American governments or from Wells Fargo in a United States court of law.

The difficulties faced by the braceros in collecting their money underline the need for effective social security arrangements to accompany reforms to temporary workers programs. The case has received a great deal of publicity and may cause temporary workers to distrust formal guest worker programs (and thus choose the illegal route) unless payroll deduction schemes are designed to avoid the problems of the past.

White-Collar Windows: NAFTA Visas in the United States

In addition to the U.S. nonimmigrant visa program, citizens of Mexico and Canada can apply for temporary entry visas under NAFTA. Generally speaking, NAFTA provisions oblige member countries to grant temporary entry visas to individuals whose activities form an integral part of trade in goods, trade in services, and foreign investment. Since NAFTA liberalizes trade in services, the agreement contains provisions to facilitate the movement of the service provider across borders. However, the cross-border movement of people is limited to temporary entry for white-collar workers (NAFTA Article 1201[3]). In addition, the NAFTA members are entitled to impose quantitative restrictions on the provision of services, with notice to other parties (NAFTA Article 1207 [3]).

Licensing and certification of service providers are often governed by independent professional organizations. For example, in Canada, membership in provincial bars is governed by independent law societies that determine who is qualified to practice law in their jurisdiction. Other self-governing professions, such as medicine and architecture, have similar independent licensing powers. Thus, in many cases the government has delegated the power to determine whether professionals from other countries are qualified to practice, whether through temporary or permanent licenses. For this reason, NAFTA only requires that governments "shall endeavor" to have self-governing professions follow certain principles in licensing and certification procedures. The endeavor is clearly nonobligatory. Those principles include transparent procedures, the least-trade-restrictive means to ensure quality, and the exhortation to not use disguised trade restrictions in setting requirements. (See Gal-Or [1998] regarding mutual recognition of professional qualification issues. McIlroy [1996] argued that it should be first based on experience and then on formal qualifications. Summers and Treacy [2002] analyze a particular profession, accounting.)

Temporary entry visas for businesspersons are covered in NAFTA Chapter 16. NAFTA requires the member governments to grant temporary entry to businesspersons (NAFTA Article 1603 [1]). "Businessperson" is defined as a citizen engaged in trade in goods, provision of services, or the conduct of investment activities. "Temporary entry" is defined as entry without intent to establish a permanent residence (NAFTA Article 1603 [8]). The principles that govern temporary entry are reciprocity, transparency, border security, and the protection of domestic labor and employment (NAFTA Article 1601). Annex 1603 contains detailed rules regarding the nature of activities and the type of documentation required to qualify for temporary entry visas under four categories: business visitors, traders and investors, intracompany transferees, and professionals. NAFTA (Appendix 1603.D.1) sets out the credentials needed to qualify as a professional, covering professions from accountant to zoologist.

Business visitors are defined as individuals whose place of business is outside the territory for which the visa is granted and who are not seeking to enter the local labor market. NAFTA (Appendix 1603.A.1) lists authorized activities in which they may engage. Traders are individuals who are engaged in trade between their home country and the country of destination. Investors are granted visas to establish, administer, or service a "substantial" investment. Visas for intracompany transferees are granted to managerial personnel, executives, or employees with specialized knowledge. In granting this type of visa, immigration authorities may require that the individual have a minimum of one year with the company in the prior three years. There are no quotas that limit the number of visas available under these categories, which reflects the central purpose of NAFTA visas—to facilitate trade and investment activities in the NAFTA region.

U.S. requirements for NAFTA visas, known as the TN visa in the United States, are different for Canadians and Mexicans. The United States imposed no limit on NAFTA visas for Canadians. However, the United States placed a limit of 5,500 visas per year for Mexican professionals. This limit is due to be phased out January 1, 2004 (NAFTA Annex 1603, Appendix 1603.D.4). The extensive list of professions that are covered means that a large number of Mexicans will soon qualify for temporary entry visas.

In addition to the numerical limit, Mexicans face more onerous requirements than Canadians to obtain the visa. Mexicans require a nonimmigrant visa, prior petition by employer, and Department of Labor certification, in addition to proof of Mexican citizenship and professional engagement in one of the listed occupations. Nonimmigrant visas are required of spouses and minor children who possess Mexican citizenship. Canadians require no nonimmigrant visa, no prior petition, no labor certification, nor prior approval, but must present appropriate documentation to the inspecting officer at the border establishing Canadian citizenship and professional engagement in one of the listed occupations. For Canadians, nonimmigrant visas are not required of spouses and minor children who possess Canadian citizenship (see North American Free-Trade Agreement Implementation Act).

With respect to professional engagement, the applicant needs an offer of employment from the U.S. employer. The applicant must also provide a copy of a college degree and employment records that establish qualification for the prospective job and a fee of U.S.$50 (see http://travel.state.gov/tn_visas.html). Both Canadians and Mexicans must have a letter offering employment in the United States. (For a sample letter, see www.stanford.edu/dept/icenter/visas/student/scholarvisas/TN/letter.html.)

In contrast to the differential treatment of the U.S. NAFTA visa requirements, Canada and Mexico apply the same requirements to professionals regardless of the NAFTA country in which they hold citizenship. Table 3.8 compares the requirements for professional visas across the three countries.

Because the NAFTA visa requirements for Canadian professionals are so simple compared to other types of U.S. visas, Canadian professionals (and their U.S. employers) now use the NAFTA visa more than any other U.S. nonimmigrant visa. Of a total 109,314 Canadians admitted under fifteen nonimmigrant visa categories in fiscal year 1999, 67,076 used the TN visa (INS, Table 38, FY 1999). Moreover, it appears that significantly more Canadians are using temporary work visas than permanent visas in the United States. In a survey of 1995 university graduates who moved to the United States, 90 percent entered with a temporary visa, of whom 72 percent used a TN visa.

Table 3.8

Requirements for Nonimmigrant Professional Visas (NAFTA)

Requirement	Canada to United States	Mexico to United States	Canada	Mexico
Proof of citizenship	Yes	Yes	Yes	Yes
Letter offering employment or contract for services	Yes	Yes	Yes	Yes
Proof of professional engagement in listed occupations	Yes	Yes	Yes	Yes
Nonimmigrant visa	No	Yes	No	No
Prior petition by the employer	No	Yes	No	No
Labor certification (United States)	No	Yes	No	No
Job Validation (Canada)				
Can apply at the border	Yes	No	Yes	No
Must apply at consulate or embassy	No	Yes	No	Yes
Limited number of visas annually	No	5500	No	No
Duration	1 year	1 year	1 year	1 year
Renewals	No limit	No limit	No limit	4 times
NAFTA visas granted (2000)	89,220	2,059	—	—

Sources: National Institute of Migration of the Ministry of the Interior (Mexico), Mexican Embassy in Canada, Citizenship and Immigration Canada, U.S. Immigration and Naturalization Service.

Notes: (1) Temporary entry means the individual has no intention to stay permanently. (2) In addition to NAFTA visa requirements, individuals must meet general entry requirements under the immigration regulations of each country, such as those relating to health, safety and national security. (3) Proof of citizenship means a passport for Mexicans. Canadians and Americans may use alternative proof in the form of a certificate of citizenship or a birth certificate together with official photo identification, such as a driver's license. (4) For occupations that require a professional license, certification, accreditation, or registration issued by a self-governing professional body (e.g., medicine or accounting), the individual must comply with the requirements. Some occupations do not impose such requirements (e.g., university professor). (5) Canada imposes no set time limit on the duration of stay for professionals, but requires employment authorization that has a maximum duration of one year. (6) Canadian requirements are the same for Mexican and U.S. citizens. U.S. requirements are different for Canadians and Mexicans. Mexican requirements are the same for Canadian and U.S. citizens. (7) Canada and the United States have a separate category for NAFTA visas and NAFTA citizens may opt for non-NAFTA visas. Mexico uses the FM3 visa for both NAFTA and non-NAFTA citizens. (8) The U.S. annual limit of 5,500 professional visas for Mexico is due to end January 1, 2004.

Of those who entered with a TN visa in 1995, only 22 percent had returned to Canada by 1999, adding to Canadian concerns about a brain drain to the United States (Human Resources Development Canada 1999).

TN authorization is valid for a maximum of one year, but can be extended indefinitely as long as the applicant maintains nonimmigrant intent. This means that Canadian professionals can renew their TN visa annually and remain indefinitely in the United States (see Nadeau et al. 2000), effectively integrating this sector of the U.S.–Canadian labor market. As of 2000, no renewal had been refused except when a TN renewal and a green card were applied for simultaneously, since applying for permanent residence negates the necessary nonimmigrant intent ("International Recruitment" 2000).

In fiscal year 1999, the United States admitted 68,354 nonimmigrant workers under the TN visa from Canada (67,076) and Mexico (1,278) (INS, Table 38, FY 1999) (see Table 3.9). In fiscal year 2000, the number granted to Canadians rose to 89,220 while those granted to Mexicans rose only to 2,059 (see Table 3.10). These numbers indicate that the additional requirements imposed on Mexicans restrict access to TN visas more than the numerical limit of 5,500 visas per year. As long as those requirements remain in place, the removal of the limit in 2004 is unlikely to result in a large increase in the number of Mexicans being granted TN visas.

Of the requirements imposed on Mexicans, labor certification is the most onerous barrier, as it requires proof that U.S. workers will not be adversely affected. Labor certification is issued by the secretary of labor. It consists of attestations by U.S. employers as to the numbers of U.S. workers available to undertake the employment sought by an applicant and the effect of the applicant's employment on the wages and working conditions of U.S. workers similarly employed. Determination of labor availability in the United States is made at the time of a visa application and at the location where the applicant wishes to work (www.ins.usdoj.gov/graphics/glossary2.htm).

Why are so few Mexicans taking advantage of the NAFTA visa? One possible explanation is that qualifications for Mexicans differ significantly from the qualifications of their peers in Canada and the United States. Another reason may be the relative lack of mutual recognition or certification procedures for Mexican professionals in the United States compared to Canadian professionals. For example, the United States has had an equivalency exam for Canadian chartered public accountants in place for some time, but only recently began to implement a similar mechanism for Mexicans. With respect to the legal profession, several state bars accept Canadian law degrees as equivalent to law degrees from schools approved by the American Bar Association (ABA), so that Canadian graduates need only write the state bar exams to be licensed to practice law. For example, common law graduates of McGill law school have their degree recognized in several states, including California, New York, and Massachusetts.

Given Mexico's civil law system, it would be difficult to grant the same status to graduates of Mexican law schools. The legal systems of Canada (except Quebec) and the United States (except Louisiana) are both based on common law, the legal system they inherited from England. Mexico's legal system is based on civil law, the system inherited from Spain. It is thus closer to the legal systems of Quebec and Louisiana, which are based on the civil law system they inherited from France.

However, accounting and law are only two of almost seventy professions listed in NAFTA as qualifying for a visa. Moreover, there is less divergence in numbers when we compare the numbers of Mexicans and Canadians granted other types of temporary entry visas in the United States, where they receive equal treatment with respect to requirements (other than the general nonimmigrant visa required of Mexicans). A more likely reason why Mexicans use the HIB visa rather than the TN visa is that the former is valid for three years, whereas the latter is valid for only one year. As a result, U.S. employers prefer to use the HIB visa for Mexican professionals, because the requirements are otherwise the same and they only have to deal with renewal procedures after three years, rather than annually. The following tables compares the number of U.S. temporary entry visas granted to skilled Mexicans and Canadians in fiscal years 1999 and 2000. These numbers indicate that when skilled Mexicans and Canadians face the same visa requirements, notably the requirement for labor certification, similar numbers qualify for entry. The removal of the labor certification requirement for NAFTA visas for Mexicans would likely have a much greater impact than the removal of the 5,500 limit.

In the short term, the removal of the labor certification requirement for Mexicans under U.S. temporary worker visa programs and NAFTA would be an important first step to legalizing the status of a large percentage of Mexican migrants. The quotas could be adjusted over time, as circumstances require. Flows of illegal immigrants from Mexico to the United States have not diminished, despite stricter immigration laws and increased border enforcement. Making existing visa programs user-friendly would increase the number of Mexican workers who opt for the legal route.

The European system of labor mobility, open borders, and harmonized security measures on external borders provides a model for the NAFTA countries to consider emulating. Existing U.S. policies regarding illegal immigration have failed to stop large numbers of illegal immigrants from crossing the border. However, they divert resources that could be used to focus border enforcement on people who pose a threat to national security. The legaliza-

Table 3.9

Temporary Entry Visas Granted to Skilled Canadian and Mexican Workers, 1999

Source	H1A	H1B	H3	J1	L1	O1	P1	TN
Canada	26	10,235	95	5,470	13,603	885	2,508	67,076
Mexico	75	12,257	574	5,538	11,387	398	8,373	1,278

Source: INS, Nonimmigrants admitted as temporary workers, exchange visitors and intra-company transferees by region and country of citizenship, Fiscal Years 1999 and 2000.

Note: H1A: Registered nurses; H1B: Workers with specialty occupations; H3: Industrial trainees; J1: Exchange visitors; L1: Intracompany transferees; O1: Workers with extraordinary ability or achievement; P1: Internationally recognized athletes or entertainers; TN: NAFTA workers.

Table 3.10

Temporary Entry Visas Granted to Skilled Canadian and Mexican Workers, 2000

Source	H1A	H1B	H3	J1	L1	O1	P1	TN
Canada	17	12,929	86	6,322	19,221	1,195	2,533	89,220
Mexico	130	13,507	307	6,295	14,516	542	9,977	2,059

Source: INS, Nonimmigrants admitted as temporary workers, exchange visitors and intra-company transferees by region and country of citizenship, Fiscal Years 1999 and 2000.

Note: H1A: Registered nurses; H1B: Workers with specialty occupations; H3: Industrial trainees; J1: Exchange visitors; L1: Intracompany transferees; O1: Workers with extraordinary ability or achievement; P1: Internationally recognized athletes or entertainers; TN: NAFTA workers.

tion of Mexican migration would allow the border patrol to focus on security threats and allow the INS to focus on resident aliens who may be security threats. It would thus reduce the cost of enhancing security.

Rising Dough: Business Implications of Labor Mobility

Legalized labor mobility between Mexico and the United States, or among all three NAFTA countries, probably will cause labor costs in Mexico to rise. However, it is unlikely that the productivity of Mexican workers will rise as quickly as labor costs under these circumstances. Indeed, the salaries of workers have risen faster than productivity in Mexico's manufacturing sector in recent years. As a result, other low-wage countries have an increasingly significant labor-cost advantage over Mexico. North American firms that rely on low-cost labor for competitive advantage will lose their competitiveness.

Already, some firms are moving their Mexican maquiladora manufacturing operations to Asia. For example, the Japanese company Canon has announced that it is shifting production of ink jet printer cartridges from Mexico to Thailand and Vietnam, a move that the company expects to reduce costs by 20 percent. According to the Mexican Center for Economic Analysis and Projections, the number of maquiladoras in Mexico declined 4 percent in 2001. Of these, 60 percent moved to Asia and 40 percent closed due to the North American recession. Between 1980 and 2000, employment in the maquiladoras grew constantly, but it then began to decline. This was due in part to a strong peso, but can also be explained by Mexican wage rates increasing faster than inflation and the rising tax burden in Mexico for firms, on top of an economic slowdown in the United States.

This trend is likely to be exacerbated by further trade barrier reductions under the GATT and other trade agreements, particularly with China as a member of the World Trade Organization. Labor mobility in NAFTA would benefit Mexican workers by giving them the one advantage other developing country workers would not have—free access to the North American labor market. This would benefit both Mexican workers and North American firms, by giving the latter an edge over Japanese and European firms that might have less access to workers to fill their own shortages. However, it would be detrimental to labor-intensive industries in Mexico.

The theory of comparative advantage favors Mexico's exploitation of its relatively cheap and plentiful labor to compete in the global marketplace. However, more recent research on the sources of competitive advantage suggests that sustained economic success depends on a more sophisticated approach to global competition. Reliance on cheap labor will not benefit Mexican business in the long run. To quote Peter Drucker, "It is no longer possible to base a business or a country's economic development on cheap labor. . . . Low labor costs no longer offset low labor productivity" (Drucker 1999, 61). Indeed, the salaries of workers have risen faster than productivity in Mexico's manufacturing sector. Mexico-based firms will increasingly have to compete with firms based in Canada and United States for labor if the free movement of labor is adopted in the NAFTA countries. Firms in Mexico already compete for knowledge workers with the United States and Canada. While the perception in both Mexico and Canada is that there is a brain drain that flows to the United States, movement of professionals between the three countries flows in all directions. Moreover, competition for talented workers has become global.

Demographic changes will intensify competition for knowledge workers long before they have an impact on semiskilled and unskilled workers. As baby boomers in Canada and the United States begin to retire over the next twenty-five years, there will be shortages first in professions such as primary, secondary, and postsecondary teaching. These demographic changes represent both an opportunity and a challenge for Mexican firms. Education and training programs in Mexico's public and private education systems, together with the human resource development policies of Mexican firms, will have a major impact on the kinds of jobs and business ventures in which Mexico will be competitive. In a 2000 OECD study of students in thirty-two countries, Mexican students ranked second-to-last in reading comprehension, mathematics, and science. The preparation that Mexico's youth receives over the next generation will determine the level of income of the nation.

Economic, demographic, geographic, and business conditions put Mexico in a position to take advantage of a real opportunity. If Mexico chooses to rely on cheap, unskilled labor to sustain its competitive advantage, it will have chosen the dead end. Other nations will have lower wages that will make any advantage unsustainable, and a cheap-labor approach will only further impoverish Mexico relative to other nations. Mexico will benefit more from North American labor mobility if the laborers it provides have the skills to demand higher wages. Mexican firms will be more globally competitive if they adopt business strategies to compensate for rising labor costs.

The achievement of greater labor mobility would dramatically change the makeup of North American labor markets. It is likely to have a particularly strong impact on firms in Mexico, be they foreign or domestic, who rely on cheap labor to remain competitive. However, the availability of Mexican labor will also affect the competitive strategies of firms in Canada and the United States. The demographic clouds on the horizon suggest that Anglo-American firms will either have Mexico's labor come to them or they will have to go to Mexico, or elsewhere. It would be beneficial to all three countries to move toward greater labor mobility in the region. It will be necessary for firms to take these trends into account in the development of their competitive strategies.

Conclusion

Illegal immigration from Mexico needs to be resolved. The U.S. and Mexican economies both benefit from Mexican migration. However, the illegal nature of this flow of people promotes more illegal activities, such as people smuggling and the abuse of undocumented workers' rights. In the long run, demographic and economic trends should reduce the wage gap between the United States and Mexico and facilitate the legalization of Mexican labor migration.

However, border issues related to the mobility of people will probably not be addressed on a trilateral basis between the members of NAFTA. Most border issues have not been addressed on a trilateral basis in the past, primarily due to the dramatic differences in standards of living. Controls at the Canada–United States border tend to be aimed at maintaining security, preventing illegal immigration from other countries, and seizing contraband that might be smuggled in either direction. Due to the similarities in wages and standards of living in Canada and the United States, in the short term labor mobility across the Canada–United States border would be more feasible politically and economically than it is across the Mexico–United States border.

Nevertheless, existing agreements and future negotiations on labor mobility in the NAFTA region appear to be moving Canada, Mexico, and the United States toward increasingly free movement of labor in the region. Demographic trends in the three countries and the needs of firms in the region will greatly contribute to the realization of this goal. Ultimately, it is likely that there will be freer movement of labor, possibly following the European model.

In the short term, however, security concerns may perpetuate the existing asymmetries in the bilateral border relationships in North America with respect to the movement of people. National security takes precedence over trade under the trade agreements that apply and is perhaps the broadest exception contained in those agreements. Despite recent advances in the relationship between Mexico and the United States, the Canadian border remains more open to the movement of people than the Mexican border and can be policed with fewer personnel. However, the tighter security on the Mexican border remains insufficient to stop the passage of 300,000 illegal migrants each year, making it a less than optimal solution over the long term.

Flows of illegal immigrants from Mexico to the United States have not diminished, despite stricter immigration laws and increased border enforcement. Despite the economic integration occurring under NAFTA, there is as yet no clear sign of convergence with respect to wages. On the contrary, the wage gap between the United States and Mexico has increased. The wage gap points to continuing flows of illegal immigrants, despite the increasingly dangerous nature of the journey and despite the recent dilution of labor rights for illegal immigrants in the United States. The illegal status of Mexican migrants has created incentives for further illegal activities on both sides of the border—the violation of labor laws on the U.S. side and the expansion of immigrant smuggling rings on the Mexican side.

Despite the apparent availability of temporary work visas under U.S. immigration programs and NAFTA, and over 2 million applications from Mexican citizens, U.S. immigration quotas are far from filled, due to restrictive labor certification requirements for Mexicans. The end of the bracero program in the 1960s sparked the beginning of the illegal immigration problem. The experience of the European Union with respect to the southern European countries suggests that legalized migration programs, combined with economic integration and vocational training programs, helped to narrow wage gaps between the north and the south and do away with the problem of illegal migration among member countries. It bears repeating that the 1.5 percent of European citizens who work legally in other member countries is roughly equivalent to the 1.3 percent of the U.S. population that is made up of Canadians and (mostly) Mexicans working illegally in the United States.

Reforms are necessary. In the short term, the removal of the labor certification requirement for Mexicans under U.S. temporary worker visa programs and NAFTA would be an important first step to legalizing the status of a large percentage of Mexican migrants. The quotas could be adjusted over time, as circumstances require. In addition, the NAFTA countries should consider funding vocational training programs to raise the skill levels of Mexicans and unskilled laborers in Canada and the United States, possibly following the European Social Fund model. This would benefit the competitiveness of both the United States and Mexico, and, to a lesser degree, Canada. However, the full integration of North American labor markets along European Union lines would require a significant reduction in the wage gap between Mexico and the United States, making it a long-term goal rather than a short-term possibility.

Appendix 3.1
Kissing Cousins: Policing the 49th Parallel

In Hollywood movies, characters fleeing American justice usually head for Mexico or Canada. The ones that head to Canada are often portrayed as misunderstood rather than real bad guys. In the age of international terrorism, however, the perception is that there may be "foreign" bad guys sneaking across the border into the United States under the noses of the unsuspecting Canadians. At the same time, legend has it that the Mounties always get their man. Here, we take a look at these two aspects of people movement between the United States and the Great White North.

Heading North: Cold Comfort for Dope Smokers and Draft Dodgers

> "Stems and seeds, stems and seeds, they sure don't deliver the kick
> that this old boy needs."
> —*Jesse Winchester, Canadian singer and songwriter, American draft dodger*

An estimated 125,000 Americans moved to Canada between 1964 and 1977, many of them draft dodgers and deserters (CBC 2002). In the 1960s and 1970s, Canada became the haven of choice for U.S. citizens who wanted to avoid U.S. military service during the Vietnam War. John Hagan (2001) estimates that more than 50,000 draft-age American men and women migrated to Canada during the Vietnam War, making this wave of emigration the largest political exodus from the United States since the American Revolution (when United Empire Loyalists also fled to Canada). Canadian immigration officials at first resisted the influx, but later gave into pressure from church and civil liberties groups to allow the draft dodgers to immigrate. During the same period, the expansion of Canadian universities produced a shortage of Canadian academics, leading to the recruitment of American professors. At the start of the 1970s, U.S. citizens constituted 21 percent of humanities professors, 20 percent of social sciences professors, and 8 percent of science professors (CBC 2002).

A generation later, most Americans who flee to Canada and file refugee claims are facing criminal charges in the United States. A new term has been coined to describe Americans who claim refugee status in Canada in an attempt to avoid jail terms for marijuana possession—"drug refugees." A small community of American drug refugees has settled on British Columbia's Sunshine Coast, where they await their immigration hearings (Ko 2002).

One drug refugee, Steve Kubby, uses marijuana to treat his adrenal gland cancer and credits marijuana with keeping the cancer at bay for twenty years. He became an advocate for medical marijuana use in California. He was acquitted of marijuana possession and possession for sale at a trial at which a doctor from the University of Southern California testified that regular marijuana use kept Kubby alive. However, he was convicted of possessing a hallucinogenic mushroom. He was sentenced to 120 days in jail (without marijuana). He fled to Canada with his wife and two daughters. When Canada denied him permanent entry because of his drug conviction, Kubby filed a refugee claim. He was subsequently charged in Canada for cultivating marijuana, and possession for the purpose of trafficking, in connection with 160 marijuana plants found in his possession (Ko 2002; "Medical Marijuana Users Take Refuge in Canada").

Another California refugee, Renee Boje, was charged with conspiring to produce marijuana for sale to Hollywood stars. Prior to her indictment, she crossed the border and claimed refugee status. She could face ten years in prison. Boje's refugee claim argues that the severity of U.S. marijuana penalties violates international law and that Boje is being persecuted for her political belief in the use of medical marijuana and her association with like-minded people. One of the grounds on which she is challenging a U.S. extradition request is that her prosecution is based in a political fight between the U.S. federal government and the state of California over the state's legalization of marijuana for medical use (Ko 2002; "Medical Marijuana Users Take Refuge in Canada").

U.S. killers facing the death penalty also see Canada as a safe haven, particularly since the Supreme Court of Canada's 2001 decision on extradition procedures in potential death penalty cases. The court ruled that two Vancouver men facing murder charges in the United States could be extradited only with guarantees that they would not face execution. Describing capital punishment as an irrevocable horror that has been discredited both as a deterrent and a punishment, the court cited a series of wrongful murder convictions in Canada and the United States as providing "tragic testimony to the fallibility of the legal system despite its elaborate safeguards for the protection of the innocent."

Aiming South: A Cold-Blooded Front from Canada

> "Canada is not any greater source of threat to the United States than
> exists within their own border."
> —*Canadian Deputy Prime Minister John Manley*

Following the attacks of September 11, the U.S. media began to ask whether the relatively open border with Canada might constitute a threat to national security. Although none of the hijackers of September 11 had entered the United States from Canada, the Canadian government found it necessary to counter the perception in the U.S. media that lax Canadian immigration laws facilitated the use of Canada as a staging ground for terrorist attacks on the United States. Canada's refugee system was placed under particular scrutiny. Table 3.11 shows the cause of U.S. concerns.

There are many arguments that support the view that terrorist activity in Canada poses no greater threat than terrorist activity in the United States itself. Canada's highly professional police and civil service are among the best trained in the world. In Transparency International's annual corruption index, Canada consistently ranks better than the United States. There is such close cooperation between U.S. and Canadian agencies that the Royal Canadian Mounted Police (RCMP) is the first and only foreign police force to be given access to the FBI's database.

However, the majority of Canada's employees working abroad are "locally engaged staff," which includes locally hired foreigners. The Canadian Bar Association has suggested that the Canadian foreign service cease hiring foreign staff for decision-making positions at missions abroad in order to eliminate corruption in the processing of visa applications. Documents obtained through Canada's Access to Information law revealed that an employee in Paris accepted bribes to expedite visa applications of people who later obtained refugee status in Canada and the United States. At Canada's mission in Hong Kong, half of the applicants under the selected worker program committed or were suspected of committing fraud by submitting fake employment records and education diplomas. The Canadian embassy in Beijing is also facing corruption allegations in the processing of visas (O'Neil 2002).

Still, the errors uncovered in Canada's management of its refugee and immigration procedures pale in comparison to those that have occurred in the United States itself. The United States did not only admit the September 11 hijackers, but trained them at U.S. flight schools and even renewed the student visas of some of them six months after their suicide attacks. That being said, coordination and information sharing, both within and between Canada and the United States, have improved since September 11. Indeed, the current location of the men listed in Table 3.11 indicates

Table 3.11

Al Qaeda in Canada

Name	Allegation	Nationality	Canadian link	Current location
Mohamed Mahjoub	Bin Laden agent	Egyptian/ Canadian	Refugee	Toronto jail
Ali Mohamed	FBI/Al Qaeda double agent	Egyptian/U.S.	Smuggling attempt	U.S. jail
Essam Marzouk	Bin Laden supporter	Egyptian/ Canadian	Refugee	Egyptian jail
Ahmed Khadr	Bin Laden lieutenant	Egyptian/ Canadian	Immigrant	Unknown/ Afghanistan?
Abdul Rahman	Khadr's son	Canadian	Father	Captured by Afghan forces
Omar Rahman	Khadr's son	Canadian	Father	Arrested by U.S. military
Abu Zubaydah	Bin Laden lieutenant	Saudi	Sought Canadian passports	U.S. jail
Ahmed Ressam	Los Angeles Airport bomb plot	Algerian/ Canadian	Refugee	U.S. jail
Fateh Kamel	Terrorist support network	Algerian/ Canadian	Immigrant	French jail
Mohamed Jabarah	Singapore Al Qaeda cell leader	Kuwaiti/ Canadian	Immigrant	U.S. jail

Sources: Mickelburgh 2002; Tu Than Ha and Freeze 2002.

that international intelligence cooperation is not only necessary but also capable of achieving the desired result.

Angry Ally: A Travel Advisory Warns Some Canadians to Avoid the United States

> "A Canadian is a Canadian for all purposes."
> —*Canadian foreign affairs minister Bill Graham*

On September 11, 2002, the Bush administration introduced a requirement that anyone born in Iran, Iraq, Libya, Sudan, or Syria be photographed and fingerprinted upon arriving in the United States—including Canadian citizens. On September 26, 2002, Canadian citizen Mohamed Arar was arrested at New York's John F. Kennedy International Airport, where he was changing planes on his way home from Tunisia to Canada. The United States deported Arar to Syria (his birthplace), where Syrian authorities put him in jail. As a result of these events, Canada's Foreign Ministry issued a travel advisory warning Canadians born in these five countries, as well as those born in Pakistan, Saudi Arabia, or Yemen, to think twice before entering the United States, including transit to and from third countries (Ljunggren 2002a).

The travel advisory sparked an uproar in Canada's Parliament. Members of Parliament were furious. One member of Parliament (MP) was particularly angry. Sarkis Assadourian, a Syrian-born MP, testified to Parliament's foreign affairs committee that the U.S. rules made him feel like a second-class citizen. He suggested that Canada respond by fingerprinting all Americans with criminal records who sought entry to Canada. Moreover, he asked rhetorically, "Why would I support U.S. policy [on Iraq] if U.S. policy does not respect my rights as a Canadian citizen?" (Ljunggren 2002b).

On October 31, 2002, the Canadian minister of foreign affairs, Bill Graham, received a standing ovation when he announced in Parliament that the U.S. ambassador to Canada had just assured him that Canadian citizens would not be questioned by U.S. officials as to their country of birth (Dunfield 2002).

Appendix 3.2
Illegal in the USA:
Conspiracies, Pepper Spray, and a Hollywood Script

Illegal immigration from Mexico to the United States is one of the most complex and challenging issues in their bilateral relationship. The following account of recent news items demonstrates that this issue continues to be not only a source of conflict, but increasingly the subject of lawsuits brought by all of the players in the drama save the employers of illegal workers. The employers are instead the ones targeted in many lawsuits.

Chickens on the Run: The Tyson Foods Conspiracy

On December 19, 2001, a federal grand jury in Tennessee indicted executives and managers of Tyson Foods, Inc., on charges of conspiring to smuggle illegal aliens to fifteen of the company's fifty-seven poultry processing plants. The indictment accused Tyson's managers of tolerating the hiring of illegal aliens to meet production goals, to cut costs, and to maximize profits. The company obtained false documents, such as fraudulent social security cards, so the illegal immigrants could work "under the false pretense of being legally employable." The company managers paid under-cover INS agents working for Tyson to recruit illegal immigrants at the U.S.–Mexi-can border and transport them to processing plants in Tennessee, North Carolina, Virginia, Indiana, Missouri, and Arkansas. Tyson often paid $100 or $200 per head to smugglers. The illegal workers were also expected to pay a fee to the smugglers.

According to James Ziglar, commissioner of the INS, the case represents the first time the INS has taken action against such a large company. Tyson Foods, Inc., is the largest meat producer and processor in the United States. The company could face sanctions and large fines if found guilty; the workers could face prison terms. Some labor organizations, such as the United Food and Commercial Workers, have been pressing the U.S. government to take action against companies for recruiting and hiring illegal immigrants at low wages for work in hazardous jobs instead of going after the undocumented workers. However, federal raids on meatpacking plants upset food companies, which have complained of disruptions. Moreover, civil rights offi-cials accused the government of harassing Mexicans and others from Central America. Midwestern politicians sometimes complained that disrupting work at meatpacking plants increased the supply of livestock and thereby harmed hog and cattle farmers, who had already been suffering from low prices for their goods (Barboza 2001a, 2001b.)

Picking an Apple Fight: Legals versus Illegals

On September 3, 2002, the federal court of appeals in Seattle ruled that companies that hire illegal immigrants can be sued by legal residents for damages allegedly caused by the competition the legal residents thus confront. Juana Mendiola and Olivia Mendoza, Mexicans working legally in the United States, allege that their employers, Zirkle Fruit Company and Matson Fruit Company, have conspired with an employ-ment agency in a scheme to hire illegal immigrants that depressed the wages paid to legal immigrants in Washington's Yakima valley. An INS investigation in 1998 and 1999 revealed that 74 percent of Matson employees were illegal immigrants, mostly from Mexico, using fraudulent documents. The case is being brought under the Rack-eteer Influenced and Corrupt Organizations Act (RICO), under which damages, if proved, could be tripled. The companies say they pay all of their workers the same wage. It remains to be seen whether the plaintiffs can prove their case in court. Even if they do not, the publicity surrounding the case may make employers more cautious about hiring illegal immigrants. Ironically, Mexico is the largest importer of apples from Washington State, one of the main products produced by the fruit companies (Fuentes and Jiménez 2002).

Rotten Eggs: The DeCoster Class Action Suit

The Mexican government has stepped in to support the rights of Mexican workers in the United States. Mexico became party to a class action discrimination lawsuit against DeCoster Egg Farm in Turner, Maine, for mistreatment of Mexican workers. While the government was later dropped from the suit, it spent about $100,000 on lawyers and mediators. Mexico's President Fox later announced that he was naming a special prosecutor who would be responsible for filing more such cases in U.S. courts in the future.

In 2001, Mexican workers in the United States sent $9 billion back to their families in Mexico, making remittances from migrant workers Mexico's third largest source of foreign exchange earnings. Remittances thus help to reduce Mexico's current account deficit, support the value of the peso, and reduce Mexico's need to borrow money abroad.

Paralyzed and Pepper-Sprayed: The Olvera-Carrera Case

On September 24, 2002, three San Antonio men—Carlos Reyna, Richard Henry Gonzales, and Louis Rey Gomez—were indicted in Houston court for their roles in beating, pepper-spraying, paralyzing, and delaying medical attention to Serafin Olvera-Carrera, a Mexican father of five. The incidents took place on March 25, 2001. The victim died February 24, 2002. The three men face prison terms ranging from ten to twenty years.

But these were no ordinary thugs. All three worked for the United States Immigration and Naturalization Service. Olvera-Carrera was working illegally as a roofer in the United States. The incidents occurred during an INS raid. The men are not charged with murder (though Olvera-Carrera's family think they should be). They are charged with civil rights violations. The family has filed a civil suit.

Following the indictment, the office of Mexican president Vicente Fox issued the following statement: "These arrests set a very important precedent, especially seeing as how it's so unusual that members of a federal organization are prosecuted for violating the civil rights of an illegal immigrant."

A Hollywood Happy Ending: The Case of the Honest Dishwasher

On August 27, 2001, a bag containing $203,000 fell out of the back of an armored truck at a bus stop in downtown Los Angeles. Ascension Franco Gonzales, a twenty-three-year-old illegal immigrant from Mexico, was waiting for the bus when the money fell out. He picked it up and stashed it in a plastic garbage bag. The next morning, he arranged to meet the police in a park, where he returned the money. Police Sergeant Rick Sanchez wanted to share the story with the media, but Franco was worried that he would run into trouble with the U.S. immigration authorities. When the policeman persisted, Franco relented. The story was picked up by media around the world. When his mother saw him on the news in their hometown of Tepeapulco, she cried with joy. "I thought it was a miracle from God, that God illuminated the path for him," she said.

As a child watching his mother work cleaning houses, Franco had dreamed of one day building her a house of her own to take care of. When he was twenty-one, he went to California to earn money for his mother's house. He found a job washing dishes in a Chinese restaurant. He worked ten hours a day, six days a week, for $1,300 a month, sending $600 to $800 a month home to his mother. The armored car company gave him a reward of $25,000, leaving him with $17,000 after taxes. He sent most of it home to Tepeapulco, enabling his parents to raise the frame for the house he had promised them as a boy.

Now two Hollywood screenwriters want to turn his story into a movie. David Freeman says, "It has the power of a fable—of myth." His colleague, Paul Mazursky, describes it as "a profoundly moving story." When last heard from, Franco was still washing dishes at the Chinese restaurant. He had not yet been rounded up and deported by the INS (Becerra 2002).

4

Doing the Laundry

Cross-Border Capital Movements

> "If you can count your money, you don't have
> a billion dollars."
> —*J. Paul Getty*

> "Not everything that can be counted counts, and not everything
> that counts can be counted."
> —*Albert Einstein*

Money makes the world go 'round—so goes the saying. Cross-border capital flows are at once the lifeblood of international commerce and the lifeblood of international crime, be it drug or people smuggling, tax evasion, or terrorism. The central issue is therefore how to strike the right balance between measures to liberalize cross-border capital flows and the restrictions that are necessary to deal with transnational crime. In this chapter, we begin by examining restrictions on capital flows for money laundering and terrorist financing. We then focus on two topics related to capital flows that affect economic integration in the NAFTA countries—the prospects for a common currency and flows of foreign direct investment. Finally, we look at how remittances from Mexicans in the United States help economic development in Mexico but may hinder the detection of illicit transfers of money across the border.

Let It Flow: NAFTA and Barriers to Capital Flows

NAFTA has done much to break down barriers to cross-border capital flows. NAFTA applies to "persons" of a NAFTA country, which means citizens or permanent residents of a NAFTA member or a business organized under the law of a NAFTA member. Thus, as long as a company from outside the NAFTA region is able to meet the requirements for incorporation (or other forms of business organization) and complies with foreign investment laws, it may become a NAFTA company. However, companies that are controlled by investors from outside the NAFTA countries may be denied NAFTA benefits if the enterprise has no substantial business activities in the territory of the country under whose laws it is constituted. Benefits may also be denied if a NAFTA country does not maintain diplomatic relations with the investor's home country or prohibits business transactions with enterprises from that country.

NAFTA prohibits restrictions on transfers of profits, proceeds, or payments unless the restrictions are due to the application of laws relating to bankruptcy, securities, criminal offenses, currency transfer reporting, or enforcement of judgments. Governments therefore remain free to restrict transfers under laws such as those relating to money laundering and those that permit the freezing of assets in litigation and bankruptcy proceedings. Following the attacks, the NAFTA governments used money laundering laws to deal with terrorist funds (see Appendix 4.1, p. 141)

NAFTA also contains a more general national security exception that applies to all of its provisions, including the treatment of foreign investors. Because it is so broad and discretionary, this exception could be used to restrict capital movements whenever one of the governments considers such restrictions necessary for the protection of its essential security interests in a time of war or other emergency in international relations.

While there have been no cases interpreting this provision under NAFTA or the equivalent provision under the General Agreement on Tariffs and Trade (GATT), capital restrictions placed on terrorist funds in the context of the September 11 attacks would very likely qualify under this exception. Support for this view may be found in the preparatory work relating to the equivalent GATT security exception. One of the drafters of the original draft charter stated:

> We gave a good deal of thought to the question of the security exception. . . . It is really a question of balance. . . . We cannot make it too tight, because we cannot prohibit measures which are needed purely for security reasons. On the other hand, we cannot make it so broad that, under the guise of security, countries will put on measures which really have a commercial purpose. (WTO 1995, 600)

In the case of restrictions on terrorist funds, the purpose of the measures would clearly be related to their security interests, not a commercial purpose.

Dirty Money: Capital Flows and Security

Canada, Mexico, and the United States are all members of the Financial Action Task Force on Money Laundering (FATF). FATF is an intergovernmental policy-making body created in 1989 by the G-7 summit in Paris. It has created a list of forty recommendations that provide a framework for policy implementation in member and nonmember countries (FATF, "More About the FATF and Its Work," May 30, 2002). There are currently thirty-one members, listed in Table 4.1, and several international organizations with observer status, listed in Table 4.2. Since 2000, FATF has published lists of countries that are not cooperative in fighting money laundering. FATF members request their financial institutions to scrutinize business transactions with individuals, companies, and financial institutions from listed countries. Table 4.3 lists those countries.

Following the terrorist attacks of September 11, FATF held an extraordinary plenary meeting on the financing of terrorism in Washington in October 2001. FATF agreed to expand its mandate beyond money laundering to include terrorist financing. The group issued a set of international standards for countries to adopt, including to criminalize the financing of terrorism, to freeze and confiscate terrorist assets, to enhance international cooperation, and to impose anti-money laundering requirements on alternative remittance systems (such as those used by Mexican migrants). FATF also agreed to identify countries that lack appropriate measures to combat terrorist financing, as was already done with respect to money laundering (FATF, "Terrorist Financing," May 30, 2002).

The Washington meeting was followed by a global forum in Hong Kong in February 2002, attended by sixty jurisdictions representing members of FATF and similar regional organizations. The Hong Kong meeting launched a process under which all jurisdictions were asked to complete a self-assessment questionnaire, the results of which FATF will use to determine what further actions are required to combat terrorist financing globally. As of September 2002, 108 jurisdictions had responded (FATF, "Overview of Steps Taken to Combat Terrorist Financing Since October 2001," September 2002).

As members of FATF, Canada, the United States, and Mexico have comparable laws in place to combat money laundering. In Canada and the United States, FATF estimated that 60 to 80 percent of money laundering transactions involved narcotics proceeds. According to FATF, the United States has a serious money laundering problem due to the size and diversity of its financial system, a plethora of state and federal laws, and its proximity to South American drug producers. Success in reducing the laundering of illegal proceeds in traditional banking institutions has led to a significant

Table 4.1

Thirty-one Members, Financial Action Task Force on Money Laundering (FATF)

Argentina	Greece	Norway
Australia	Gulf Co-operation Council (GCC)	Portugal
Austria	Hong Kong, China	Singapore
Belgium	Iceland	Spain
Brazil	Ireland	Sweden
Canada	Italy	Switzerland
Denmark	Japan	Turkey
European Commission	Luxembourg	United Kingdom
Finland	Mexico	United States
France	Netherlands	
Germany	New Zealand	

Source: OECD, www1.oecd.org/fatf/Members_en.htm.

Notes: The members of the GCC are Bahrain, Kuwait, Oman, Qatar, Saudi Arabia, and the United Arab Emirates. While the GCC is a member of the FATF, its member countries are not.

Table 4.2

Observers, Financial Action Task Force on Money Laundering (FATF)

FATF-style regional bodies
  Asia/Pacific Group on Money Laundering (APG)
  Caribbean Financial Action Task Force (CFATF)
  Council of Europe PC-R-EV Committee
  Eastern and Southern Africa Anti-Money Laundering Group (ESAAMLG)
  Financial Action Task Force on Money Laundering in South America (GAFISUD)
Other International organizations
  African Development Bank
  Asia Development Bank
  The Commonwealth Secretariat
  Egmont Group of Financial Intelligence Units
  European Bank for Reconstruction and Development (EBRD)
  European Central Bank (ECB)
  Europol
  Inter-American Development Bank (IDB)
  International Monetary Fund (IMF)
  Interpol
  International Organisation of Securities Commissions (IOSCO)
  Organization of American States/Inter-American Drug Abuse Control
    Commission (OAS/CICAD)
  Offshore Group of Banking Supervisors (OGBS)
  United Nations Office for Drug Control and Crime Prevention (UNODCCP)
  World Bank
  World Customs Organization (WCO)

Source: OECD, www1.oecd.org/fatf/Members_en.htm.

Table 4.3

Thirteen Countries Listed as Noncooperative in Fight against Money Laundering

Cook Islands	Indonesia	Russia
Dominica	Marshall Islands	St. Vincent and the Grenadines
Egypt	Myanmar	Ukraine
Grenada	Niue	
Guatemala	Philippines	

Source: OECD, Third FATF Review to Identify Non-Cooperative Countries or Territories: Increasing the Worldwide Effectiveness of Anti-Money Laundering Measures (June 21, 2002), www1.oecd.org/fatf/pdf/NCCT2002_en.pdf.

Notes: Cayman Islands, Panama, and Liechtenstein were removed from the list in June 2001. Hungary, Israel, Lebanon, and St. Kitts and Nevis were removed from the list on June 21, 2002.

increase in cash smuggling out of the United States, particularly on the border with Mexico. Mexico's money laundering problem stems from its strategic geographic location between the South American drug producers and American drug consumers. In Canada, the problem stems from its location next to the United States (FATF, "Mutual Evaluations of Canada, United States and Mexico, 1997–2000").

In May 1996, the Mexican congress modified the penal code to make money laundering a punishable offense, independent of other monetary violations (Article 400 *bis*). Article 400 *bis* is broad enough to apply to all criminal activities. To combat money laundering, banks, stock brokers, and exchange houses have been required since May 1997 to confidentially report suspicious financial activities involving $10,000 or more. Mexico established a Special Prosecutor's Office for Crimes Against Health under the attorney general in April 1997 to spearhead antinarcotics investigations. In addition, Mexico has added a Financial Intelligence Unit to the Finance Ministry's Directorate General for the Investigation of Transactions (FATF, "Mutual Evaluations").

Around the same time, Canada introduced several changes to its money laundering regime, beginning with new anti-money laundering guidelines published by the Superintendent of Financial Institutions in 1996. In May 1997, Canada enacted organized crime legislation that expanded the scope of money laundering offences. All serious crimes are now covered. In June 2000, Canada enacted the Proceeds of Crime (Money Laundering) Act, which established the Financial Transaction and Reports Analysis Centre of Canada (Section 41). The act applies mandatory record-keeping and reporting rules regarding suspicious activity to banks and nonbank financial institutions and sets out new search and seizure and forfeiture laws (FATF, "Mutual Evalua-tions"; Proceeds of Crime [Money Laundering] Act).

In the United States, money laundering regulations are issued by the di-rector of the Financial Crimes Enforcement Network (FinCEN) under the Bank Secrecy Act (BSA), enacted in 1970. More than 220,000 financial in-stitutions are subject to BSA reporting and record-keeping requirements, in-cluding banks and nonbank financial institutions. A very extensive list of crimes is covered, including terrorism, health care, and immigration offences.

Smurfing USA: A Money Laundering Example

Street-level narcotics sales occur frequently in the United States. Naturally, cash is the preferred method of payment for these transactions. The cash from one or multiple sales locations is collected at a safe or "stash" house for processing. The cash is then taken to a remittance business for transmission out of the country.

To avoid scrutiny by law enforcement or bank regulatory authorities, the cash may be divided into amounts less than $10,000 and "smurfed." Smurfing is a process that uses a large number of individuals to make small deposits and withdrawals (transfer of amounts below federal reporting requirements) at a remittance business. The funds are sent by the U.S.-based remitter to a Mexican-based counterpart. The remittance company will normally utilize an offsetting book entry transfer or conduct a bank wire transfer in order to move the money out of the United States.

The remittance business in Mexico pays out in Mexican pesos. This is the most common method applied to avoid detection of money movement at either end (Molander et al., 1998).

Icing on the Layer Cake: The General Process of Money Laundering

In the initial or placement stage of money laundering, the launderer intro-duces the illegal profits into the financial system. This might be done by breaking up large amounts of cash into less conspicuous smaller sums that are then deposited directly into a bank account, or by purchasing a series of monetary instruments (checks, money orders, etc.) that are then collected and deposited into accounts at another location.

After the funds have entered the financial system, the second, layering stage takes place. In this phase, the launderer engages in a series of conver-sions or movements of the funds to distance them from their source. The funds might be channeled through the purchase and sales of investment instruments, or the launderer might simply wire the funds through a series of accounts at various banks across the globe. This use of widely scattered accounts for laundering is especially prevalent in those jurisdictions that do not cooperate in anti-money laundering investigations. In some instances, the launderer might disguise the transfers as payments for goods or services, thus giving them a legitimate appearance.

Having successfully processed the criminal profits through the first two phases of the money laundering process, the launderer then moves them to the third stage—integration—in which the funds reenter the legitimate economy. The launderer might choose to invest the funds into real estate, luxury assets, or business ventures (Molander et al., 1998).

Banking on Supervision: Regulation in North America

In a series of tables (Table 4.4a to Table 4.4g), we compare and contrast banking regulation and supervision in the NAFTA region. Table 4.4a tells us that even though in Canada and Mexico the licensing authority rests with their respective ministries of finance, it is not so in the United States, where licensing is done state by state by the comptroller of currency. Given the existence of the Glass-Steagall Act, which restricted expansion of banks across states for over seven decades, the United States ended up with more than 10,000 banks compared to fifty odd banks in Canada and Mexico. Given the relative sizes of the economies, there should not be more than 500 banks in the United States (Table 4.4a).

Legal submissions required for banking licenses are virtually the same across the three NAFTA partners (Table 4.4b). The only difference is that in the United States banks are not required to submit their intended organizational charts. The use of risk management is also similar except for one item with one exception. In Canada, the capital required to be held by banks does not vary with the riskiness of the banks whereas in Mexico and United States it does (Table 4.4c). The requirements for capital structure vary widely across countries. For example, in Mexico and the United States, the use of securities (that is, stocks of corporations) is severely restricted whereas in Canada it is not. Moreover, the use of insurance instruments is prohibited in Mexico but fully permitted in Canada and restricted in the United States. In addition, the use of real estate as an asset is unrestricted in Canada but not in the other two. On the other hand, banks' ownership of non-financial firms is fully permitted in Mexico but highly restricted in Canada and the United States (Table 4.4d). Audit requirements for the banks are very similar across the three countries (Table 4.4e). It appears

Table 4.4a

Banking in NAFTA

	Licensing authority	Number of banks	Minimum capital entry requirement in millions	Is information on source of funds for capital required?
Canada	Ministry of Finance	55	CDN $10	Yes
Mexico	Ministry of Finance	52	U.S. $6.5	Yes
United States	Office of the Comptroller of the Currency	10,500	No absolute minimum	Yes

Source: Bank Supervision Database, World Bank, Special Tabulation, 2001.

Table 4.4b

Legal Submissions Required for Banking License

	Canada	Mexico	United States
Draft by-laws	Yes	Yes	Yes
Intended organization chart	Yes	Yes	No
First three-year financial projections	Yes	Yes	Yes
Financial information on shareholders	Yes	Yes	Yes
Background and experience of future directors	Yes	Yes	Yes
Background and experience of future managers	Yes	Yes	Yes
Sources of funds in capitalization of new bank	Yes	Yes	Yes
Intended market differentiation of new bank	Yes	Yes	Yes

Source: Bank Supervision Database, World Bank, Special Tabulation, 2001.

Table 4.4c

Use of Risk Management

	Canada	Mexico	United States
Minimum capital-asset ratio requirement (percent)	8	8	8
Is it risk-weighted in line with Basle guidelines?	Yes	Yes	Yes
Does the ratio vary with a bank's credit risk?	No	Yes	Yes
Does the ratio vary with market risk?	No	Yes	Yes
Actual risk-adjusted capital ratio (percent)	11	13	12

Source: Bank Supervision Database, World Bank, Special Tabulation, 2001.

Table 4.4d

Structure of Capital

	Securities	Insurance	Real estate	Regulatory restrictiveness of bank ownership of nonfinancial firms
Canada	Unrestricted	Permitted	Unrestricted	Restricted
Mexico	Restricted	Prohibited	Restricted	Permitted
United States	Restricted	Restricted	Restricted	Restricted

Source: Bank Supervision Database, World Bank, Special Tabulation, 2001.

Table 4.4e

Auditing Banks

	Canada	Mexico	United States
Is an external audit compulsory?	Yes	Yes	Yes
Are there specific requirements for the extent of the audit?	No	Yes	Yes
Are auditors licensed or certified?	Yes	Yes	Yes
Is auditor's report given to supervisory agency?	Yes	Yes	Yes
Can supervisors meet external auditors to discuss report without bank approval?	Yes	No	Yes

Source: Bank Supervision Database, World Bank, Special Tabulation, 2001.

Table 4.4f

Additional Supervisory Issues

	Canada	Mexico	United States
Are auditors legally required to report misconduct by managers/directors to supervisory agency?	Yes	No	No
Can legal action against external auditors be taken by supervisor for negligence?	No	Yes	Yes
Has legal action been taken against an auditor in last five years?	—	No	No
Can supervisors force banks to change internal organizational structure?	No	Yes	Yes
Has this power been utilized in last five years?	—	Yes	Yes

Source: Bank Supervision Database, World Bank, Special Tabulation, 2001.

Table 4.4g

Asset Allocation by Banks

	Are there guidelines for asset diversification?	Are banks prohibited from making loans abroad?	Minimum liquidity requirement (percent)
Canada	Yes	No	None
Mexico	No	No	Not reported
United States	No	No	None

Source: Bank Supervision Database, World Bank, Special Tabulation, 2001.

that the supervisory body has more teeth for forcing additional actions in the United States and Mexico compared to Canada (Table 4.4f). Finally, asset allocation requirements are similar across NAFTA countries, with the exception of an asset diversification rule imposed in Canada (Table 4.4g).

Hidden Treasure: Mexico's Bank Secrecy Act

A crucial provision of the Mexican law regulating financial groups relates to secrecy. Commonly called the law of *secreto bancario* (although it applies to all financial groups, not only banks), the rule prohibits a financial holding company from disclosing information relating to its operations or to the operations of any member of its group, other than to the legally empowered government agencies. This prohibition includes board members, officers of the company, and any company agent or employee. The legally empowered agency means the relevant Mexican federal regulator. The main concerns raised so far by this secrecy law are related to money laundering. A more mundane (but no less important) concern is that the secrecy law could exclude revelation of information to an adversary in a lawsuit as part of the standard U.S. process of discovery. Also, it is not clear that a U.S. regulatory agency inspecting or evaluating the operations of a U.S. subsidiary in Mexico would be able to obtain the information it requires in spite of this provision. However, Mexican officials say that *secreto bancario* does not stand in the way of access to information in criminal investigations.

Shell Games: Unilateral Actions by the United States

After the September 11 attack on the World Trade Center in New York, the United States government moved swiftly to take actions to starve the terrorist organizations of funds. In a bill passed by Congress in October 2001

(H.R. 3162/P.L. 107–56), a section called "Shell Bank Ban" (Sec. 313) prohibited U.S. banks and securities firms from opening accounts for foreign
shell banks that have no physical presence anywhere and no affiliation with
another bank, and required closure of any existing shell bank account by
December 2001.

This led to a huge protest by U.S. banks. On September 20, 2002, the U.S.
Treasury reversed course. The reversal, which came after pressure from U.S.
banks and other financial institutions with global operations, means new prohibitions aimed at excluding so-called shell banks from U.S. financial markets will apply only to bank operations within the United States.

The prohibitions on U.S. financial institutions dealing with shell banks—
usually small banks with nothing but a post office drop in an offshore banking secrecy haven—indicate a dilemma. Such shell banks are seen as
particularly vulnerable to money laundering, and the United States is seeking to ban all dealings between U.S. financial institutions and shell banks.
But the United Kingdom and European countries do not have similar restrictions, leading U.S. officials to worry that shell banks will find new ways to
move money. The Treasury had originally proposed including foreign
branches of U.S. banks under the prohibition in an effort to extend the reach
of the new regulations beyond U.S. shores.

My Beautiful Launderette: Business Implications of Money Laundering Rules

The financial services industry plays a central role in the detection of proceeds of crime. However, the industry's role consists mainly in scrutinizing
and reporting suspicious transactions, not conducting investigations. Instead,
the reports sent to the financial intelligence authorities in each country trigger investigations on the part of the authorities. The industry needs to famil-
iarize itself with the types of activities that should trigger greater scrutiny as
part of general due diligence procedures. The industry also needs to remain
up to date with respect to lists of countries and persons identified as meriting
added scrutiny.

FATF recognizes that it will be difficult for financial institutions to detect
terrorist financing as such and it is not the role of the industry to determine
the legality of the source or destination of the funds. Moreover, the guidelines that have been developed are not intended to discourage transactions
with legitimate clients. While money laundering laws are being modified to
cover terrorist financing, the activities that should trigger added scrutiny will
be similar to those involved in money laundering in general. There are two
main sources of terrorist funds—first, governments (so-called state-sponsored

terrorism) and organizations (such as Al Qaeda) and, second, revenue-generating activities of terrorist groups. These latter activities may be criminal in nature (kidnapping, extortion, smuggling, fraud, theft, and drug trafficking) or consist of legitimate activities (fund-raising for charitable organizations where some funds are later diverted to terrorist groups). When the funds derive from criminal activities, the methods used to launder funds do not differ from those used by nonterrorist activities and the task of financial institutions does not differ greatly from their duties with respect to money laundering in general.

However, the size and nature of terrorist financing may make detection more difficult. With the September 11 hijackers, for the most part money was sent in small sums by wire transfer and appeared to be for the purpose of supporting students studying abroad. Thus, the size of the transfers fell below the normal cash transaction reporting threshold of $10,000 and the nature of the transactions did not trigger financial institution guidelines for greater scrutiny. FATF has developed a list of characteristics of transactions that may be cause for greater scrutiny as possible terrorist financing that should be followed by financial institutions (see FATF, *Guidance for Financial Institutions on Detecting Terrorist Financing*, April 24, 2002, especially Annex 1).

Dollars, Dollars, Everywhere: The Prospects for a Common Currency

Other than removing one step from the international money launderers' smurfing process discussed above, the creation of a common currency in the NAFTA region would not have a major impact on the monitoring of illegal money transfers. If anything, a common currency would make it easier to launder money in the region. The idea of a common currency relates more to the issue of economic integration and business in the region. There has been some discussion of a European-style monetary union among NAFTA countries. Unlike in Europe, however, this would probably entail the adoption of the U.S. dollar in Canada and Mexico rather than the creation of a new currency.

A company is sitting on a pile of cash it wants to invest. The common method is to take on additional projects in the same geographical region. A less traveled road is to expand in foreign countries. The lure of foreign expansion is enormous. Many companies get much higher returns on their investments from foreign operations. Generally, the risks in foreign countries are higher as well.

Even if there were no political and other risks associated with foreign countries, there is always the risk of currency fluctuations unless the other country also uses the same currency. In the European Union, twelve member countries (all but Denmark, Sweden, and the United Kingdom) have adopted a new currency that eliminates this source of uncertainty. Others have tried to eliminate the fluctuations by pegging their currencies to others. But without the explicit elimination of their own currency, there is always the problem of long-term commitment to such a strategy. The crisis in Argentina in 2002 is a clear demonstration. There, the local currency once traded at par with the U.S. dollar but fell by 75 percent in six months.

Moreover, moving to a common currency in North America would prove difficult to manage politically. Nevertheless, former U.S. ambassador to Mexico Jim Jones has predicted a "de facto monetary union" between the United States and Mexico in ten to fifteen years. He believes that "people and events will run ahead of the politicians," citing a poll taken in Mexico on "dollarizing" the Mexican economy. The poll showed that about 80 percent of the Mexican people favored using the U.S. dollar as their currency. Jones said the poll indicates that the Mexican peso, which has long been one of the major symbols of Mexican sovereignty, "is no longer an important issue." However, he said he doubted that Canada would join such a monetary union because Canadians attach much more importance to the Canadian dollar than Mexicans do to their peso (Green 2000). While it is difficult to predict political sentiments, exchange rates probably influence Mexican attitudes to dollarization. Decades of devaluation may have weakened political support for the currency. However, the peso has been much stronger in recent years and that may increase Mexicans' desire to retain the peso.

Economists are divided on the issue of dollarization. Some argue that such a move would reduce transaction costs and reflect the existing bookkeeping practices of many North American firms (Courchene and Harris 1999). Others argue that the structure of the Canadian and Mexican economies is sufficiently different from that of the United States to require independent monetary policies (Laidler and Poschmann 2000). However, the three economies are becoming increasingly integrated as a result of NAFTA, particularly in key sectors such as manufacturing and financial services.

Is formal monetary union necessary? Countries that have adopted other currencies formally have not necessarily fared well without explicit policy coordination. For the European Union, the adoption of a common currency has come after three decades of policy coordination in different spheres. In the case of Argentina, de facto adoption of the U.S. dollar in 1991 (in the form of a currency board) was not accompanied by fiscal restraint and debt reduction. Not surprisingly, Argentina was unable to sustain the situation in the long run.

Summarizing their views regarding the adoption of another currency or the introduction of a currency board (equivalent to a dollarization), Greenwood and Allen state the following:

> Successful adoption and maintenance of a currency board comes with a serious list of requirements. Some of these are painful, costly, and difficult to implement. As such, currency boards may not be appropriate for many, even most, countries. A currency board is like the "silver bullet" antibiotic given by doctors only in rare circumstances. They are powerful and effective when used appropriately, but lose their potency if over-used. Currency boards will lose their effectiveness if more countries follow in Argentina's footsteps and misuse this strong but demanding antidote to economic ill health. (2002, 2)

In Mexico, successive devaluation crises in the 1980s and 1990s resulted in the partial dollarization of some parts of Mexico, notably the U.S. border region and major tourist resorts. Devaluation problems increased calls for dollarization in some Mexican corners, particularly following the currency crisis of 1994–95. However, the floating of the peso, together with a smooth political transition from the Partido Revolucionario Institucional (PRI) to the Partido Acción Nacional (PAN) in the 2000 presidential election, has increased the stability of the peso.

Mexico has had a long history of devaluation. Figures 4.1 and 4.2 illustrate the situation. Between 1921 and 1981, the Mexican peso fell from 2.06 to 23.08 per U.S. dollar. This may sound like a big fall in the exchange rate, but what followed over the next eighteen years was much more spectacular: *the Mexican peso fell from 23.08 to 9,550 per dollar.* This fall made the previous sixty years pale in comparison. To accommodate such a change in a graph, we have put the changes in a logarithmic scale (see Figure 4.2). To simplify matters, Mexico decided to chop three zeros off its currency in 1992. Thus, in 2002, instead of seeing 10,000 pesos to the dollar, the "new" peso was valued at 10 to the dollar.

Canada has not seen the dramatic devaluation experienced in Mexico. However, the value of the Canadian dollar has fluctuated against the U.S. dollar over the past nine decades (see Figure 4.3). If we look at the interval 1913–91, one U.S. dollar has been worth 0.96 Canadian dollar (1956, 1959) and 1.39 in 1986. The value of one U.S. dollar was 1.15 in 1991. Since then, the Canadian dollar has seen a decade-long fall against the U.S. dollar. In Canada, this has caused concern in some quarters that the rise in Canadian export competitiveness has been induced by exchange rates rather than based on improvements in productivity in recent years.

Figure 4.1   **Mexico–U.S. Exchange Rate, 1921–82**

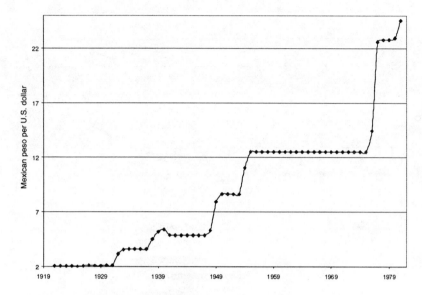

Source: www.eh.net, Economic History website.

Figure 4.2   **Mexico–U.S. Exchange Rate, 1982–99**

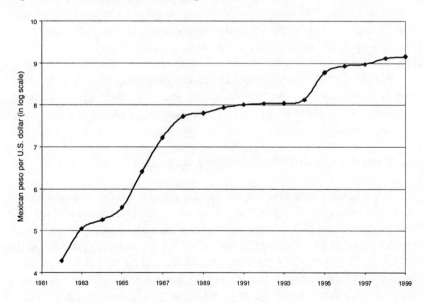

Source: www.eh.net, Economic History website.

Figure 4.3   **Evolution of Canadian Dollar Against U.S. Dollar, 1913–99**

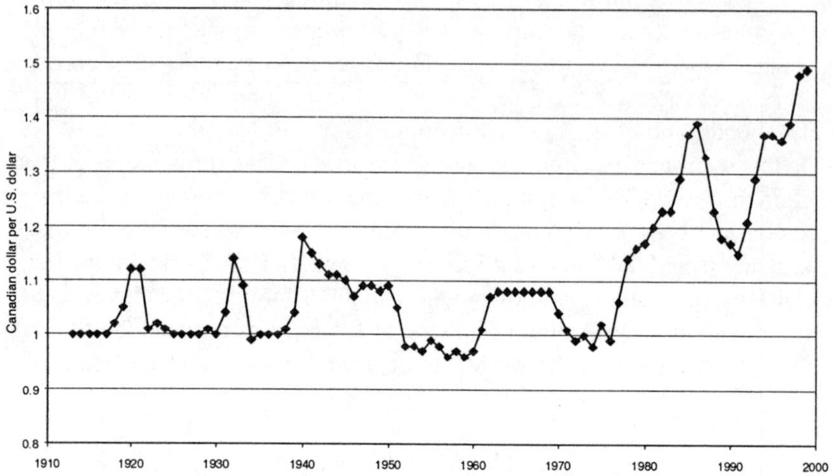

Source: www.eh.net, Economic History website.

Those who argue in favor of a common currency or dollarization in both Canada and Mexico do so for three principal reasons. First, they see it as a way to induce firms to rely on strategies other than devaluation to maintain the competitiveness of their exports. Second, they see it as a way to reduce cross-border transaction costs. Third, they see it as a way to reduce currency risk. However, we believe that a common currency is not in the cards at present. Relatively stable currencies in Canada and Mexico make the political obstacles difficult to overcome. The failure of the Argentine dollarization experiment also militates against dollarization in the NAFTA region. Moreover, such a move is not necessary to address security issues relating to capital movements in the region.

The Aliens Are Coming: Foreign Direct Investment

Flows of foreign direct investment play an integral role in integrating the economies of the NAFTA countries. Foreign direct investment may be defined as "capital invested for the purpose of acquiring a lasting interest in an enterprise and of exerting a degree of influence on that enterprise's operation" (OECD 1998). The degree of control exerted by the investor is what distinguishes foreign direct investment from portfolio investment, with ownership of 10 percent of the shares of a corporation used as the benchmark for classifying the investment as foreign direct investment. The degree of influence a given percentage of shares provides will depend on the size of the company. A controlling interest may require a majority of shares in a small company or a substantial minority in a large company. Portfolio investment refers to investments that do not result in a controlling interest, such as stocks (less than 10 percent of the outstanding shares of the company), bonds, and other financial instruments.

In this section, we examine economic theories and business strategies that explain the growth of foreign direct investment flows in recent decades. We then consider how NAFTA protection for foreign investors reduces political risk, using the Metalclad case to illustrate how NAFTA works in practice. We also examine statistics showing the growth of foreign direct investment. We end with an examination of how security concerns affected the foreign investment decisions of the world's top corporations in 2002 and Mexico's strategy for attracting foreign direct investment.

Fine in Theory: Orthodox, Eclectic, and Strategic

Orthodox trade theory (for example, Krugman and Obstfeld 1994) assumes that the direction and magnitude of capital flows are determined by differences in factor proportions among countries. A difference in factor proportions between countries forces an adjustment of real exchange rates between them. Therefore, it encourages countries with abundant capital and scarce labor to invest in countries with abundant labor and scarce capital.

Unfortunately, in real life, international capital flows are volatile and factor endowments are stable. Empirical studies have shown that exchange rate movements strongly affect foreign direct investment. Foreign direct investment is just one form of capital inflow from other countries (others are foreign loans and portfolio investments).

According to Krugman and Obstfeld, "[t]he distinct feature of direct foreign investment is that it involves not only a transfer of resources but also the acquisition of control" (1994, 223). This argument is used as a justification for the movement of foreign direct investment inconsistent with the direction implied by the law of factor proportions.

Market imperfections, such as the merits of "internalization," often become key concepts in explaining the motives of multinational firms to extend their control. According to the theory of internalization, "the key ingredient for maintaining a firm-specific competitive advantage is possession of proprietary information and control of the human capital that can generate new information through expertise in research, management, marketing, and technology" (Eiteman et al. 1995, 183).

This internal market of multinational firms is "an efficient response to the given exogenous market imperfection in the determination of the price of information" about their operations, which is created through the process of research and ordinal operations (Rugman 1981, 41).

John Dunning's "eclectic theory" synthesizes a number of paradigms derived from three areas: industrial organization, neoclassical trade theory, and the theory of the firm. Eclectic theory proposes that the extent of a firm's international involvement depends on the presence, or lack thereof, of three types of advantages: (1) ownership (proprietary intangible assets such as trademarks and technical know-how); (2) location (exogenous characteristics of the foreign market and government policies); and (3) internalization (the ability of a firm to internalize transactions within the firm and across countries in order to have greater control over ownership advantages and to gain from economies of scale and scope). Thus, Dunning's theory embodies a number of different strands of literature from international trade and international business (Dunning 1995).

There are two types of foreign direct investment. The first is vertical integration. A firm exploits the natural resources in the host country required for its final products. The second is horizontal integration. A firm builds plants for producing lines of products similar to those produced in the home country. The main purpose is to capitalize on the cheap labor of developing countries.

Vertical integration explains the presence of U.S. car manufacturing companies in Canada. Horizontal integration explains the presence of the U.S. car manufacturing companies in Mexico (see Appendix 4.2, p. 144).

Horizontal integration is likely to increase exports from home to host country as well as imports from host to home country, since integrated assembly lines in host countries require imports of intermediate goods for their production. Further, this type of investment may attempt to shift the export base for third markets from home to host country, leading to a decrease of exports from the home country and an increase of exports from the host country.

The strategic goals served by foreign direct investment vary considerably depending on the sector, the target client, and the strategic purpose of the investment. Foreign direct investment in the manufacturing sector may serve different strategic objectives than foreign direct investment in the services sector. Firms that provide support services to multinationals or firms from their home country may use foreign direct investment abroad to enhance services for those clients, while other firms may seek customers in the host country. The strategic purpose of the investment may be to secure resources or to serve the host market. Similarly, an investment in a joint venture may provide a vehicle to gain market access or may be designed to gain access to new technology that the partner has.

For several reasons, it is important to distinguish between foreign direct investment that sets up manufacturing facilities and foreign direct investment that establishes a commercial presence for service firms. First, trade in services and trade in goods are governed separately, and differently, in international trade agreements. Secondly, manufacturing is more likely to be seeking resources and services are more likely to be seeking markets.

Where there are low barriers to trade in goods, manufacturers no longer have to set up a factory in each market in order to serve the market, as they can export from a location that is most cost-effective. Thus, foreign direct investment in manufacturing chooses that location based on the attractiveness of factor costs and other variables, such as proximity to markets, labor cost and quality, natural resources, and the competitive structure of the market. Depending on the type of resource the manufacturer seeks, the foreign direct investment may be long-term or short-term. If the resource is specific to the location (for example, oil in Saudi Arabia) or the location enjoys a long-term advantage over other locations, manufacturing foreign direct investment may be long-term. However, where the resource, such as cheap labor, is generally available, and the location quickly loses its cost or quality advantage to other locations, the foreign direct investment in manufacturing may be short-term, as the firms seek the same resource elsewhere at a better price.

Foreign direct investment in manufacturing may be a market entry strategy rather than a resource-seeking strategy in three sets of circumstances. First, when transport costs are high and the product has to be customized to suit local preferences, it may be better to manufacture the product in the target market. However, the market would have to be sufficiently attractive to justify the cost of the investment, for example due to its size, purchasing power, the sophistication of its consumers, its demographic profile, or its future growth potential. Second, trade barriers may make foreign direct investment the only strategy available for market entry, and minority stake in a joint venture with a local firm may be the only way to penetrate the market due to investment restrictions. Third, a firm may choose to enter a market through an equity-based joint venture to achieve technological innovation that provides the firm with a strategic advantage over competitors. Sometimes, a combination of strategic goals and trade or investment restrictions may be the motivating force.

Manufacturing foreign direct investment may serve the firm's home market, the host market, other markets, or all of the above. When the foreign direct investment is purely resource-seeking, producing goods for export rather than for the host market is the main strategic goal being served. The Mexican maquiladora zone provides a good example. Initially, Mexican law allowed the duty-free import of inputs as long as most of the production was then exported, after Mexico added labor to the value chain. U.S. firms invested in assembly plants, seeking Mexico's cheap labor to produce products for sale in the U.S. market. However, Asian firms also used Mexico as an assembly location, to exploit the cheap labor and Mexico's proximity to the United States, with the final products destined for the U.S. market. Finally, with the removal of Mexico's domestic sales restrictions under NAFTA, these firms also were able to serve the growing Mexican market from the same plants. However, the initial raison d'être of these plants was to exploit cheap labor and proximity to the U.S. market, not to serve the Mexican market.

Foreign direct investment in the services sector is more likely to be a market entry strategy than a resource-seeking strategy (Birkinshaw and Hood 1998). There are two principal reasons for this. First, many services require a commercial presence in the target market, which means foreign direct investment is a necessary entry strategy. For example, retail banking services cannot be provided without establishing branches in the target market, through mergers, acquisitions, joint ventures, or new investments. Secondly, most countries still limit the ability of firms to engage in cross-border trade in services. In North America, for example, cross-border trade in financial services (without the establishment of a commercial presence) is subject to many restrictions in Canada, Mexico, and the United States.

A distinction may be made between services firms that enter the market to serve local firms versus those that enter to serve other multinationals operating in the market. When manufacturers integrate their operations on a regional or global basis, service firms may set up regional or global operations to better serve their multinational clients. For example, the Bank of Montreal invested in banks in the United States and Mexico in order to provide North American banking services for the rapidly growing cross-border trade and investment in the region (although it later sold its stake in Mexico's Bancomer). Similarly, Canadian National Railway acquired assets in the United States and Mexico in the face of increasingly north-to-south movement of goods in the region. On a global scale, Citibank is pursuing a strategy of building a global brand in banking, while AT&T does the same in telecommunications.

Risky Business: Reducing Political Risk for Foreign Investors

Political risk refers to actions by the host country government that reduce the value of the foreign company's investment. There are three broad categories of political risks: (1) confiscation, expropriation, and nationalization, (2) contract repudiation and frustration, and (3) currency risk. There are many historical examples of confiscation, expropriation, and nationalization. In Mexico, oil companies were nationalized in 1938. In Russia, after the revolution of 1917, all foreign companies were confiscated.

All three categories are similar but they might differ in terms of compensation. At one extreme, no money might be paid to the foreign company. At the other, a full market value would be paid to the foreign company. In reality, most foreign companies are compensated at a value somewhere between these two extremes. There could be many reasons for contract repudiation.

NAFTA Chapter 11 requires governments to treat investors in accordance with international law, which includes fair and equitable treatment and full protection and security (Article 1105). While a government's treatment of its own nationals may fall below this standard, its treatment of foreign investors may not. NAFTA Chapter 11 allows foreign investors from one NAFTA country to sue the host government of another NAFTA country for compensation or restitution in the event of expropriation or measures equivalent to expropriation.

NAFTA Article 1110(1) states:

> No Party may directly or indirectly nationalize or expropriate an investment of an investor of another Party . . . or take a measure tantamount to nationalization or expropriation . . . except: (a) for a public purpose; (b) on a nondiscriminatory basis; (c) in accordance with due process of law and [international law]; and (d) in payment of compensation [at fair market value, plus interest].

Article 1139 provides a very broad definition of the kinds of investments that are protected, including, among other things, "property, tangible or intangible, acquired in the expectation or used for the purpose of economic benefit or other business purpose." The definition thus has the potential to cover investments in intellectual property, such as trademarks and patents. However, Article 1110 does not apply to the issuance of compulsory licenses granted in relation to intellectual property rights or other measures that are consistent with NAFTA Chapter 17 (Intellectual Property). This provision is especially significant for the pharmaceutical industry, both in the NAFTA region and in the rest of the world, where NAFTA Chapter 11 may serve as a precedent for future agreements. In emergencies, government may issue compulsory licenses to allow generic drug manufacturers to produce patented medicines without the patent holder's consent. For example, in the aftermath of the anthrax attacks, the Canadian government was ready to do so with respect to Bayer's drug, ciprofloxacin, to ensure an adequate supply in the event of widespread anthrax infections.

The definition in Article 1139 may also cover intangible property such as the goodwill and reputation of a company. Indeed, Ethyl Corporation sought compensation from the Canadian government for expropriation of goodwill based on statements of government officials in the media alleging that the company's product was harmful to the environment and health (*Ethyl* v. *Canada*). However, since the case was settled before a tribunal could rule on that aspect of the claim, it remains unclear whether such a claim could succeed.

Chapter 11 provides NAFTA investors with the power to demand compensation whenever government measures interfere with business activities to such an extent that it amounts to expropriation. The responsibility of federal governments includes measures of state and local governments, as well as courts. In the case of courts, the decision of the court must be clearly incompatible with a rule of international law, constitute a denial of justice, or, in exceptional circumstances, be contrary to the law of the country in question. This does not mean that court decisions can be appealed to international investment tribunals. Rather, it means that a claimant must show either a denial of justice or a pretense of form to achieve an internationally unlawful end (*Robert Azinian et al.* v. *Mexico*).

The crucial question is how to define the term "tantamount to expropriation." A measure that prevents the use, enjoyment, or disposal of the property may qualify, but a mere reduction in profits does not constitute a sufficient degree of interference to constitute expropriation. However, government regulations can be applied in a way that would constitute "creeping expropriation," where they have the effect of "taking" the property in whole or in large part, outright or in stages (*Pope & Talbot* v. *Canada*).

In the Metalclad case (see Appendix 4.3, p. 145), the tribunal gave an interpretation of expropriation under Article 1110 that was sufficiently broad to include a legitimate rezoning of property by a municipality or other zoning authority, and therefore too broad, in the opinion of the British Columbia Supreme Court. The tribunal concluded:

> . . . [E]xpropriation under NAFTA includes not only open, deliberate and acknowledged takings of property, such as outright seizure or formal or obligatory transfer of title in favour of the host State, but also covert or incidental interference with the use of property which has the effect of depriving the owner, in whole or significant part, of the use or reasonably-to-be-expected economic benefit of property even if not necessarily to the obvious benefit of the host State. (*Metalclad* v. *Mexico*, Paragraph 103)

The British Columbia Supreme Court also ruled that transparency is not an obligation contained in Chapter 11. An official interpretation of the Free

Trade Commission regarding the minimum standard of treatment later confirmed this interpretation.

An important issue is whether the term "tantamount to expropriation" makes NAFTA governments liable for the economic impact of regulatory action. The answer appears to be that it does not. The Myers tribunal, after noting that the primary meaning of the word "tantamount" is "equivalent," concluded that something that is equivalent cannot logically encompass more (*S.D. Myers* v. *Canada*). The Myers tribunal agreed with the Pope & Talbot tribunal that the drafters of NAFTA intended the word "tantamount" to embrace the concept of "creeping expropriation," rather than to expand the internationally accepted scope of the term "expropriation."

The general body of international legal precedent does not normally treat regulatory action as amounting to expropriation. The Myers tribunal therefore concluded that regulatory conduct is unlikely to provide a legitimate basis for complaints under Article 1110. In this regard, the tribunal stated:

> Expropriations tend to involve the deprivation of ownership rights; regulations a lesser interference. The distinction between expropriation and regulation screens out most potential cases of complaints concerning economic intervention by a state and reduces the risk that governments will be subject to claims as they go about their business of managing public affairs. (*Myers* v. *Canada*, paragraph 282)

The claims that have been successful, through negotiation or favorable tribunal decisions, provide examples of the kinds of measures that may be covered. Canada settled a claim by Ethyl Corporation of the United States by paying U.S.$13 million in compensation and repealing legislation banning trade in the gasoline additive MMT that Ethyl processed and sold in Canada. Ethyl Canada's MMT business constituted 50 percent of the company's activity. Mexico was ordered to pay U.S.$15,626,260 to Metalclad Corporation of the United States after the state government of San Luis Potosí declared an ecological zone to prevent the operation of the company's hazardous waste disposal facility in the state. (For a more detailed discussion of the Metalclad case, see Appendix 4.3. p. 145.) However, the Pope & Talbot lumber company was unsuccessful when it sought compensation from Canada after Canada restricted lumber exports to the United States under a bilateral trade agreement.

Chapter 11 claims for compensation represent a powerful tool that companies may use to dissuade NAFTA governments from implementing legislation that causes significant harm to their cross-border investments. Even if a claim is ultimately unsuccessful, the mere threat of a claim can be used as a bargaining tool, particularly at this early stage before enough cases have been settled to clarify what claims might succeed. Indeed, the Canadian government has publicly expressed its desire to renegotiate Chapter 11 in order to limit the kinds of claims that may be brought. The threshold requirements for seeking arbitration are sufficiently low that firms may abuse the process in order to harass a government. However, launching claims for compensation for ordinary regulatory actions that diminish the value of investments to a relatively small degree will not only be likely to fail, but result in the claimant paying the legal costs of the government, as well as its own.

Number Crunching: Statistics on Capital Movements

In the last two decades of the twentieth century, worldwide production and consumption of goods and services has become increasingly internationalized. Curiously, foreign direct investment has grown four times as fast as the international trade in goods. In 1980, foreign direct investment stock abroad accounted for only 5 percent of world GDP. By 2000, this number had tripled to 15 percent. In the seven-year period from 1993 to 2000, world foreign direct investment flows increased from just over U.S.$200 billion to around U.S.$1 trillion. A distinguishing characteristic of world investment is that the vast majority is among OECD countries. More than 90 percent of foreign direct investment world outflows originates in OECD countries, and in recent years the OECD has accounted for around three-quarters of foreign direct investment inflows as well.

The dramatic increase in foreign direct investment since the 1980s reflects the globalization of business and the increasing integration of the global economy. There are three major reasons for the growth in foreign direct investment. First, many governments removed barriers to foreign investment, both unilaterally (for example, Mexico) and through regional initiatives (such as NAFTA). Second, many governments decreased government involvement in the economy through deregulation, privatization, and demonopolization. Finally, foreign direct investment played a major role in the global business strategies of large corporations aimed at reducing costs by globalizing production and expanding into new or growing markets. The growth of international cooperation between firms, such as licensing agreements, joint ventures, strategic alliances, mergers, and acquisitions, has further increased foreign direct investment flows.

According to Rugman, foreign direct investment by multinational enterprises (MNEs) drives international business and 90 percent of foreign direct investment (as well as over half of world trade) is dominated by the 500 largest MNEs. Most of that trade and investment occurs between firms and is

Table 4.5

Inflow of Foreign Direct Investment (in millions of U.S. dollars)

	Canada	United States	Mexico	Brazil	China
1970	1,823	1,260	323	392	—
1975	3,387	2.560	609	1,203	—
1980	5,807	16,918	2,090	1,910	57
1985	.1,372	20,490	1,984	1,418	1,659
1990	7,582	48,422	3,374	989	3,487
1995	9,255	58,772	9,552	4,405	35,849
2000	66,617	300,912	14,706	32,779	40,772
2001	27,465	124,435	24,731	22,457	46,846

Source: World Investment Report, UNCTAD, version released September 17, 2002.

Table 4.6

Foreign Direct Investment as a Percentage of Fixed Capital Formation

	1997	1998	1999	2000
Canada	9.7	19.4	18.7	47.3
United States	7.8	11.9	18.0	17.5
Mexico	18.0	13.6	12.3	12.2

Source: World Investment Report, UNCTAD, version released September 17, 2002.

regionally based. More than 90 percent of MNE manufacturing is regional rather than global (with notable exceptions, such as consumer electronics), and in services over 95 percent of employees are local, not global (again, with notable exceptions in certain industries and professions). Rugman thus concludes that "operating globally for an MNE really means operating regionally" (Rugman 2001, 4).

Inflows of foreign direct investment have become extremely large in all the NAFTA countries in recent years. Table 4.5 illustrates this fact. Since 1995, Mexico has become the second largest destination of foreign direct investment among the developing countries (only after China). The only other country that comes close to Mexico is Brazil. However, the flow of capital to Brazil is much more erratic than to Mexico. The reason can clearly be traced to NAFTA.

As a critical part of the gross fixed capital formation in the country, foreign direct investment has become very important for all the three NAFTA countries. In Mexico, it seems to have fallen from 18 percent to 12 percent. In the United States, foreign direct investment is close to 20 percent; in Canada it is a whopping 47 percent of fixed capital formation (see Table 4.6).

Table 4.7

U.S. Direct Investment Abroad (USDIA) in Canada and Mexico and in Other Countries

	1994	2000	Growth rate
Total, all countries	612,893	1,244,654	12.5
Canada	74,221	126,421	9.3
Mexico	16,968	35,414	13.0
NAFTA partner totals	91,189	161,835	10.0
NAFTA partner share of total USDIA (percent)	14.9	13.0	
Investment in Mexico relative to investment in Canada (percent)	22.9	28.0	
Europe	297,133	648,731	13.9
Latin America and other Western Hemisphere countries	116,478	239,388	12.8

Source: U.S. Department of Commerce, Bureau of Economic Analysis, International Accounts Data, "U.S. Direct Investment Abroad," available at www.bea.doc.gov/bea/di/dia-ctry.htm as of July 25, 2001.

Note: The Bureau of Economic Analysis defines U.S. direct investment abroad as the ownership or control, directly or indirectly, by one U.S. person of 10 percent or more of the voting securities of an incorporated foreign business enterprise or the equivalent interest in an unincorporated foreign business enterprise.

More than 70 percent of banking capital in Mexico is under foreign control. The capital, management expertise, and technology that foreign banks have brought to Mexico's banking sector should facilitate bringing their ability to monitor suspicious transactions up to the same standard as Canada and the United States. The largest bank in Mexico, Banamex, was taken over by Citigroup in the middle of 2001. Citigroup took the unprecedented step of listing itself on the Mexican Stock Exchange—the first foreign company ever to do so. As shown in Table 4.7, U.S. foreign direct investment in Mexico increased at an annual rate of 13 percent in the first seven years of NAFTA from 1994 to 2000 as opposed to 9.3 percent per annum in Canada. What is surprising is that U.S. investment in Europe has outpaced the investment in NAFTA countries over the same period.

Canada is the largest foreign real estate owner in the United States. The United States is the largest source of foreign investment in Canada. Recently, there has been a flurry of cross-border mergers and acquisitions in the financial sectors of the United States and Canada, further blurring financial borders. For example, the Canadian firm T.D. Waterhouse handles investments in both countries.

Capital movements are basically free between the NAFTA member countries. There are, however, a few remaining impediments to capital flows. Tax regulations may impede capital flows, such as withholding taxes on payments to nonresidents. Subsidiaries may not be able to claim full tax deductions for payments made to a foreign parent under rules designed to prevent using transfer pricing to avoid taxes (International Bureau of Fiscal Documentation 1999). In addition, foreign investment restrictions remain in place for some industries in each country. A few other barriers also need to be addressed, such as Canadian residency requirements for account holders at Canadian banks and securities firms, and Mexico's prohibition on foreign currency accounts.

In and Out: Flows of Capital

Sometimes it is forgotten that foreign direct investment is not a one-way street. If inflows of capital are counterbalanced by an equal outflow of capital at the same time, there may not be much of a quantitative gain. However, the larger volume of cross-border capital flows that comes with increasing amounts of foreign investment makes it harder to sift through transactions to detect illicit funds.

How exactly does foreign investment flow in the three countries in question? We have noted earlier that most foreign investment tends to move between developed countries. The following series of tables shows how inward flows of foreign investment compare with outward flows in the region.

Several important characteristics should be noted in the data. (1) For the United States, since 1980, the outflow of foreign direct investment has *always* exceeded the inflow. However, the difference between inflow and outflow has narrowed as a percentage of GDP. (2) The largest inflow has come from the United Kingdom and Japan. In recent years, these countries outside NAFTA have set up wholly owned subsidiaries in the United States. This has partly been a reaction to NAFTA. These countries correctly concluded that it would be less advantageous to export directly than to make investment commitments when the full force of NAFTA came into play. (3) For Canada, inward investment always exceeded outward investment until 1999. (4) The main source of inward investment to Canada had traditionally been the United Kingdom. In recent years, the United States has replaced the United Kingdom as the main source of investment. (5) A new trend emerged in the 1990s, with the United States becoming a big destination for Canadian investment. As a consequence, for the first time in its history, the outward flow of Canadian investment has now exceeded the inward investment into Canada. (6) The foreign direct investment pattern in Mexico stands in sharp contrast to

Table 4.8a

Foreign Direct Investment Stock as a Percentage of GDP in Canada

	1980	1985	1990	1995	2000
Inward	20.4	18.4	19.6	21.1	28.8
Outward	8.9	12.3	14.7	20.3	32.4

Source: World Investment Report, UNCTAD, version released September 17, 2002.

Table 4.8b

Foreign Direct Investment Stock as a Percentage of GDP in Mexico

	1980	1985	1990	1995	2000
Inward	3.6	10.2	8.5	14.4	16.9
Outward	0.1	0.3	0.2	1.4	1.4

Source: World Investment Report, UNCTAD, version released September 17, 2002.

Table 4.8c

Foreign Direct Investment Stock as a Percentage of GDP in the United States

	1980	1985	1990	1995	2000
Inward	3.0	4.4	6.9	7.3	12.4
Outward	7.8	5.7	7.5	9.5	13.2

Source: World Investment Report, UNCTAD, version released September 17, 2002.

that in both the United States and Canada. Inward foreign direct investment to Mexico has far outweighed outward foreign direct investment from Mexico since 1980. Mexico has become a big destination for foreign investment for both the United States and Canada (although U.S. investment to Mexico is ten times higher than that of Canada in absolute terms).

Given that the OECD countries account for most of the capital flows (more than 90 percent) of the world, it is appropriate to take a closer look at the inflows and outflows of the OECD countries (see Table 4.9). The United States occupies the first place in both inflows and outflows of capital over the decade from 1992 to 2001. However, it also occupies the last place in terms of the net flow (a negative number implies an inflow). Mexico occupies the second to last place, making it the second most favorite destination of foreign investment in absolute terms among the OECD countries. Canada does not play a prominent role in any of the categories. The United Kingdom occupies the second place in both inflows and outflows. But it occupies the first place in terms of net outflow of capital. Not surprisingly, two big destinations for foreign investment for the United Kingdom are the United States and Canada.

Table 4.9

**Cumulative Foreign Direct Investment Flows in OECD Countries,
1992–2001** (in billions of U.S. dollars)

Inflow		Outflow		Net flow	
United States	1,274.2	United States	1,145.5	United Kingdom	389.8
United Kingdom	444.4	United Kingdom	834.1	Japan	349.7
Belgium	422.3	France	583.9	France	291.6
Germany	342.6	Germany	477.7	Germany	135.1
France	292.3	Japan	455.9	Switzerland	120.2
Netherlands	238.3	Belgium	414.1	Netherlands	80.8
Canada	186.7	Netherlands	319.1	Italy	37.1
Sweden	157.4	Canada	200.2	Spain	36.7
Spain	138.6	Switzerland	182.8	Finland	35.6
Mexico	127.3	Spain	175.3	Canada	13.5
Japan	106.1	Sweden	130.3	Portugal	0.8
Australia	69.6	Italy	97.7	Iceland	0.3
Ireland	64.3	Finland	71.9	Norway	−1.0
Switzerland	62.6	Australia	49.6	Slovak Republic	−4.9
Italy	60.6	Denmark	41.5	Greece	−6.2
Denmark	48.5	Norway	33.0	Denmark	−7.0
Poland	47.2	Korea	25.7	Belgium	−8.3
Korea	38.5	Portugal	24.2	Turkey	−8.4
Finland	36.3	Austria	23.9	Austria	−12.0
Austria	35.9	Ireland	22.1	Korea	−12.8
Norway	34.0	Mexico	3.7	New Zealand	−19.2
Czech Republic	26.8	Turkey	3.4	Hungary	−19.9
Portugal	23.4	Greece	3.3	Australia	−19.9
Hungary	22.1	New Zealand	2.8	Czech Republic	−26.0
New Zealand	22.0	Hungary	2.2	Sweden	−27.1
Turkey	11.8	Iceland	1.1	Ireland	−42.2
Greece	9.4	Czech Republic	0.8	Poland	−46.5
Slovak Republic	4.9	Poland	0.6	Mexico	−123.6
Iceland	0.8	Slovak Republic	0.0	United States	−242.6

Source: OECD International Direct Investment Database; OECD International Investment Perspectives, September 2002.

Instilling Confidence: Measuring Foreign Direct Investment Attractiveness

In an annual survey that has run for five years, consulting firm A.T. Kearney surveyed top corporate decision makers of the world's 1,000 largest firms in 2002 regarding their views of the relative attractiveness of different countries and what is influencing their foreign direct investment strategy. The corporations surveyed accounted for 70 percent of global foreign direct investment flows and represented forty-one countries and twenty-four different industries. The survey examined sixty countries that receive 90 percent

Figure 4.4   **A.T. Kearney Foreign Direct Investment Confidence Survey, 2002, Top Ten Countries**

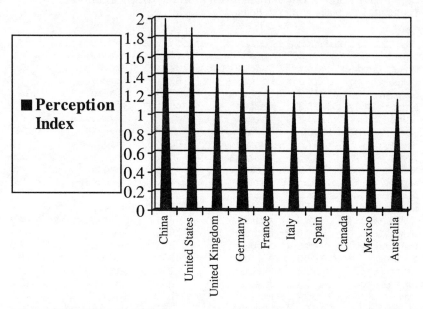

Source: A.T. Kearney, 2002.

of global foreign direct investment flows. As Figure 4.4 shows, all three NAFTA countries ranked in the top ten. What is interesting is that Canada and Mexico ranked about the same (A.T. Kearney 2002).

At the beginning of the twenty-first century, Mexico's attractiveness declined globally. This appeared to be largely due to the decline of Europe's interest in foreign direct investment in Mexico in 2002. This was in part due to the impending expansion of the European Union to include Eastern European countries, scheduled to begin in 2004. Outside Europe, however, Mexico remained a highly attractive destination for foreign direct investment. Canada ranked Mexico number two, the United States ranked Mexico number six, and Japan ranked Mexico in the top five. Mexico's attractiveness was linked to NAFTA and the performance of the U.S. economy. The 2002 survey showed a marginal decline in Mexico's attractiveness (A.T. Kearney 2002). However, over the long term it will remain a highly attractive destination due to its geographic location, the size and potential of its internal market, its relative attractiveness compared to other Latin American countries in the wake of economic turbulence in Brazil and Argentina, and its network of free trade agreements.

Figure 4.5   **Free Trade Agreements Signed by Countries in the Western Hemisphere**

Source: www.sice.oas.org/tradee.asp.

Note: Caricom stands for a group of countries in the Caribbean region. The countries are Antigua and Barbuda, the Bahamas, Barbados, Belize, Dominica, Grenada, Guyana, Haiti, Jamaica, Montserrat, St. Kitts and Nevis, St. Lucia, Suriname, St. Vincent and the Grenadines, and Trinidad and Tobago.

One-Horse Race: Mexico's Free Trade Network

If there is a race on to set up free trade agreements, Mexico certainly wins it hands down. Mexico's network of free trade agreements covers thirty-two countries, accounting for more than 60 percent of the world's GDP, and provides preferential access to a potential market of over 870 million consumers. Mexico's free trade strategy helps to explain its attractiveness as a destination for foreign direct investment. Figure 4.5 identifies the free trade agreements that Mexico has signed in recent years in the Western Hemisphere and with the European Union.

In the 1990s, Mexico did not stop with joining the OECD and NAFTA. It continued to pursue free trade negotiations with other countries in the region (the smaller Central American countries), with the economies of South America (such as Chile), and with the second largest economic bloc in the world—the European Union. As a result, Mexico has a huge network of free trade agreements in place. This gives Mexico a unique position in the world, which it hopes to cash in on over the next several decades. Mexico also decided to pursue free trade negotiation in Asia, notably with Japan. It wants to serve as the hub of business activities that stretch across East Asia, Western Europe, and North America.

The Color of Money: Remittances as a Source of Mexican Capital

As we noted in Chapter 3, remittances from Mexicans working in the United States are one of Mexico's biggest sources of foreign exchange income. This money is building dreams for millions of Mexican families who would otherwise live in grinding poverty. At the same time, however, the flow of remittances has expanded the financial services sector that moves this money across the border. This money tends to be transferred in small amounts. Thus, while they represent an important source of income for Mexico, remittances provide a cross-border flow of money that makes it easier to hide illicit transfers, which are also sent in small amounts to avoid detection. Moreover, the increase in the number and type of money transfer services further complicates the supervision of financial institutions with respect to money laundering and terrorist financing laws.

Mexicans working in the United States are most likely to send their money home using wire transfers or money orders. Many migrants also take the money home themselves or send it by check or cash. Banco de Mexico estimated that in 1995 almost 40 percent of these remittances came in the form of money orders, 27 percent were electronic transfers, almost 25 percent were via telegraph, 8 percent were pocket and in-kind remittances, and less than 1 percent were personal checks (Lozano-Ascencio 1998). Wire transfer services receive a lot of business transferring money to Mexico despite the high fees they charge for two principal reasons. In addition to the security of the transfer, Mexican banks charge high fees for cashing checks and money orders for those without bank accounts, and many of the recipients of remittances fall into this category.

Responding to the increased volume of remittances, money transfer services expanded noticeably in the 1990s, especially in the nonbank financial institution (NBFI) sector. In a summary of these activities, Orozco (2002) noted:

These institutions (NBFI) manage the majority of remittances. International money orders, the next most frequent means of transferring remittances, grew at about 7 percent a year in the same period. Today, at least 90 percent of all remittances are transferred electronically or via money orders.

Western Union, for instance, typically charges $29 for the average electronic transfer of $300 that is completed within fifteen minutes. Moreover, its agent in Mexico, Elektra, generally exchanges the money at 10 percent less than the interbank rate, meaning that up to 20 percent of the remittance is lost in transfer costs. Elektra also encourages those receiving the money to spend it in Elektra stores by providing a discount on goods bought with the remitted money. Elektra alone transferred U.S.$100 million in 1994, $400 million in 1995, and about $700 million in 1996 (Lozano-Ascencio 1998). Other partnerships in Mexico include the U.S. Postal Service and Bancomer, which teamed up in May 1997 to provide their *Dinero Seguro* service, which charges $15 for up to $250 remitted from a U.S. post office to any of Bancomer's branches, though it takes a few days. Wells Fargo and Banamex offer similar services, as do U.S. Bank and Banca Serfin, who charge $25 for any money transfer to Mexico and promise the interbank exchange rate and no extra pickup charges (Orozco 2002). Numerous other small money transfer businesses tend to focus on specific immigrant groups and generally charge more per transaction.

The channel Mexican emigrants choose depends on various factors: whether a modern banking and financial infrastructure is present, the efficiency of the delivery system, and the educational and income status of the recipient and sender. Many migrants were forced to pay these fees because they could not perform an interbank transfer. The reason they could not send the money through the banks is that they lacked bank accounts in the United States. The reason they lacked bank accounts was that most of them lacked official documents to open a bank account (due to the illegal nature of their stay in the United States). Thus, paying high transmission fees seemed to be a vicious circle.

Remittances are now Mexico's third largest source of income, exceeding local and state budgets in much of rural Mexico. They amount to U.S.$10 billion, approximately the same order of magnitude of foreign direct investment to Mexico in recent years. Mexican immigrants across the United States have organized themselves in the last decade into powerful hometown clubs that finance public works projects and small businesses in Mexican communities that would otherwise languish. When the Mexican political scene was dominated by the old guard of the Institutional Revolutionary Party of Mexico

(PRI), Mexicans who migrated to the United States (or other developed countries) were treated with contempt (so much so that many politicians in Mexico called them "traitors"). Abandoning the attitudes of past governments who viewed emigrants as an embarrassment, Mexico's current president, Vicente Fox, has hailed them as "national heroes" (Thompson 2002). The government of Mexico now recognizes that the money sent by migrants is a major source of investment. However, the vast majority of remittance amounted to $250 or less.

In the wake of the attacks of September 11, the Mexican government began to distribute new, digitally coded consular identification cards. These cards check an applicant's information against computerized census and voter rolls in Mexico. Mexican consulates in the United States issue the identification cards to Mexican migrants in order to facilitate this flow of money and to capitalize on its potential to bring economic development to communities all over the Mexican countryside. These cards enable undocumented workers to open bank accounts, acquire ATM cards, and reduce the cost of sending money home. And that means higher foreign exchange receipts for Mexico.

The Mexican government also negotiated with banks and wire transfer agencies in the United States to make it cheaper for immigrants to send money home. Beginning in December 2001, some fifteen NBFIs and regular banks all over the United States agreed to allow immigrants from Mexico to use identification cards they receive from Mexican consulates to open bank accounts, irrespective of their legal status in the United States. This process of "regularization" has produced positive results for charges paid: there has been a decline of some 30 percent (Thompson 2002). However, these cards could also facilitate illicit transfers of money unless they are designed and monitored to prevent such abuse.

Conclusion

For security purposes, each of the three NAFTA governments may exercise a lot of discretionary power in the financial sector. Moreover, the active membership of all three in international organizations and agreements that deal with money laundering and terrorist financing facilitates cooperation in this area. However, corruption (the topic of the next chapter) may impede the effective application of Mexico's international obligations in this regard and complicate cooperation.

Flows of foreign direct investment have increased dramatically both worldwide and among the NAFTA members, playing a crucial role in economic integration. However, foreign direct investment cuts both ways with respect to security. On the one hand, the integration of the banking sector should facilitate compliance with money laundering rules while the integration of the manufacturing sector facilitates the secure movement of goods (as we discussed in Chapter 2). On the other hand, foreign direct investment flows increase the number of transactions that need to be monitored. Similarly, the flow of migrant remittances has its good and bad side. This source of foreign capital helps economic development in Mexico but also provides a cover for illicit money transfers.

NAFTA has made Mexico a top destination for foreign direct investment worldwide. The proliferation of Mexican free trade agreements, together with its geographic proximity to the U.S. market, its wage rates, and the potential of its internal market, means that Mexico will continue to attract large amounts of investment. Today, Mexico is running neck and neck with Canada in attracting investment. In the future, Mexico may very well pull ahead. Moreover, capital flows to Mexico, together with better economic policies in recent years, have stabilized the peso. In the wake of the Argentine crisis, a stable peso lessens the prospects for dollarization in the region.

Appendix 4.1
Freezing Their Assets Off: Terrorist Financing

"Canada as a separate but dominated country has done about as well under the U.S. as women, worldwide, have done under men; about the only position they've ever adopted toward us, country to country, has been the missionary position, and we were not on top. I guess that's why the national wisdom vis-à-vis Them has so often taken the form of lying still, keeping your mouth shut, and pretending you like it."
—*Margaret Atwood*

Cracking Down

In November 2001, the Bush administration froze the assets of two suspected bin Laden financial networks, Al-Taqua and Al-Barakaat, and affiliated organizations in Minnesota, Massachusetts, Ohio, and Washington. Both are money exchanges, known as "hawalas," suspected of channeling funds to Al Qaeda through businesses and charities. The affiliates include Aaran Money Wire Service, Inc., of Minneapolis; Al-Barakaat Wiring Service of Minneapolis; Barakaat Boston of Dorchester, Massachusetts; Barakaat Enterprise of Columbus, Ohio; Barakaat North America, Inc., located in Ottawa and Dorchester, Massachusetts; Barakat Wire Transfer Co. of Seattle; Global Service International of Seattle, and the Somali International Relief Organization of Minneapolis ("U.S. Moves Widely..." 2001).

Cracking Up

On August 22, 2002, the United States requested that a United Nations panel remove four individuals and two businesses from a sanctions list after European countries and Canada criticized the lack of evidence that they were linked to the Al Qaeda network. The U.S. Treasury Department maintains a list of individuals and groups that allegedly support Al Qaeda, which it submits to the United Nations Security Council sanctions committee. At the end of August 2002, more than 215 names were on the U.S. list. The United Nations collects such lists from its members and then asks all United Nations members to block the transfer of those funds. However, there is no formal United Nations system to determine whether those on the list should be.

Three of the individuals (Somali-born Swedes) worked for the Al-Barakaat Bank and exchange company, which is used by expatriate Somalis to send remittances home to their relatives. However, the United States alleges that the bank was also used to channel Al Qaeda funds. A fourth individual, a Somali-born American citizen, ran Aaran Money Wire Service in Minneapolis. The two businesses removed from the list were Global Services International U.S.A, of Minneapolis, and Barakaat Enterprise, of Columbus, Ohio. The individuals signed sworn statements with the U.S. Treasury Department declaring that they would not participate in banned organizations. Their assets had been frozen for several months (Leopold 2002).

All Aboard

The Canadian Superintendent of Financial Institutions maintains a list of terrorist suspects, based on a list established under the United Nations Suppression of Terrorism Regulations. The Canadian cabinet must approve additions to the Canadian list. Under Canadian Proceeds of Crime legislation, financial institutions must scrutinize their records and freeze the assets of suspected terrorists on the list.

In December 2001, Canada added three groups allegedly linked with Hamas (a Palestinian organization) to its list, hours after the United States froze the assets of some of the same groups. The previous week, Hamas had claimed responsibility for suicide attacks in Israel. The three groups were Al-Aqsa Islamic Bank; Beit El-Mal Holdings Co., a Palestinian-based investment group; and the Holy Land Foundation for Relief and Development, of Richardson, Texas. The latter says it is the largest Muslim charity in the United States and is not a front for Hamas. As of December, Canada had frozen C$344,000 in suspected terrorist assets in twenty-eight accounts ("Ottawa Freezes Assets" 2001).

Probing the Aliens

While Canadian and American authorities cooperate closely with each other, there are limits to Canadian cooperation, notably when U.S. authorities forget that U.S. jurisdiction ends at the border. In July 2002, a Canadian judge denied the United States access to evidence in a probe of a Vancouver, British Columbia, resident due to possible misconduct by U.S. tax agents. The judge ruled that the U.S. government's refusal to allow Internal Revenue Service (IRS) agents to testify in court about their actions raised questions about whether the rights of author Jerome Schneider had been violated in a search last year. Schneider writes books and articles on how U.S. citizens can establish private offshore banks to avoid paying taxes. Schneider had not been charged with any criminal offense. However, the United States alleged that he had committed fraud and wire fraud and conspired to defraud the U.S. government.

A Canadian search warrant authorized the Royal Canadian Mounted Police (RCMP) to conduct a search of Schneider's premises and authorized IRS agents to be present "for the purpose of observation only at the time of execution of the search warrant." The RCMP seized boxes of documents, including files of Schneider's clients in the United States. At a hearing to determine whether to release the evidence to the United States, Schneider's lawyer argued that the U.S. agents had actively participated in the search, rather than just observing. One of the IRS agents later acknowledged in an affidavit that they had also searched through and copied documents in the weeks after the raid, without the consent of Canadian police. The agent said that they had not used the material after learning that their conduct may have been improper.

The judge ruled that Schneider's lawyer had the right to cross-examine the two IRS agents. Since the U.S. government refused to allow them to testify, the judge ordered the evidence returned to Schneider, stating, "While the court obviously lacks jurisdiction to enforce attendance of the IRS agents, the court can, and I think should, deny the requesting state its sending request" ("Canadian Judge . . ." 2002).

Systems Friction

A perception exists in the United States that weaknesses in the Canadian system complicate the fight against terrorism, especially when terrorism suspects are deported instead of being charged with crimes. In one case in November 2001, authorities accused Hassan Almrei of being involved in financing Osama bin Laden's terrorist network, first in Saudi Arabia and later in Toronto, where he arrived with a false passport from the United Arab Emirates on January 2, 1999. Almrei was also alleged to be connected with Nabil al Marabh, whom the FBI arrested in the United States on September 19, 2001, on suspicion that he might have provided false documents used by the September 11 hijackers.

Judges in the United States and Canada have also reached different decisions regarding bail. Liban Hussein, a Somali-born resident of Ottawa, was accused by American authorities of managing an international money-transferring operation that channeled $3.8 million to Al Qaeda. His brother, Mohammed M. Hussein, was arrested in Boston. In November 2001, a Canadian judge released Liban Hussein on $8,000 bail. Mohammed Hussein was denied bail in the United States.

Another source of systems friction is the difference in the way the two countries treat refugee claimants. The United States detains them. Canada detains them only if there is a risk of flight. That left the refugee system subject to abuse by those who claimed refugee status in order to gain legal residency while awaiting their refugee hearing. Until Canada streamlined its system in 2001, such individuals could remain in Canada for years while their cases worked their way through hearings and appeals. However, some U.S. officials still think that Canada's refugee law is inadequate because detention is not mandatory (DePalma 2001).

Appendix 4.2
Baby, You Can Drive My Car: Mexico's Assembly Plants

The presence or absence of trade barriers and trade-related investment barriers has become an important consideration in the foreign direct investment decisions of firms that base location of manufacturing on worldwide or regionwide sourcing of inputs and export of finished products. For example, Mexico has attracted considerable foreign direct investment in automobile production, for several reasons. Initially, Mexico attracted automobile producers by making access to its market conditional upon foreign direct investment and the use of local inputs. As the investment and trade regimes were liberalized, car manufacturers chose to locate or expand operations in Mexico for other reasons.

First, Mexico's geographic location is attractive for a product that is expensive to transport. With its proximity to the wealthy markets of North America and the growing markets of Latin America (including Mexico), Mexico's location is strategic. Moreover, with ports on both the Atlantic and Pacific oceans, Mexico is relatively close to both Asia and Europe, in terms of transporting both inputs and finished products.

Second, Mexico has pursued a "hub-and-spoke" strategy (a term coined by Richard Lipsey) by aggressively seeking free trade agreements with North America, Latin America, Europe, and Asia. This strategy makes Mexico the most attractive location for foreign direct investment in car manufacturing because it is the only country that provides preferential access to all markets.

Third, Mexico enjoys a labor cost advantage over other members of NAFTA and the Mexico–European Union Free Trade Agreement.

Fourth, the rules of origin that apply to automobiles in NAFTA require an increasingly higher percentage of NAFTA content to qualify for duty-free treatment. This was designed to give North American–based manufacturers an advantage over those based in Europe and Asia. To level the playing field in the North American market, European and Asian car manufacturers had to produce cars in North America. While many already did, those who did not, or who chose to expand North American production, had a strong incentive to choose Mexico over the United States or Canada. For example, Volkswagen expanded its foreign direct investment in Mexico, not only to serve the North American market in certain makes, but also to serve the global market in the popular new Beetle.

Finally, Mexico has improved treatment of foreign investors through amendments to its Foreign Investment Law, the signing of NAFTA, and the negotiation of foreign investor protection agreements, all of which provide better property rights for inves-

tors. Other changes in Mexico have reduced political risk (through democratic reforms prior to the 2000 election) and economic risk (through the introduction of a
floating exchange rate in 1994).

Appendix 4.3
Ironclad Guarantees: Metalclad in Mexico

Metalclad, a U.S. company, purchased COTERIN, a Mexican company, on September 10, 1993, together with its hazardous waste landfill site in Guadalcazar, in the
state of San Luis Potosí, and associated permits. Metalclad relied on assurances from
Mexican federal officials that COTERIN had all the authorizations required to undertake the landfill project. The director general of the federal environmental agency also
told Metalclad that the federal government was responsible for obtaining support for
the project in the state and the local community.

Shortly after Metalclad purchased COTERIN, the governor of San Luis Potosí
began a public campaign to denounce and prevent the operation of the landfill. After
negotiations, Metalclad believed it had secured the governor's support and began
construction in May 1994. During construction, federal and state officials inspected
the site and Metalclad provided them with written progress reports. However, in October 1994, construction was halted abruptly when the municipality of Guadalcazar
ordered building to cease due to the absence of a municipal construction permit. In
November 1994, after federal officials said Metalclad had all the authority necessary
to build and operate the landfill, Metalclad resumed construction and applied for the
municipal permit in order to facilitate relations with the municipality. In the spring of
1995, an independent university study and a federal audit of the site both confirmed
that the site was geographically suitable for a hazardous waste landfill.

You Can't Fill My Hole

In March 1995, Metalclad completed construction of the landfill and held an inauguration that was attended by dignitaries from the United States and Mexico's federal,
state, and local governments. However, the inauguration was disrupted by demon-
strators who blocked the entry and exit of buses carrying guests and workers. Metalclad
said that the state and local governments helped to organize the demonstration and
that state troopers helped to block traffic. Thereafter, Metalclad was prevented from
operating the landfill, despite efforts to negotiate a solution.

In November 1995, Metalclad signed an agreement with federal environmental agencies under which the company agreed to follow an action plan, including the setting
aside of fourteen acres (thirty-four hectares) of its property to conserve local species.
The agreement allowed Metalclad to operate the landfill for a renewable five-year term.
However, the state governor immediately denounced the agreement. In December 1995,
the municipality denied Metalclad's application for a construction permit.

The municipality did not notify Metalclad of the town council meeting at which the permit application was discussed and rejected, nor allow Metalclad to participate in the process. Moreover, there was no evidence that the municipality had ever required or issued a municipal construction permit or even had an administrative process in place to do so. In January 1996, the municipality launched legal challenges to Metalclad's agreement with the federal agencies, which ended unsuccessfully in May 1999.

From May to December 1996, Metalclad negotiated with the state government, without success. On January 2, 1997, Metalclad began legal proceeding against the Government of Mexico under Chapter 11 of NAFTA. In September 1997, three days before the end of his term, the governor issued an ecological decree declaring a "natural area" for the protection of rare cactus, which included Metalclad's landfill, permanently preventing the operation of the landfill. Metalclad added this ecological decree to its NAFTA claim.

Transparent Denial: The Decision of the Chapter 11 Tribunal

The three-person NAFTA tribunal held that the federal government was responsible for the actions of the state and local governments and that those actions violated NAFTA Article 1105(1) requirement to treat investors in accordance with international law. Mexico failed to ensure the transparency required by NAFTA because there was no clear rule as to whether or not a municipal construction permit was required. The municipality improperly required and denied a construction permit after construction was virtually complete and the federal permit had been granted. Its reasons for denying the construction permit had nothing to do with any defects in construction, and the municipality gave Metalclad no opportunity to participate in the decision. Finally, NAFTA Article 1114, which allows members to ensure that investment activity is undertaken in an environmentally sensitive matter, could not affect the outcome because the federal permits and agreements demonstrated that Mexico was satisfied that the project was consistent with its environmental concerns.

The tribunal held further that, under NAFTA Article 1110, Mexico took a measure tantamount to expropriation by acquiescing in the denial of the municipal permit when the federal government had exclusive authority for siting and permitting a hazardous waste landfill. The tribunal identified the governor's ecological decree as a further ground for a finding of expropriation because it had the effect of barring forever the operation of the landfill.

The tribunal held that Metalclad has lost 100 percent of its investment. In its calculation of the compensation payable under NAFTA Article 1110(2), the tribunal decided that fair market value should be determined by reference to Metalclad's actual investment, less the cost of site remediation that the Mexican government would incur. In addition, the tribunal awarded Metalclad interest at 6 percent per year, compounded annually, from the date on which the municipality wrongly denied Metalclad's application for a construction permit. Mexico was ordered to pay U.S.$16,685,000, plus 6 percent interest compounded monthly until the compensation was paid.

Denying Transparency: The Decision of the Supreme Court of British Columbia

Because the arbitration took place in Vancouver, British Columbia, Mexico appealed the tribunal's decision in the Supreme Court of British Columbia (BCSC). The court overturned the tribunal's decision regarding the actions of the municipality, ruling that there are no transparency obligations contained in Chapter 11. However, the court ruled in favor of Metalclad's claim based on the ecological decree. Because the ecological decree occurred later than the refusal to issue the municipal permit, the court reduced the award of interest by calculating the interest from the date of the ecological decree (September 20, 1997), rather than the date the municipality refused to issue a permit (December 5, 1995). Because Mexico succeeded in its legal arguments regarding transparency and in reducing the interest payable, the court required Mexico to pay only 75 percent of the legal costs Metalclad incurred in the appeal.

Following the court's decision, Metalclad's president, Grant Keseler, said that the ruling on the transparency issue violated the spirit of NAFTA and would discourage foreign investors fearful of secretive and arbitrary government actions. He said that the company had liquidated all of its Mexican holdings and would not invest in Mexico until the legal protections for foreign investors improve. The company once had the largest waste collection operation in Mexico, with sites in eleven states (Iritani 2001).

The Mexican government was pleased that the judge had set limitations on the rights of private investors under NAFTA and hoped that the case would set a precedent for future Chapter 11 cases (Iritani 2001). Both sides later agreed not to appeal the court's decision after Metalclad accepted Mexico's offer to pay U.S.$15, 626,260 plus daily interest of $2,559 after June 1, until the settlement was paid in full ("Metaclad Reaches . . ." 2001).

Metalclad began legal action against the Mexican government at the beginning of October 2001 because the payment had not been made. The Mexican government paid the company by check on October 26, 2001, and received the deed to the property from Metalclad. Mexico issued a statement that the government "honors its international obligations, even when it does not agree with the findings of the international tribunal nor with the way the tribunal works" ("Eye on Investors," 2001).

5

Invisible Elephants

Corruption and Cooperation

"The King shall protect trade routes from harassment by
courtiers, state officials, thieves and frontier guards . . .
[and] frontier officers shall make good what is lost. . . . Just
as it is impossible not to taste honey or poison that one
may find at the tip of one's tongue, so it is impossible
for one dealing with government funds not to taste,
at least a little bit, of the King's wealth."
—*Kautilya*

"A dog with a bone in his mouth cannot do two things.
He cannot bark and he cannot bite."
—*Porfírio Diaz*

"My mother said that you should never expect recognition for
doing your duty. That was what I did, my duty."
—*Ernesto Zedillo*

There is a joke told in Mexico that goes as follows. In Canada, when there is
a crime being committed, you call 911 and the police are there in ten minutes. In the United States, when there is a crime being committed, you call
911 and the police are there in five minutes. In Mexico, when there is a crime
being committed, you don't have to call the police. They are already there!
Unfortunately, police corruption in Mexico is no laughing matter (see Appendix 5.1, p. 169).

Corruption is neither new nor novel. It has existed for millennia. In fact,
the first complete treatise on corruption was written by Kautilya (chief minister to the king in ancient India), in *The Arthashastra* (around 300 B.C.).

Plato talked about corruption in Greece around the same time. Over seven centuries ago, Dante put bribers in the deepest parts of Hell. The U.S. constitution explicitly makes two crimes an impeachable offence for the U.S. president: treason and bribery.

In the NAFTA countries, corruption is not a problem that is limited just to Mexico (see Appendix 5.2, p. 171), although it is more widespread in Mexico today than in the United States or Canada. In the Canadian province of Quebec, electoral corruption under Premier Maurice Duplessis from the 1930s to the 1950s was comparable to the electoral corruption Mexico experienced under the Partido Revolucionario Institicional (PRI). In the Duplessis era, voter turnout exceeded 100 percent. Premier Duplessis was so popular that even the dead voted for him. Before rising to political prominence as prime minister of Canada, Pierre Trudeau gained prominence in Quebec writing articles that criticized the corrupt electoral practices of the Duplessis regime, such as the theft of ballot boxes by armed thugs. More recently, in the province of British Columbia, two premiers have resigned due to corruption scandals. In the 1980s, Premier Bill Vander Zam resigned amid allegations that he had misused the office of premier to gain financial benefits in a real estate transaction. After leaving office, former Premier Glen Clark was acquitted in 2002 of corruption charges involving a neighbor who helped build decks at his house and cottage before being awarded a gambling license by the government. Effective opposition parties and vigilance on the part of police have thus greatly reduced corruption in Canada over time.

In international surveys and studies, the United States always ranks worse than Canada in corruption. In prohibition-era Chicago, police corruption was such that it became the subject of popular television shows and movies. Police corruption in New York, Los Angeles, and New Orleans similarly became fodder for screenwriters. More recently, the mayor of Providence, Rhode Island, was involved in a corruption scandal. Thus, contrary to the general perception that the Deep South is the home of political corruption, it affects the northern states as well.

Why does corruption matter? A study by the U.S. Department of State summarizes the impact of corruption in no uncertain terms:

> Corruption has a corrosive impact on both market opportunities overseas and the broader business climate. It also deters foreign investment, stifles economic growth and sustainable development, distorts prices, and undermines legal and judicial systems. More specifically, corruption is a problem in international business transactions, economic development projects, and government procurement activities. (U.S. Department of State 2001, 2)

Corruption in government costs business money in five principal ways. First, there is the cost of providing bribes when companies choose to engage in bribery to secure government contracts or to secure permits or licenses to do business. Second, there is the loss of the investment made in attempting to secure government contracts when companies choose not to engage in bribery or are out bribed by competitors, thereby losing out on government procurement bids. Third, when corruption in the police force creates a security problem, the company incurs the cost of hiring private security and higher insurance costs to protect employees against security risks such as kidnapping. Fourth, judicial corruption can increase the costs and risks associated with litigation. Fifth, when companies engage in corrupt payments, they run the risk of fines, imprisonment of employees, civil penalties, and other sanctions.

Corruption also robs citizens of the benefits they would otherwise receive for the taxes they pay. When the costs of government procurement contracts are inflated to include illicit payments to politicians, it is the taxpayer who gets less for the taxes paid. When police corruption and involvement in criminal activities increase the personal security risks to the individual, citizens not only lose the value of the money paid in taxes that support the police force but incur extra security costs too. In the end, corruption may cause citizens to feel less protected from other security threats, including terrorist attacks.

In the NAFTA context—and indeed globally—corruption is an international problem that requires cooperation across borders. When companies from the United States or Canada bribe officials in Mexico, they contribute to the problem. Thus, Canadian and U.S. governments can contribute to the solution of the problem in Mexico by enforcing antibribery laws against their own citizens. Other forms of international cooperation have already borne fruit in Mexico, notably the reform of Mexican electoral practices that produced cleaner elections in 2000 and led to the defeat of the PRI by Vicente Fox. Reforms to Mexico's electoral laws made by former Mexican president, Ernesto Zedillo, made this dramatic event possible. Zedillo was also instrumental in making sure the transition went smoothly. When Vicente Fox won the election, Zedillo said on television, "I've told Fox that I will personally take charge of insuring that the handover of power will be transparent, tidy and efficient." Nevertheless, corruption in Mexico remains a matter of personal, national, and international security that has serious implications for the process of economic and security integration that is taking place in the region.

The Nature of Things: Defining Corruption

Exactly what constitutes corruption? One researcher noted that corruption is like an elephant. It may be difficult to describe but it is not difficult to recognize

once it is observed (Tanzi 1998). The World Bank uses the following definition of corruption: *the abuse of public power for private benefit.* The OECD
uses a similar definition: the use of public office for private gains. Both definitions presuppose that corruption is a public sector phenomenon.

We can view the problem of corruption as a problem of principal-agent. If
there is a difference in the information set that the principal has and the
information set that the agent has, we are likely to see that the agent will try
to exploit the situation for gaining resources. The principal is defined as the
top level of government and the agent is a government official designated to
carry out a specific task. In the case of high-level corruption—perpetrated at
the center by the elite of the political or administrative structures—one might
consider the citizens who elect a politician as the principals and the politician as the agent.

For the manifestation of corruption, three elements are crucial: (1) there
has to be some monopoly power of government officials; (2) there has to be
a degree of discretion that officials are permitted to exercise; and (3) there
have to be some problems with the systems of accountability and transparency in the government institution.

Take the example of a license. If there is more than one government agency
that can issue a license, the bribe "price" will be driven to zero. However, the
argument does not apply in the case of corruption involving theft, as when
an official accepts a bribe in exchange for nonpayment of an import duty. In
this case, corruption reduces overall costs for businesses in addition to lining
the pockets of government officials, so businesses have an incentive to seek
out corrupt state agents. It is also important to note that competition among
businesses in this case will lead to the spread of corruption, since businesses
that do not reduce costs through bribery will be at a disadvantage.

If there is no discretion involved in a decision by a government official,
there is no case for corruption. The more discretion a government official
has, the more favorable a decision (for the businessperson) can be taken by
the official in exchange for a bribe. This may prompt us to believe that more
detailed regulations are better. But if there are too many detailed rules set by
government, they will lead to noncompliance and thereby defeat the whole
purpose of rules and regulations. Simple, transparent rules function better.

If government institutions are transparent and accountable, there will be
little scope for corruption. In many developing countries, the functioning of
the government at various levels is extremely opaque.

In developing countries, the size of the government has been linked with
corruption. Bigger government means more tax revenue and therefore more
leeway to evade taxes. Also, larger government spending lends itself to more
abuse with respect to how the money is spent. This observation has led Nobel

laureate Gary Becker to proclaim that if we abolish government, we abolish corruption! However, such a lofty claim does not sit well with the real-life observation that some developed countries with very large government sectors, such as Finland, Denmark, and New Zealand, are also the countries with the least amount of corruption in the world (see Table 5.1).

Transparency International surveys the perceptions of businesspeople and risk analysts regarding the degree of corruption that exists in various countries. In its corruption perception index, Mexico ranks far below Canada and the United States (see Table 5.1). In terms of corruption (a low number implies low levels of corruption), Canada ranked seventh in the world, the United States ranked sixteenth, and Mexico had a lowly rank of fifty-seven. Mexico's score was less than half of the U.S. number. We also note that the only Latin American country to be in the top twenty is Chile.

The Jet Set: International Suppliers and Demanders

Rapid growth of international business has created opportunities for "grand corruption" across countries. Bribes are paid by international companies to secure contracts for construction or arms. Of course, such bribes are illegal in most countries. Therefore, it is hard to come by concrete figures to measure the extent of the problem. Some intermittent reports by investigative journalists give us a glimpse of the problem. For example, on March 17, 1995, *Le Monde* reported that French companies have paid some 10 billion French francs (U.S.$2 billion) to secure foreign contracts. On March 4, 1996, *World Business* reported that German firms paid over U.S.$3 billion to get overseas contracts in 1995.

The developed countries are home to big companies capable of mounting large infrastructure projects. The developing countries have a heavy demand for such projects. This creates an opportunity for developing country officials to demand bribes and for multinational companies from developed countries to pay bribes. With NAFTA, Mexico trades mostly with the United States and Canada. Many big projects in Mexico are being undertaken by American and Canadian firms. Thus, the U.S. and Canadian governments have a significant role to play in containing corruption in Mexico.

The Girl Next Door: Domestic Suppliers and Demanders

Of course, much corruption (especially small-scale corruption) does not originate from transactions between foreign companies and host governments. It arises domestically. Instead of paying a fine for going through a red light or speeding, the citizens simply pay a bribe to the police. The bribe they pay

Table 5.1

Transparency International Score of Corruption Perception Index, 2002

Rank	Country	CPI
1	Finland	9.7
2	Denmark	9.5
2	New Zealand	9.5
4	Iceland	9.4
5	Singapore	9.3
5	Sweden	9.3
7	Canada	9.0
7	Luxembourg	9.0
7	Netherlands	9.0
10	United Kingdom	8.7
11	Australia	8.6
12	Norway	8.5
12	Switzerland	8.5
14	Hong Kong	8.2
15	Austria	7.8
16	United States	7.7
17	Chile	7.5
18	Germany	7.3
19	Israel	7.2
20	Belgium	7.1
20	Japan	7.1
20	Spain	7.1
...	...	...
57	Colombia	3.6
57	Mexico	3.6

Source: www.transparency.org, Transparency International website.

Note: CPI stands for Corruption Perception Index. CPI 2002 score relates to perceptions of the degree of corruption as seen by businesspeople and risk analysts, and ranges between 10 (highly clean) and 0 (highly corrupt). A more detailed description of the CPI methodology is available at www.transparency.org/cpi/index.html#cpi or at www.gwdg.de/~uwvw/2002.html. The CPI 2002 is based on 2000-02 data. Since fundamental changes in the levels of corruption in a country evolve only slowly, while public perceptions may change more swiftly and be influenced to some extent by short-term events, Transparency International determined to base the CPI on a three-year rolling average. Hence, 2002 CPI is based on survey data collected exclusively between 2000 and 2002.

usually is much smaller than what they would have paid as a fine. Thus, the citizens lose less. Of course, the bribe money lines the pockets of the police officer. The authorities lose. This kind of petty corruption is extremely common in Mexico but not in the United States or Canada.

In 2001, the Mexico City government decided to replace all the policemen who fine the public for traffic violations with policewomen. The logic was that women are less corrupt than men. Therefore, this action was expected to reduce corruption. There have not been any substantive reports whether the program has been a success. However, cross-country evidence indicates that higher women's participation in government tends to reduce corruption in government (Dollar et al. 1999).

Tales from the Corrupt: Mexican Cases

If we were to catalog all of the corruption that takes place in Mexico, it would fill several volumes. Instead, we will set out just two cases to illustrate the problem. The first, the so-called PEMEX-gate scandal, shows how corruption leads to illegal movement of capital between the United States and Mexico. The second case, involving an elephant, shows how corruption leads to illegal movement of goods between the United States and Mexico.

Oily Characters: The PEMEX-Gate Scandal

In 2001, after the new federal government of Vicente Fox came into power, sensational allegations surfaced from the Mexico's attorney general's office (PGR) regarding the losing candidate for the Institutional Revolutionary Party (PRI). Francisco Labastida had reportedly received U.S.$162 million for his election campaign, diverted through the government-owned Mexican petroleum monopoly, PEMEX. In the year 2000, PEMEX and the Mexican Union of Workers of the Petroleum Industry allegedly colluded in illegally embezzling from the company and then contributing to his political campaign. Immediately afterwards, the erstwhile managing director of PEMEX, Rogelio Montemayor, fled the country.

The PRI has vigorously denied any wrongdoing. Its leader, Dulce Maria Sauri, declared on August 31, 2002, that the government should either produce evidence for the case or apologize to the PRI.

However, Montemayor later resurfaced in Houston, Texas, arguing that he had been the victim of a political witch-hunt. Surprisingly, the attorney general's office had not issued any extradition request for him with the U.S. government (as of September 7, 2002). Since the funds were allegedly used for election purposes, the Federal Electoral Commission decided on June 2, 2002, to investigate the case.

There are many loose ends in this particular case. For example, on February 11, 2002, Geri Smith, a reporter from *Business Week,* reported an amount of U.S.$120 million. On July 2, 2002, Ross Milloy of the *New York Times* put the figure at U.S.$200 million. On September 5, 2002, the respected daily *La Reforma* indicated that the amount of money involved was about U.S.$161 million. Whatever the amount, it still is large when we consider that the amount of funds officially received by the PRI from the Federal Electoral Commission was U.S.$91 million for its campaign.

In this case, large quantities of money moved effortlessly between the United States and Mexico without raising red flags anywhere. Nobody questioned whether the money was serving an illicit purpose.

Three Tons of Fun: The Case of the Invisible Elephant

In March 2000, a three-ton, ten-foot, nine-year-old Indian elephant named Benny was smuggled into Mexico from Texas. Benny changed both his identity (he is now called Dumbo in Mexico) and his nationality. For nine months, Benny performed circus tricks like playing the harmonica and riding the bicycle.

Indian elephants are an endangered species. Trade in endangered species is regulated by an international agreement—the Convention on International Trade in Endangered Species (CITES). Canada, Mexico, and the United States, who are among the more than 150 countries that are members of the CITES agreement, have stipulated that its provisions take precedence over NAFTA. Thus, it is illegal to export Indian elephants from the United States without a permit. Nevertheless, nobody "saw" the elephant crossing the border— apparently the customs agents were paid $4,500 to make him "invisible" (Sullivan 2001). *La Reforma,* the Mexico City newspaper that broke Benny's story, called him "the biggest wetback in the history of the Mexico–U.S. border" (quoted in Sullivan, 2001).

The story went that Guillermo Vazquez, a Mexican circus owner, bought Benny for $40,000. He then applied for a license to export an endangered species from the United States to Mexico. After two months, when no reply from the U.S. authorities was forthcoming, Vazquez took matters into his own hands. He paid the Mexican customs officials at the border $4,500. So Benny came across the border into Matamoros, Mexico, in a wooden box on a flatbed truck. Vazquez said Mexican customs agents, with his $4,500 bribe in their pockets, "did not see a thing." What is even more alarming, the truck did not attract any scrutiny on the U.S. side of the border.

Crime and Punishment: The Big Picture in Mexico

There were 214 million acts of "small scale" or "petty" corruption in Mexico in 2001, adding up to a figure which represents about 1 percent of Mexican GDP (Lizarraga 2001). On average, each family (and that means *all* families in Mexico and not just the ones that paid the bribe) paid some 110 pesos in bribes in 2001. Of those who reported paying a bribe, some 6.9 percent of their income went to paying bribes. Among low-income families, the number jumped to 13.9 percent of family income (Anti-corrupcion informes).

Corruption under the PRI regime, which governed Mexico for seventy-one years until losing the presidency in the year 2000, caused the United States to have little trust in Mexico. In the past, corruption has complicated efforts to cooperate on drug trafficking when corrupt officials in Mexico passed on information to the drug traffickers. Mexican customs officials also have a bad reputation for corruption. It hit a nadir when Benny the elephant was smuggled into Mexico from Texas in 2000.

Since 2000, however, there has been an unprecedented level of cooperation between the U.S. Drug Enforcement Agency (DEA) and its Mexican counterpart. The Federal Bureau of Investigation (FBI) has begun to send agents to investigate drug-related crimes in Mexico. Some opposition members of the Mexican congress have attacked the Mexican federal government for letting the FBI make arrests on Mexican soil (Notimex 2001).

In Mexico, corruption and incompetence in the police force are legendary. For example, more than 90 percent of reported crimes never get solved (Craddock 2001). This record makes willingness to report crime a low priority. A survey by the Fundación Rosenblueth in 2000 found that less than 20 percent of people from Mexico City are willing to report criminal activities. Other questions reveal why. In Mexico City, when people were asked why they do not report crime to the police, 79 percent said that it "does not make a difference." Some 29 percent added that they did not trust the police (www.rosenblueth.mx).

The procedures involved in filing criminal charges are lengthy and time-consuming, involving several half-day visits to the police station over a period of several months. Once the procedure for filing the charges is completed, the police will not investigate unless they are paid a bribe. If the suspect pays the investigating police a larger bribe, they will not investigate further. Even when the case makes it to court, the judge may be bribed or threatened and rule in favor of the accused. If the accused is jailed, the jail keepers may be bribed or threatened and allow an "escape" to occur. Under these circumstances, it is no wonder that people see the process of reporting crime as a waste of time.

Crime statistics in Mexico are staggering. For example, reported annual kidnappings in Mexico soared from 150 in 1993 to 600 in 1998. It is estimated that only 20 percent of actual kidnapping cases get reported to the police (Sistema Nacional de Seguridad Pública, Annual Report 2000). Other types of criminal activities are equally startling. In Mexico, 400 cars get stolen every single day, with 40 percent in and around the Mexico City area (Policía Federal Preventiva, Annual Report 2000). The rates are (as a percentage of total number of cars) at least twice as high as in the United States. Very few of the cars are ever found (unlike in the United States and Canada).

Table 5.2

Reported Crime in Mexico City and in New York City

	New York City	Mexico City
Homicide rate	7.9	9.4
Auto theft rate	365.7	445.8
Crime rate	1998.8	1993.8

Source: New York City and Mexico City Police Departments, 2002.
Notes: Rates are per 100,000 people.

All these statistics are indications of national (and international) bands that operate in the business of kidnapping people and stealing cars.

There is one cautionary note about using Mexican crime statistics. In Table 5.2, we compare reported crime statistics between Mexico City and New York City. Homicide rates are marginally higher in Mexico, as is the rate of auto theft. However, the crime rate in Mexico City actually appears lower than in the City of New York. This does not coincide with perceptions regarding crime rates in Mexico City.

Many homicides in Mexico City are reported as suicides. A classic example was that of the human rights lawyer, Digna Ochoa, who was shot to death at close range in her office in Mexico City in 2001. City police concluded that she killed herself. The fact that she had gunshot wounds on her knees as well as on her head apparently escaped the investigators. When the news caused outrage and it emerged that Ochoa had received death threats for her work on human rights violations, the police changed their story.

Auto theft rates are calculated per 100,000 people and not per number of cars. Car ownership is five times higher in New York City than in Mexico City. Thus, the theft rate (per 100,000 cars) is six times higher in Mexico City. Moreover, the crime rate is calculated on a reported basis. It is well known in Mexico City that citizens usually do not report crime to the police. The reason is simple. Many people believe (and, in most cases, quite rightly) that the police are working hand in hand with the criminals. Quite frequently, when groups of robbers or kidnappers are caught, some members turn out to be police officers. As a consequence, Mexico's human rights agency estimates that at best about 20 percent of crimes are ever reported to the police.

Crime statistics in Mexico clearly point to one uncomfortable reality: Mexico could be a fertile ground for the operation of international terrorist groups that can strike at the heart of any North American target.

Corruption will not be eliminated overnight and will likely continue to complicate the information sharing and trust required for Mexico and the United States to cooperate closely on security issues. The U.S.–Mexico

Table 5.3

Country Breakdown of Amounts Raised by Privatization

	1990	1991	1992	1993	1994	1995	1996	1997	1998	1999	2000
Canada	1,504	808	1,249	755	490	3,998	1,768	—	11	—	—
Mexico	3,124	10,757	6,864	2,531	766	170	73	2,670	988	279	406
United States	—	—	—	—	—	—	—	3,650	3,100	—	—

Source: OECD unpublished database.
Note: Amounts in millions of U.S. dollars.

relationship improved with the election of Vicente Fox in 2000. The U.S. foreign relations committee, headed by Senator Jesse Helms, held its first ever meeting outside of the United States in May 2001. In a letter published in the influential Mexico City daily *La Reforma,* Helms wrote, "The United States recognizes Fox as a genuinely democratic leader and a true reformer— and U.S. leaders of all stripes as more than disposed to work with him." But the reaction of the "man in the street" in Mexico to the September 11 attacks demonstrates that the relationship needs to improve much more than it has. A mutual lack of trust endures between the countries.

Does corruption in Mexico rest with the party (PRI) that ruled Mexico for seventy-one years? The answer is a definite no. There have been a number of cases in which leaders of the current ruling party have been implicated on corruption and bribery charges. One recent case illustrates the point. In September 2001, Maria de los Angeles Tames, a twenty-seven-year-old lawyer and recently elected member of the city council, was gunned down in front of her home in Atizapan, a wealthy suburb of Mexico City. Later, the police arrested the mayor of Atizapan for masterminding her murder. Apparently, Tames got "too close" with her investigation into corruption in the mayor's office. In 2002, the Corruption Perception Index of Transparency International showed that there had been no abatement of corruption since the election of the new federal government in Mexico.

Your Money is My Money: Privatization in Mexico

Privatization in Mexico produced huge resources for the government through rapid-fire sale of banks, the telephone monopoly, and other enterprises in the early 1990s (see Table 5.3). In 1991 alone, more than U.S.$10.7 billion was raised through privatization (mainly of banks). In the following year, another U.S.$6.8 billion was raised (mainly from the sale of the state monopoly of the telephone giant, TELMEX). The pace of privatization slowed considerably over the following years only to rise again after the new government came in.

The rapid sale of government assets always creates a danger that money could be siphoned off, directly or indirectly. For example, during the privatization process in Russia, most of the profitable resources were quickly bought by the "oligarchy" (friends and family of the Communist Party of the Soviet Union).

Privatization brought its own scourge to Mexico. In November 1995, Mexican officials announced that they had uncovered forty-five bank accounts belonging to Raul Salinas, the brother of former President Carlos Salinas, or his wife. These accounts were located in several countries in the Caribbean islands (which have what are described as "the best governments that money can buy"). Suspicions surrounded the ability of Raul Salinas to amass a fortune of over U.S.$120 million while serving as a public official. Raul Salinas transferred U.S.$80 to $100 million in alleged drug money out of Mexico between 1992 and 1994 through Citibank accounts. He claimed that it was payment for his services. But exactly what "services" he provided (other than a direct ear to the president of the republic) remained unclear.

There were many theatrical elements to the escapades of the brothers Salinas. Raul has been jailed for fifty years for masterminding the murder of their sister's ex-husband. Carlos Salinas, once feted around the world by the leaders of developed countries and once a serious contender for the position of director general of the World Trade Organization, fell from grace very quickly after his departure from the president's office. His departure also ended on a comic note when he staged a brief hunger strike in the cinderblock home of a political supporter to protest the sullying of his reputation and later drove off in a beat-up Dodge Dart. Less funny was the fact that Carlos Salinas bequeathed to Mexico the country's worst economic crisis since World War II. He went into a self-imposed exile, first to Miami and then to Dublin (though he was also rumored to have taken refuge early on in Montreal). In 2000, the wife of Raul was prevented from withdrawing U.S.$80 million from a Swiss bank account which she and her husband held under a false name.

I'll Show You Mine: Comparing Corruption

Recent studies have shown that corruption can impose large costs on doing business. How large is the cost? Sjaifudian (1997) reported that bribery costs for small business can be 20 percent of the turnover in Indonesia. Similar ballpark figures have been suggested by other researchers.

In 1995–96, for the World Development Report of 1997, the World Bank undertook a massive study to investigate obstacles to doing business. The exact data description and the methodology are discussed by Brunetti et al (1997). The questionnaires were distributed by the World Bank through its own channel of contacts. A total of nearly 4,000 questionnaires were administered in sixty-nine countries. Managers were asked to judge on a four-point scale how problematic various obstacles are for doing business. The four points range from "no obstacle" and "moderate obstacle" to "strong obstacle" and "major obstacle." Some other parts of the questionnaire will be analyzed in Chapter 6. Here, we have used the survey results for selected questions, as shown in Table 5.4, to draw out the differences among the NAFTA countries in the realm of corruption. Many questions concerned obstacles to doing business that are not necessarily related to corruption. We discuss each question in detail to contrast the three countries. There were approximately one hundred respondents for each country.

Question 56 (variable code "corr") asked if corruption of bank officials posed an obstacle (with 1 = no obstacle, 4 = major obstacle). We expected that Mexico would produce a higher obstacle than in the United States and Canada. This is indeed the case. It is somewhat surprising to see the difference between the United States and Canada. Corrupt bank officials posed a far greater obstacle to doing business in the United States than in Canada. The differences between all three countries are statistically significant at 1 percent.

Question 93 (code "scri") asked if street crime posed a major obstacle for doing business. The results show that street crime is the biggest problem in Mexico. It also is a substantial problem in the United States.

Question 94 (variable code "ocri") asked if organized crime posed a major obstacle to doing business. The results show that organized crime is the biggest problem in Mexico. It also is a substantial problem in the United States.

Question 96 (variable code "gcorr") asked if the general level of corruption posed an obstacle. Once again, we find statistically significant differences between all three countries, with Canada faring the best and Mexico the worst. Note that businesspeople perceive the general level of corruption as a much bigger problem than corruption among bank officials for doing business.

Question 142 (variable code "licpy") asked to what extent payments to licensing authorities (in the form of bribes) are a problem. For this question, the difference between the United States and Canada is not statistically significant. The difference with Mexico (both for the United States and Canada) is statistically significant. The surprising element here is that payment for licensing in Mexico is much lower than many in Mexico normally believe it to be. This implies that there is little difference across these three countries in terms of bribes for licensing. Whatever the dimension of the problem in Canada and the United States, the size of the problem is virtually the same in Mexico.

Question 143 (variable code "taxpy") asked if payments to tax authorities (in the form of bribes) are an obstacle to doing business. Here, too, we find

Table 5.4

Corruption Survey Results

Country	corr	scri	ocri	gcorr	licpy	taxpy	cuspy
Mexico	2.04	3.38	3.31	3.33	0.68	0.80	0.35
Canada	1.07	1.30	1.28	1.31	0.01	0.02	0.01
United States	1.51	2.15	1.51	1.84	0.19	0.23	0.23

Source: Tabulated from the results of World Bank Survey of businesses; see also, Brunetti et al. (1997).
Key to variables:
corr = corruption of bank officials
scri = street crime
ocri = organized crime
gcorr = general level of corruption
licpy = payments to licensing authorities (in the form of bribes)
taxpy = payments to tax authorities (in the form of bribes)
cuspy = bribes to customs officials

the expected result that they are a problem in Mexico. The difference with Mexico (both for the United States and Canada) is statistically significant.

Question 145 (variable code "cuspy") asked if bribes to customs officials are viewed as an obstacle to doing business. Surprisingly, there does not seem to be any difference in this respect among the three countries.

In general, as expected, we find Mexico to be at the top of the corruption list among the NAFTA countries in most areas. However, in some categories, Mexico did not appear way out of line with its biggest trading partners. We also find Canada to be much cleaner in various aspects of corruption than the United States. These results are consistent with the overall ranking provided by Transparency International.

But Curiously, Folks: Mexican Perceptions

Latinbarómetro is an organization that surveys public opinion on a variety of issues in seventeen Latin American countries. In 2000, it conducted a poll to find the attitude of people toward corruption in the seventeen countries. The specific question asked was the following: "Thinking about the problem of corruption in [country] today, would you say that the problem is 'very serious,' 'serious,' 'not very serious,' or 'not at all serious'?" The percent that responded with "very serious" is reported in Table 5.5. Among the seventeen countries, Mexico has the lowest percentage of respondents who see corruption as a very serious problem. Given the level of corruption that exists in Mexico, this is very surprising. For example, Chile is by far the least corrupt

Table 5.5

Perception of Corruption in Latin America

Country	Percent
Argentina	88
Bolivia	67
Brazil	73
Chile	65
Colombia	87
Costa Rica	82
Ecuador	74
El Salvador	55
Guatemala	54
Honduras	77
Mexico	47
Nicaragua	80
Panama	68
Paraguay	77
Peru	66
Uruguay	57
Venezuela	79

Source: Marta Lagos, 2000, "Assessing Perceptions of Corruption in Latin America," Latinobarómetro Research Group.

Question asked: "Thinking about the problem of corruption in [country] today, would you say that the problem is 'very serious,' 'serious,' 'not very serious,' or 'not at all serious'?" The table shows the percentage of the population that considers the corruption problem to be "very serious."

country in Latin America. Yet 65 percent of Chileans find corruption is a very serious problem, whereas only 47 percent of Mexicans do (Lagos 2000). This percentage shows that the level of awareness of the corruption problem is very low in Mexico. Thus, for the policy makers, there is a lot of work to be done to change this attitude.

Changing Channels: Fixing Domestic Corruption

Fixing domestic corruption requires action in three principal areas: civil service reform, tax collection capacity, and "grand corruption." We discuss each in turn.

Many countries that are now developed once had a great deal of corruption in the civil service. They have dealt with the problem through two methods: raising pay for the civil servants and establishing merit-based promotion systems. In Sweden, in the nineteenth century, corruption was rampant among civil servants. A decisive moment came in the early 1800s when the government decided to raise the salary level fourfold for all the civil servants. This raised the salary of high-level administrators (*generaldirektörer*) to fifteen to twenty times the average wage of an industrial worker. Of course it would be naive to believe that raising the salary alone would root out corruption. High-level administrators should have the power to reward honest underlings and punish dishonest ones. If, for example, dishonest workers in the government sector can hide behind the cloak of worker unions, this method is defeated.

In Mexico, high-level officials are always under pressure. It is a common practice for these officials to sign two documents when they join the civil service. First, they sign a contract with a date of joining. Second, they sign an undated document of resignation. The government wields this document like a sword to keep these officials in line.

Improving tax collection capacity is another good route to follow. If income tax becomes the main source of revenue for the government, it does not have to rely on sales tax, import duties, and other forms of taxation that are much more prone to tax evasion and corruption to avoid payment. However, if the informal labor market is large (as in the case of Mexico), income tax collection is a daunting prospect.

Reforms to increase the capacity, independence, and honesty of the justice system are critical in any honest government. If judges can be bought, there is very little hope of legal punishment for corrupt civil servants.

Governments of developing countries engage in big projects (such as building power plants and dams or buying armaments for the military) that involve large multinational companies and foreign governments of developed countries. This is a very good recipe for breeding corruption. This kind of corruption is sometimes known as "grand corruption" (OECD 2000). It often involves the ruling elite in the developing countries.

In its most extreme form, grand corruption can amount to state capture, where corrupt interests control the state itself and manipulate the machinery of government to serve their private interests. This form of corruption has taken on a grotesque dimension in some countries. In Zaire, former President Mobutu Sese Seko's "salary" was reported at one point as equaling 17 percent of the national budget and his "personal allowance" exceeded the combined expenditure on education, health, and social services. Sese Seko followed a long and illustrious tradition of corrupt leaders, including President Suharto of Indonesia, President Ferdinand Marcos of the Philippines, and President François "Papa Doc" Duvalier of Haiti.

International organizations such as the World Bank and the International Monetary Fund (IMF) can play a big role in stemming the tide of grand corruption. In the past, their roles have been rather dubious. These international bodies have facilitated projects in countries that were well known for their corrupt practices that directly affected these projects. For example, during the regime of Benazir Bhutto of Pakistan, the government signed so many contracts with power companies (some of which were for installations in totally inappropriate locations) that Pakistan was set to produce far more energy than it could possibly consume until 2010. Yet the government was contractually bound to buy all the electricity produced. This was encouraged by the World Bank and the IMF (Kielmans 1998). Privatization advocacy by these international organizations has at least contributed to the problem of grand corruption.

Multinational banks have contributed their part (sometimes unwittingly) in the business of tainted money. For instance, Citibank established private banking services for Raul Salinas, brother of former Mexican president Carlos Salinas, without following its own internal rules on due diligence for starting such accounts. Raul Salinas then laundered tens of millions of dollars (estimates range from U.S.$80 million to $120 million through Citibank accounts alone) in drug money (Zagaris and Ehlers 2001).

Carcinogenic Culture: Corruption and the Rule of Law

NAFTA adds a new layer of law to the existing legal systems and legal cultures of Canada, Mexico, and the United States. To what extent will NAFTA affect the evolution of law in the NAFTA countries? How will differences in legal culture affect the enforcement of security measures in a North American common perimeter?

The purpose of trade agreements is to impose the rule of law on the management of international trade relations, the logic being that the rule of law is preferable to the arbitrary exercise of economic power or influence in governing international economic relations. However, the rule of law is not firmly entrenched in all nations. The legal cultures of Canada and the United States are based on the rule of law. While the legal systems of these countries are not perfect, as a general rule the law is applied in a predictable manner and enforced by the police and the courts. While gaps in the law ("loopholes") are exploited by lawyers for the benefit of their clients, such exploitation is conducted within the system and interpretive arguments are presented to an independent judiciary to rule on each case.

In Mexico, the rule of law is not firmly entrenched. While Mexico has a sophisticated body of law, made up of civil codes, legislation, and international agreements, the rules may be applied, or not applied, in an arbitrary manner. Economic power and political influence determine outcomes often enough that one cannot predict outcomes based solely on an interpretation of formal law (see, for example, Appendix 5.3, p. 173). Widespread corruption in the police and government, and the lack of an independent judiciary, remain serious obstacles to the development of a legal culture based on the rule of law.

Corruption has become a part of Mexican culture that is accepted by both the corrupters and the corrupted. It has spread like a cancer, with legislators placing private interests above the public good, judges turning the law on its head and police allying themselves with organized crime. A senior official in the PGR identified increasing levels of impunity arising from corruption as the central problem facing his department. Since amending the Penal Code to criminalize bribery of foreign officials by the private sector in 1999, as of September 2002 not a single complaint has been filed with the PGR. Mexico needs to develop a culture of reporting corruption in order to make anticorruption laws effective. Combating corruption in Mexico requires a transformation in the attitudes of Mexican citizens regarding the filing of complaints, investigations, and punishment. Thus, the current buzzword in Mexican government circles is "coresponsibility"—corruption cannot be successfully tackled without all citizens taking responsibility for their own contribution to the problem.

The Mexican government has undertaken several anticorruption initiatives in the form of new legislation and electronic processing. Legislative initiatives include the Federal Law on Responsibilities of Public Servants of the Zedillo administration, the Federal Law on Transparency and Access to Government Information passed by the Fox administration in June of 2002, and a new government procurement law being developed by the Fox administration with the aim of reducing opportunities for corruption. Electronic processing initiatives include tracking activities of public servants (www.claranet.gob.mx), information and electronic processing for government licenses (www.tramitanet.gob.mx), and electronic government procurement (www.compranet.gob.mx). In addition, Mexico has implemented the OECD bribery agreement, which is discussed below.

Greasing the Big Wheels: Bribery Laws in the NAFTA Countries

In many countries, government policies can be influenced by financial contributions from firms. These contributions may take the form of campaign contributions or bribes. Campaign contributions have come under close scrutiny in recent years, precisely due to the perception that they have a corrupting effect on government decision making. Nevertheless, large campaign contributions can buy access to key politicians and permit a firm to raise government policy issues that are relevant to its industry.

Bribery can be distinguished from campaign contributions in that it is generally illegal and the transaction is not recorded. It remains common, particularly in the developing world. In some countries, it is difficult to do business without resorting to bribery. However, an increasing number of countries are trying to discourage bribery through laws that make it illegal for their citizens to engage in this practice in order to secure commercial advantages from domestic and foreign government officials. The best known example is the U.S. Foreign Corrupt Practices Act.

Canada, Mexico and the United States have all implemented the OECD Convention on Combating Bribery of Foreign Public Officials in International Business Transactions. All three also make bribery of domestic public officials a criminal offence. As a result, their laws in this regard have been largely harmonized, with some modifications that take into account differences in their respective legal systems. Table 5.6 provides a comparative overview of the laws of the three countries. Each country has its own procedures for enforcing these laws. As noted earlier, enforcement of laws in general remains problematic in Mexico.

The rationale for the negotiation of the OECD convention is that corruption distorts international competition and trade and undermines economic development. The goals of the convention are to reduce the international flow of corrupt payments, enhance the competitiveness of industries, and set high standards for global governance. As of September 2002, thirty-four countries had ratified the convention.

The convention criminalizes bribery of foreign public officials and provides legal definitions of acts that constitute bribery and public officials. It thus focuses on the supply side of the equation—active, as opposed to passive, bribery committed by natural or legal persons (that is, corporations).

The convention sets out guidelines for sanctions, requirements for corporate accounting procedures, and rules on jurisdiction, mutual legal assistance, and extradition. It sets standards for criminal sanctions without specifying what they must be, seeking sanctions for bribery of foreign officials that are comparable to each country's sanctions for bribery of domestic officials. The convention has led to a degree of harmonization of national laws regarding the criminal responsibility of corporations. Moreover, it has led to the further development of international law regarding national jurisdiction over international crimes.

The convention provides for monitoring the compliance of signatories in order to measure progress and expose gaps to public criticism. In phase one, the OECD published reports on the implementation of the convention by the signatories, which moved several countries to introduce improvements to meet criticism in the reports. Phase two got under way in 2002 and will

Table 5.6

NAFTA Countries' Implementation of the OECD Convention on Combating Bribery of Foreign Public Officials in International Business Transactions

Provisions	United States	Mexico	Canada
OECD in force	11/10/98	5/18/99	2/14/99
Domestic law	FCPA (1)	FCC (2)	CFPO (3)
Domestic officials	Yes	Yes	Yes
Foreign officials	Yes	Yes	Yes
Maximum fine, foreign	$100,000 (4)	$1,800 (5)	No limit
Maximum fine, domestic	3 times the bribe	$1,800	No limit
Maximum prison, foreign	5 years	14 years	5 years
Maximum prison, domestic	15 years	14 years	5 years
Other sanctions	SEC, Government benefits (6)	Corporate dissolution	
Government job (7)	None		
Private civil actions	RICO (8)	FCC/Civil Code	Unclear
Corrupt intent required	Yes	Yes	Yes
Via intermediary	Yes	Yes	Yes
Benefit to third party	Yes	Yes	Yes
Defenses	FCPA specific (9)	General FCC	CFPO specific (10)
Gratuities exception	Yes (11)	No	Yes
Corporate liability	Yes	Non-government corps	Yes
Prohibit tax deduction	Yes	Yes	Yes
Extraditable offence	Yes	Yes	Yes
Prohibit false accounting	Yes	Yes	Yes

Source: OECD Review of Implementation of the Convention and 1997 Recommendations.

Notes: (1) FCPA: Foreign Corrupt Practices Act, 15 U.S.C., enacted 1977, amended 1998. (2) FCC: Federal Penal Code, Article 222 bis, enacted 1999. (3) CFPO: Corruption of Foreign Public Officials Act, S.C. 1998, c. 34, enacted 1998. (4) If the bribe causes a monetary gain or loss, the fine can be twice that amount. (5) Fine for natural person, calculated at 500 times the prevailing daily minimum wage. Figure calculated based on November 1999 wage and exchange rate. For legal person, maximum fine is 500 times the daily net income of whoever commits the crime. (6) Indictment may cause ineligibility for U.S. government contracts, financing, and export licenses. (7) Dismissal and disablement from holding public post or commission for one to twenty years. (8) Private civil actions possible under the Racketeer Influenced and Corrupt Organizations Act, 18 U.S.C. chapter 96. (9) FCPA has two specific defenses permitting: (a) payments that are lawful under the laws of the foreign official's country and (b) payment of a foreign official's expenses that are directly related to the sale of products or services or the execution/performance of a contract. (10) Canadian law provides virtually the same defenses as U.S. law. (11) The FCPA permits gratuities to expedite processing of nondiscretionary permits or licenses or other routine documentation, provided the company is entitled to the action in question and the amount is not inappropriately large.

examine whether countries are effectively applying the law in practice. Phase two will consider factors such as whether prosecutions or investigations are under way and whether governments have achieved an adequate level of awareness regarding the convention. The priority of the OECD is to secure adequate enforcement of the convention and other related initiatives before tackling the issue of extending the rules to cover corrupt transactions between private firms.

The $64,000 Toilet Seat: Government Procurement in NAFTA

A central objective of the OECD convention is to promote a culture of honesty and integrity on the part of companies pursuing government procurement contracts internationally. Government purchases of goods and services represent a significant portion of total government expenditures. It is estimated that government procurement represents 10 to 15 percent of GDP. Opening government purchasing to foreign suppliers can thus have a significant impact on international trade and competition.

NAFTA Chapter 10 partially opens government purchasing to foreign suppliers. It applies to federal contracts for goods, services, and construction, but not to government procurement by provinces or states. Some sectors have exemptions—for example, Canadian shipbuilding and U.S. military supplies. Chapter 10 applies only to contracts over certain threshold amounts—U.S.$25,000 in Canada and the United States and U.S.$50,000 in Mexico. These amounts are adjusted for inflation, using a specific formula that is set out in NAFTA Annex 1001.1c.

The thresholds are higher for some government corporations, such as Mexico's oil company PEMEX and Mexico's electricity utility, but they are phased out over time.

Detailed rules cover bidding procedures, advertising, breaking up contracts to lower the amount below thresholds, and factors used to evaluate bids. A key provision requires governments to award contracts based on price and compliance with the specific evaluation criteria set out in the notices or tender documentation (Article 1015[4]). Governments must provide suppliers with procedures for challenging bid procedures when there are irregularities (Article 1017). Their governments can seek additional information on the award of the contract to determine whether the procurement was made fairly and impartially, in particular with respect to unsuccessful tenders (Article 1019[3]). These rules were engaged at the highest levels when the prime minister of Canada called the president of Mexico to complain about the awarding of a natural gas contract to a firm whose bid was significantly higher priced than that of a Canadian competitor.

The purpose of the detailed rules of Chapter 10 is to make government procurement practices transparent in the NAFTA countries. Transparency is a procedural principle that requires countries to ensure that their laws and administrative practices are accessible. Countries must publish laws and regulations so that they may be located easily. Countries must make administrative decision making "transparent" by ensuring that decisions are based on recorded evidence and arguments, not corruption or nepotism. For this reason, transparency is also known as the "sunshine" principle. When government affairs must be conducted in the light of day for all to see, some practices that might have occurred in the shadows happen less frequently.

Conclusion

Generally speaking, corruption remains a far more serious problem for Mexico than it is for Canada and the United States. Nevertheless, corruption in Mexico is also a problem for its NAFTA partners. For Canada and the United States, corruption in Mexico means more opportunities for their own firms to engage in corrupt practices, which in turn requires more vigilance on their part in the enforcement of their anticorruption laws. Corruption in Mexico also complicates cooperation on security measures and transnational crime.

Nevertheless, Mexico is making some progress in this area. The election of an opposition party to the presidency in 2000 will mean greater vigilance from opposition parties. Moreover, the administration of President Vicente Fox appears to be making a serious effort to enhance transparency and accountability in government operations. But Mexico cannot wipe out corruption on its own. It will need assistance and cooperation from both Canada and the United States in this area.

Appendix 5.1
Kidnapping, Mexican Style:
Thalía and Her Sisters

Laura Zapata, the star of a play in Mexico City, drove away from the theater after a standing ovation for her performance on September 22, 2002. But the drama of her life was just beginning. She drove the car in which her sister, Ernestina Sodi, was the only other passenger. Some half-dozen men stopped their car at a stoplight, smashed the windows, and drove away with the two sisters. The kidnappers knew precisely who the two women were—sisters of a famous soap opera star turned singer called Thalía. Thalía is not just rich and famous in her own right. She is also married to the wealthy president of Sony Music, Tommy Mottola (Ferriss 2002).

The next day the abandoned car was found on the outskirts of Mexico City. No charges were filed with the police about the kidnapping. Mexico City attorney general

Bernardo Batiz told news reporters that he "respects" the decision of relatives "to negotiate directly with the kidnappers." There were rumors that somewhere between U.S.$2–$10 million were demanded as ransom (Ferriss 2002). There were also rumors that Mottola hired private negotiators to secure the release of his sisters-in-law. Laura Zapata reappeared on October 10 and Ernestina Sodi on October 26. In a telephone interview the following day with the television news presenter Joaquin Lopez Doriga, Zapata declared, "It totally changed our lives. There is the us of before the twenty-second of September and the us of after the twenty-second of September." They both reportedly flew out of Mexico the weekend after the interview.

This is just one incident in what is widely perceived to be a Mexican kidnapping epidemic. Hard reports on kidnapping are hard to come by. Families of victims rarely file charges for fear that the victim might be killed in a botched rescue attempt, or worse, that the police might be the kidnappers. Two years earlier, in the state of Morelos (just a short drive south of Mexico City), numerous police officers were found to be ringleaders of kidnapping gangs. Some of the police involved held a unique qualification for this job—they formed part of special police squads that were supposed to be dedicated to arresting kidnappers. The commander of one such antikidnapping squad lost his job after he was caught dumping barrels containing chopped-up body parts of kidnap victims off a hillside highway.

Mexico has the second largest market in the world in one line of insurance business: kidnap and ransom (the first place is occupied by Colombia). Many of Mexico's rich and famous hire bodyguards and drive around in bulletproof vehicles. They do not announce their daily schedule in the hope of not becoming the target of an attempted kidnapping.

Not only high-profile people get kidnapped. There are low-level kidnappings too, which involve paying ransoms at budget rates. The most common ones are referred to as "kidnap express." So-called pirate taxis serve as the vehicle for the perpetrators. They drive the victims to the nearest deserted automated teller machine and force them to draw out the maximum amount of money permitted by the bank's daily withdrawal limit. Sometimes, victims are held for several days so that the kidnappers can maximize their take by making daily withdrawals up to the limit. Incredibly, until September 2002, the law did not recognize such short-term kidnapping as kidnapping. Such incidents were treated as robbery. Of course, robbery is a much lesser offense than kidnapping.

Executives visiting from other countries are routinely warned not to catch the ubiquitous green-and-white Volkswagen taxis in the streets of Mexico City. Pirate taxis typically pick up accomplices with weapons who are stationed at a prearranged location. The driver feigns engine trouble and stops the taxi and the accomplices pile in. Alternatively, the accomplices, following behind in another vehicle, pull up and pounce when the taxi "stalls." Since these taxis have only two doors, it is hard for a passenger to escape. This problem has prompted the Mexico City government not to give any more permits to taxis with two doors. The hope is that there will be fewer express kidnappings with four-door taxis.

Kidnapping is an extreme consequence of Mexico's lack of law enforcement and police corruption.

Appendix 5.2
Subnational Shenanigans and Other Trilateral Affairs

The following three vignettes are all cases of corruption: one involves a Mexican governor, one a member of the U.S. House of Representatives, and one is a case of private sector corruption. The scales of corruption are different. The U.S. prosecutors went after corruption that involved tens of thousands of dollars. This strongly suggests that for the U.S. government (and more so for the Canadian government), relatively small corruption is not tolerable. In contrast, Mexico is still struggling with corruption that nets millions of dollars.

The Governor, the Broker, and the Cocaine Trader

In April 1999, the governor of Quintana Roo (the state of Mexico where Cancun is located) handed over power to his successor and moved away from the limelight. There were two odd things about his exit. First, he handed over power by sending a fax instead of doing so publicly. Second, he not only disappeared from the limelight, but disappeared from Mexico altogether.

Mario Villanueva knew that he would be arrested once he had lost his immunity upon handing over office to his successor. He had been shipping cocaine through his state for the Colombian drug cartels for years, at times even using his official plane. He charged the cartel a mere $495 per pound ($1,000 per kilogram) of cocaine shipped. Over a year after he had left office, he was tracked down and arrested in Managua, Nicaragua, and extradited to Mexico. He is now in La Palma jail in Mexico waiting to be extradited to the United States, where he faces a number of drug-related charges.

This would have been a simple story of a crooked politician had it ended there. (Indeed, Villanueva has a nickname befitting his action—"el chueco"—the crooked one, but the name comes from his facial features, not his activities.) But it didn't end there.

One of the consequences of the U.S. Patriot Act of October 2001 is a new requirement for financial disclosure by brokerage firms. Prior to the passage of the Patriot Act, brokerage houses, unlike banks, didn't have to report to the government their clients' activities and therefore could potentially serve as the backdoor gateway to America's financial system.

In 1995, Consuelo Marquez was a broker for Lehman Brothers. So if you happened to be a Mexican state governor with a pile of drug money, an obliging Ms. Marquez could be much more helpful than a regular bank employee. Now U.S. federal prosecutors have charged the former Lehman Brothers broker with helping to launder $15 million for Mario Villanueva from 1995 to 2000. For those millions and more, Villanueva, who was governor of Quintana Roo from 1993 to 1999, helped usher through 200 tons of cocaine into the United States, via his governor's airplane and bribes to police officers (DeBaise 2002).

The prosecutions of Villanueva and Marquez are an unexpectedly positive fallout from two things: closer scrutiny of dealings of U.S. financial institutions as a consequence of the events of September 11 and the change of government at the federal level in Mexico.

The Porn Star Mistress, Pillowtalk, and Insider Trading

Kathryn Gannon, the Canadian-born porn actress, was the mistress of James McDermott Jr., former head of Keefe, Bruyette & Woods. McDermott admitted that he gave Gannon tips about a potential takeover of Barnett Banks by SunTrust Banks in August 1997. Gannon then purchased 1,800 shares of Barnett stock. In addition, she shared the information with another lover, Anthony Pomponio. Later, in 1999, McDermott and Pomponio were arrested. McDermott was not charged with making any money from the illegal trades. However, he and Pomponio stood trial together in Manhattan federal court. They were both convicted. Gannon (who went by the name of Marilyn Starr in the porn industry) fled to her hometown, Vancouver, Canada.

It would be two years before the U.S. prosecutor could have Gannon extradited to the United States to face charges. Finally, she was extradited, tried, and sentenced on October 24, 2002, to three months in prison for trading on inside stock tips. Immediately afterward, Gannon told reporters, "I did a lot of wrong things, but I'm an adventurous Aries and a Canadian. There is going to be a movie made about my life story. Jail time actually promotes it even better—ching, ching! There's no fear here. I'm from Canada and I can handle it" (Appleson 2002).

Jim Traficant: The Man with the Funny Hair

On July 24, 2002, James A. Traficant Jr., the former representative in the U.S. House of Representatives for Youngstown, Ohio, was sentenced to eight years behind bars and said he intends to run for election from his prison cell—and expects to win. Mr. Traficant was an oddball in the House. He wore a crooked toupee, and cheap polyester suits. A week before, he had been expelled from the House. For only the second time since the Civil War, the House of Representatives expelled a member from its ranks (voting 420 : 1) for official misconduct. (The first instance was the case of Michael "Ozzie" Myers, expelled in 1980 for accepting money from FBI agents posing as Arab sheiks seeking favors from Congress in the Abscam scandal. Myers was convicted on bribery and conspiracy charges.)

The violation of ethics by Traficant came in the form of nine different charges: (1) Receiving from Anthony Bucci, Robert Bucci, and companies in their control free labor and materials for his horse farm in exchange for his using his official influence on their behalf; (2) Accepting free labor and materials from Honey Creek Contracting Co. and its owner, Arthur Sugar, in return for several favors; (3) Accepting numerous meals, use of automobiles, and money for repairs to his boat from John Cafaro, whose U.S. Aerospace Group was seeking Traficant's help in seeking Federal Aviation Administration certification of the company's laser-guided aircraft landing technology; (4 and 5) Hiring as a member of his congressional staff Allen Sinclair in exchange for favors, including preferential rental rates for office space and kickbacks of $2,500 from Sinclair's monthly congressional paychecks; (6) Trying to persuade Sinclair to destroy evidence and provide false testimony to a federal grand jury; (7) Requiring his congressional staff in Washington to maintain and repair his personal boat and directing members of his congressional staff in Ohio to perform work at his farm; (8 and 9)

Reporting with his wife to the IRS income of $138,985 in 1998 and $140,163 in 1999 when the amounts were substantially greater.

As the case against Traficant was being built, he was reelected in 2000. He told a reporter, "Why would you want to do a piece on a jackass like me? Though I am at the zenith of my jackasshood, I want you to know" (Jacoby 2002).

Appendix 5.3
The CNI Drama: A Very Hostile Takeover

On December 27, 2002, CNI, a small independent television station in Mexico City, started telecasting the signal of a rival television station, TV Azteca (the second largest Spanish language television group in the world). The viewers were informed that two years of litigation had led to a court ruling in early December 2002 giving TV Azteca 51 percent of TVM (the parent holding company of CNI), as well as control over CNI's output. To prove the legitimacy of the handover of the television signal, TV Azteca showed video footage of people (presumably TV Azteca employees) entering the signal-generating complex of CNI, showing CNI workers documents, and peacefully taking over the signal station.

The true story began to emerge the following day. The BBC News described TV Azteca's seizure of the CNI installation as "the most hostile takeover ever." CNI said it had testimony from seven employees that TV Azteca's takeover had been enforced not by lawyers, but by armed guards in ski masks who held CNI staff hostage for several hours. The video footage aired by TV Azteca turned out to be a staged event. The staff of CNI were told what to do in front of the camera after TV Azteca's hired commandos took over the transmission station at gunpoint. The CNI staff were also given large sums of money to "compensate" them for the "scare."

It became clear within forty-eight hours that the takeover was completely illegal. However, the Mexican federal government did nothing. This was curious because the federal government is the technical owner of the signal stations and concession holders like CNI merely lease the facility. The first reaction of the federal government was even more bizarre. Mexico's secretary of communications and transport simply washed his hands of the matter, declaring that the dispute was between private parties and therefore the government had no responsibility to intervene. Even Mexican president Vicente Fox, when asked about it, said (half jokingly), "What does this have to do with me?"

After ten days of inaction (and much public criticism), the federal government decided to arrange a meeting between the parties to resolve the matter. Two days of talks yielded no solution. On January 9, 2003, by order of the interior secretary, federal agents took control of the signal station, forcing the station off the air and ending the transmission of TV Azteca's programs on CNI's channel.

On January 24, a Mexican district judge ordered the government to restore the broadcasting facilities to CNI and rebuked the federal government for its inaction. On January 29, 2003, CNI was back on the air. It was only then that the other side of the story came out in the mass media. The news media reported the story as a win for the underdog in a battle of David and Goliath. For example, Inter Press Services dispatched a report with the heading, "Independent Station Defeats Giant."

Regardless of the merits of TV Azteca's claim against CNI, its forcible capture of the transmission tower was a gross violation of the law. TV Azteca took the law into its own hands to achieve what it had been unable to achieve through litigation. Even more alarming was that the federal government allowed TV Azteca to do so. This event raises serious questions about the enforcement of property rights in Mexico and the general state of the rule of law in the country.

6

Three's Company

NAFTA as a Bloc

"It is said that the present is pregnant with the future."
—*Voltaire*

"My brain is filled with questions marks."
—*Hal Saijo*

"Snap out of it!"
—*Cher*

Exactly six months after the attack on the World Trade Center, Rudi Dekkers, president of Huffman Aviation in Venice, Florida, received a letter from the Immigration and Naturalization Service (INS) saying that Mohammad Atta's application to change his status from a "visitor" to a "student" had been approved (Johnson 2002). Atta was one of the masterminds who coordinated the attack on the World Trade Center and was on one of the planes. Huffman Aviation was the place where he trained to fly airplanes. This incident produced a ripple effect through various parts of the U.S. government, prompting President Bush to order an inquiry into the matter immediately (Mitchell 2002). It also led to some reshuffling at the INS (Schmitt 2002).

This episode underscores the problem of coordination, not just among the federal (and state) agencies in the United States, but among the government agencies of all three NAFTA countries. Coordination of activities has to be extended further between the three governments along with the private companies that make movement of people and goods possible—trucking companies, airlines, shipping companies, among others.

The central purpose of NAFTA is to remove barriers to cross-border business. However, NAFTA is just a beginning. The elimination of tariffs does not eliminate other costs associated with the cross-border movement of goods. The creation of new visas to facilitate the movement of businesspeople in the region does not resolve the issue of illegal migration. The creation of institutions to resolve trade and investment disputes does not solve the problem of coordination among government agencies within and between the three countries. The removal of barriers to foreign investment does not by itself make a country an attractive location for foreign investment. Much work remains to be done to further enhance the business environment in the NAFTA countries. Some of that work requires close international cooperation. However, each country can do a lot on its own—particularly when it comes to removing obstacles to doing business in the region.

Three-Country Circus: Hoops for Businesses

How do Canada, Mexico, and the United States differ in terms of obstacles to doing business? Some specific issues involving corruption were discussed in Chapter 5. Here, in order to compare and contrast the NAFTA countries, we critically examine a broader group of issues that impede business activities in the region, such as government regulation, intervention, and availability of credit.

Starting a business requires going through a number of steps in any country. However, the process varies enormously across countries. In Table 6.1, we compare this process in the NAFTA countries. We have also included Denmark as an extreme case where it costs literally nothing to register a business with the government.

In a comparison of the three NAFTA countries, several striking facts emerge. First, it takes a few days to start a business in Canada and the United States, but it takes two months to start one in Mexico just going through bureaucratic hoops. Second, the difference in the cost of starting a business is also striking. In absolute terms, it costs more to start a business in Mexico (almost five times as much in as the United States and eight times as much as in Canada). The discrepancy becomes even starker when we calculate the cost as a percent of per capita GDP. The absolute cost may not be all that important if per capita income is correspondingly high. But the reality is exactly the opposite. Mexico has lower per capita income as well as higher absolute cost of registering a business. The net result is that, while it costs less than 1 percent in the United States and Canada (in terms of per capita GDP), it costs almost 21 percent in Mexico. Not surprisingly, most businesses that operate in Mexico are not registered with the government.

Another important aspect of running a business is enforcement of contracts (Table 6.2). The number of procedures required in Mexico is much

Table 6.1

Starting a Business: Procedure, Delay, and Cost in NAFTA

Country	Number of Procedures	Duration (days)	Cost (U.S.$)	Cost* (percent)
Canada	2	2	125.62	0.59
Denmark	3	3	0.00	0.00
Mexico	7	51	1,058.51	20.88
United States	5	5	210.00	0.69

Source: Entry regulation data from the World Bank, rru.worldbank.org/DoingBusiness/
SnapshotReports/EntryRegulations.aspx

Note: Duration stands for the number of days it takes for the new business to register. Cost* measures the cost as a percent of per capita GDP. Measuring the cost: The text of the company law, the commercial code, or specific regulations are used as a source for the costs associated with starting up a business. If there are conflicting sources and the laws are not completely clear, the most authoritative source is used. The constitution supercedes the law and the law prevails over regulations and decrees. If the sources have the same rank, the source indicating the most costly procedure is used, since an entrepreneur never second-guesses a government official. In the absence of express legal fee schedules, we take a governmental officer's estimate as an official source. If several sources have different estimates, the median reported value is used. In the absence of a government officer's estimates, estimates of incorporation lawyers are used instead. If several incorporation lawyers have different estimates, the median reported value is computed. In all cases, the cost estimate excludes bribes. Measuring time: Time is recorded in calendar days. One week has seven calendar days, one month has 30.5 calendar days. For the sake of uniformity, for all countries it is assumed that the minimum time required to fulfill a procedural requirement is one day. Therefore, the shortest procedure lasts one calendar day. The time variable captures the average duration that incorporation lawyers estimate is necessary to complete a procedure. If a procedure can be speeded up at additional cost, the fastest procedure, independent of cost, is chosen. It is assumed that the entrepreneur does not waste time, committing to the completion of each remaining procedure from the previous day, unless the law stipulates the contrary. When estimating the time needed for complying with entry regulations, the time that the entrepreneur spends gathering information is ignored. The entrepreneur is aware of all entry regulations and their sequence from the very beginning. The study collects information on the sequence in which the procedures are to be completed, as well as any procedures that lend themselves to being carried out simultaneously.

higher than in the United States and Canada. However, legal processes move faster in Mexico than in Canada, but slower than in the United States. The last index (formalism) refers to procedures to resolve disputes. The higher the formalism, the more the cost. On this count as well, Mexico fares far worse than either the United States or Canada.

It is not surprising that Mexico ranks below Canada or the United States in almost all areas. After all, we are comparing a middle-income country, where more than half the labor force works in the informal sector, against

Table 6.2

Contract Enforcement in NAFTA

Country	Number of procedures (1)	Duration (days)(2)	Formalism index (3)
Canada	17	421	2.09
Mexico	47	283	4.71
United States	12	54	2.61

Source: rru.worldbank.org/DoingBusiness/Methodology/ContractEnforcement.aspx. The data are for January 2002.

Notes: (1) The first indicator is the number of independent procedural actions, where each action is defined as a step of the procedure, mandated by law or court regulation, that demands interaction between the parties or between them and the judge or court officer. (2) The second indicator of efficiency is an estimate—in calendar days—of duration of the process of dispute resolution by the lawyers who completed the questionnaires. Duration is measured as the number of calendar days counted from the moment the plaintiff files the lawsuit in court until the moment of actual payment. This measure includes both the days when actions take place and waiting periods between actions. The participating firms make separate estimates of the average duration until the completion of service of process, the issuance of judgment (duration of trial), and the moment of payment or repossession (duration of enforcement). To the extent that database users are interested in the ability of an ordinary person to use the legal system, these estimates of duration are highly relevant for efficiency. (3) The third indicator is an index of the degree of formalism in the procedures to resolve disputes. This index measures substantive and procedural statutory intervention in judicial cases at lower level civil trial courts.

two highly developed countries with the highest standards of living in the world. Nevertheless, the comparison shows how far Mexico has to travel to join the club to which its neighbors in the north belong.

In 1995–96, the World Bank investigated obstacles to doing business around the world. The study used nearly 4,000 questionnaires in sixty-nine countries. As we noted in Chapter 5 in our analysis of the questions relating to corruption, managers rated obstacles on a four-point scale, ranging from "no obstacle" and "moderate obstacle" to "strong obstacle" and "major obstacle."

In Table 6.3, we compare five different types of government regulation from the World Bank study. First, we look at business regulation (variable "blreg"). All three countries differ in statistically significant ways. The difference between the United States and Canada is smaller than the difference between Mexico and the United States or Canada. Nevertheless, they are all statistically significant. Customs regulations (variable "cusreg") is the same. Labor regulation (variable "labreg") and environmental regulation (variable "envreg") also follow the same pattern. Although Canada is generally perceived to be more sympathetic to labor conditions and more environmentally friendly, it scores better than the United States on both counts in terms of the

Table 6.3

Regulatory Differences in NAFTA

Country	blreg	cusreg	labreg	envreg	hitreg
Mexico	3.17	2.82	2.82	2.61	3.52
Canada	1.84	2.01	1.82	1.80	3.04
United States	2.07	1.87	2.32	2.55	2.95

Source: Tabulated from the results of World Bank Survey of businesses; see also, Brunetti et al. (1997).
Key to variables:
blreg = business regulation
cusreg = customs regulation
labreg = labor regulation
envreg = environmental regulation
hitreg = high taxes

impact on business. This is somewhat surprising. High taxes are disliked by businesses the world over. Companies in the NAFTA region are no exception. The difference in the degree to which tax regimes are an obstacle to doing business (variable "hitreg") is not significant between the United States and Canada. However, the difference between Mexico and Canada and between Mexico and the United States is substantial.

The next set of questions explores different types of government intervention (Table 6.4). Once again, government intervention in investment decisions (variable "ginv") differs significantly across countries, with Canada ranking as the most friendly to business and Mexico the worst. Once again, the United States is much closer to Canada than to Mexico. With respect to government intervention in employment decisions (variable "gemp"), the United States and Canada switch positions. The United States is viewed as more business-friendly than Canada in this regard. Government intervention in sales (variable "gsle") occurs the least in Canada and the most in Mexico. Government intervention in pricing (variable "gpce") does not differ at all between the United States and Canada, whereas in Mexico pricing intervention differs substantially compared to both of its NAFTA partners.

Government intervention in mergers and acquisitions (variable "gmaq") is a study in contrasts. Here, the United States and Mexico are in the same ballpark whereas Canada is in a league of its own. This outcome was a surprise. In terms of government intervention in dividend decisions (variable "gdvd"), Mexico and the United States are in the same league but Canada fares better. Finally, the problem of violation of patents (variable "cmpe") produces another surprise. Businesses put the United States and Mexico in the same position whereas Canada fares much better. The similarity of the United States

Table 6.4

Differences in Government Intervention in NAFTA

Country	ginv	gemp	gsle	gpce	gmaq	gdvd	cmpe
Mexico	3.07	2.73	2.79	2.10	2.65	2.44	2.58
Canada	1.81	2.01	1.84	1.74	1.79	1.57	1.84
United States	2.13	1.92	2.33	1.74	2.57	2.32	2.56

Source: Tabulated from the results of World Bank Survey of businesses; see also, Brunetti et al. (1997).
  Key to variables:
  ginv = government intervention
  gemp = government intervention in employment decisions
  gsle = government intervention in sales
  gpce = government intervention in pricing
  gmaq = government intervention in mergers and acquisitions
  gdvd = government intervention in dividend decisions
  cmpe = problem of violation of patents

Table 6.5

Financial Constraints for Doing Business in NAFTA

Country	coll	papr	spcn	lckm	acfk	expf	acnb	lesf
Mexico	2.72	2.08	2.34	3.47	2.82	2.66	2.56	2.05
Canada	1.88	1.73	1.61	2.95	1.83	1.91	2.07	1.69
United States	2.32	1.78	2.34	3.06	2.19	2.35	1.93	1.81

Source: Tabulated from the results of World Bank Survey of businesses; see also, Brunetti et al. (1997).
  Key to variables:
  coll = "collateral" for business
  papr = problem with paperwork
  spcn = special connections needed for business
  lckm = lack of business loans
  acfk = access to foreign banks as a source of capital
  expf = access to export financing
  acnb = access to nonbank equity
  lesf = access to lease financing

and Mexico for the last three variables was completely unexpected given the difference in the level of development in the three countries. We would have expected that the United States would be closer to Canada on all counts than to Mexico. However, the results reveal that this was not so.

In Table 6.5, we compare the NAFTA countries in terms of various financial constraints for doing business. Problems with collateral for business (variable "coll") are bigger both in the United States and Mexico than in Canada.

Table 6.6

Legal, Central, and Local Governmental Differences in NAFTA

Country	lawpred	nghelp	lghelp	avlreg	intlrg
Mexico	2.58	2.51	1.96	2.46	2.47
Canada	1.88	1.96	1.61	1.97	2.01
United States	2.25	1.97	1.87	2.19	1.95

Source: Tabulated from the results of World Bank Survey of businesses; see also, Brunetti et al. (1997).
Key to variables:
lawpred = predictability of legal regime
nghelp = helpfulness of national government
lghelp = helpfulness of local government
avlreg = ease of obtaining laws and regulation
intlrg = consistency of regulation

Problems with paperwork (variable "papr") are very similar between the United States and Canada but not so for Mexico. Curiously, having special connections (variable "spcn") matters equally in the United States and in Mexico. Mexico is well known for this particular constraint. Finding the same for the United States is surprising.

Lack of business loans (variable "lckm") is a problem of similar magnitude in the United States and Canada. Not surprisingly, the problem is much worse in Mexico, as is access to foreign banks as a source of capital (variable "acfk). Access to export financing (variable "expf"), access to nonbank equity (variable "acnb"), and access to lease financing (variable "lesf") are all bigger problems in Mexico.

With respect to the predictability of legal regime (variable "lawpred"), Mexico and the United States rank far lower than Canada. As for the helpfulness of national government (variable "nghelp"), there is no difference between the United States and Canada. However, with respect to the helpfulness of local government (variable "lghelp"), there is no statistically significant difference between the United States and Mexico. Regarding the ease of obtaining laws and regulation (variable "avlreg"), Canada again ranks higher than the United States. In the final variable of consistency of regulation (variable "intlrg"), there is no statistically significant difference between the United States and Canada, but Mexico is a distant third. Thus, in all the variables in Table 6.6, Canada fares better than the other two countries and Mexico trails behind on all measures.

Substantial differences exist in how businesses regard court systems in the three NAFTA countries. In judging whether courts are fair and impartial (variable "ficrt"), Canada comes out on top. In judging the honesty of the

Table 6.7

Differences in Court Systems in NAFTA

Country	ficrt	hucrt	cstcrt	enfcrt	cfcrt
Mexico	2.40	1.96	2.39	2.35	1.93
Canada	2.07	1.66	2.01	2.07	1.66
United States	2.27	1.79	1.99	2.31	1.82

Source: Tabulated from the results of World Bank Survey of businesses; see also, Brunetti et al. (1997).
Key to variables:
ficrt = courts fair and impartial
hucrt = honesty of the court system
cstcrt = consistency of courts
enfcrt = enforceability of court rulings
cfcrt = confident that legal system will uphold my rights today

court system (variable "hucrt"), Mexico does not trail too far behind. Given widespread reports about judges being bribed in Mexico, this is somewhat surprising. As for the consistency of courts (variable "cstcrt"), the United States and Canada are statistically indistinguishable. With respect to the enforceability of court rulings (variable "enfcrt"), the United States does just as badly as Mexico. For the item entitled "confident that legal system will uphold my rights today" (variable "cfcrt"), Mexico is not too far off from the United States. However, Canada once again ranks higher.

The World Bank survey results show that each of the NAFTA countries retains a great deal of control over several factors that influence the business climate in the region. As a result, there is much that each country can do on its own to enhance the competitiveness of its business environment both with respect to its NAFTA partners and with respect to countries outside the region. However, enhancing the competitiveness of the regional business climate vis-à-vis other regions of the world requires cooperation on border management. And that requires cooperation on border security measures.

It's the Money, Honey: Cost of Doing Business in NAFTA

In the previous section, we have discussed obstacles to doing business. That discussion does not make it clear how NAFTA is shaping up as a place for doing business in terms of actual dollars and cents. In this section we compare wages in manufacturing, labor productivity, and unit labor costs in the three countries.

Our first point of comparison is the evolution of the hourly wage rate in manufacturing. Comparable tables for the three NAFTA countries with similar

Table 6.8

Hourly Wage in Manufacturing

Year	Mexico	United States	France	Chile
1993	2.1	11.7	7.5	1.7
1994	2.1	12.0	7.9	2.0
1995	1.3	12.3	8.8	2.3
1996	1.3	12.7	8.7	2.4
1997	1.6	13.1	7.9	2.6
1998	1.6	13.4	8.0	2.5
1999	1.9	13.8	7.9	2.3
2000	2.2	14.3	7.2	2.3
2001	2.5	14.8	7.2	2.1
2002	2.5	15.1		2.0

Source: Instituto Nacional de Estadística, Geografía e Informática (INEGI) website, www.inegi.gob.mx, 2002.
Note: Hourly wage measured in U.S. dollars per hour.

base are not readily available. So we use France (for which we have available data) as a proxy for Canada. The wage structure in manufacturing in France and Canada has been similar in recent years. Table 6.8 shows that the Mexican manufacturing wage rate is about one-sixth of its counterpart in the United States (2002). Thus, Mexico offers a tremendous advantage in terms of labor cost. Canada's labor cost (using France as a proxy) is almost half of that of the United States. It also provides an advantage in terms of labor cost for manufacturing. Not surprisingly, manufacturers in the United States with high labor cost content tend to relocate in Mexico and Canada. Chile provides a point of comparison for Mexico. It also provides cost advantage in the same order of magnitude as Mexico. Mexico has the edge over Chile in geographical proximity. Thus, for manufacturers in the United States with just-in-time requirements, Chile does not offer an alternative to Mexico.

Labor productivity offers another point of comparison (see Table 6.9). During the time since the implementation of NAFTA, Mexico has had stellar performance in terms of productivity gains. The gain over ten years has been over 50 percent (with an annual rate of 4.15 percent). This gain in productivity has slightly edged out the productivity gain in the United States. Surprisingly, none of this has rubbed off in Canada. Canada has had a slow growth in productivity (in the same mold as Europe).

Unit labor cost provides another point of comparison among NAFTA countries in terms of doing business (Table 6.10). The first important feature of the table is that in all three countries the unit costs are down in the neighborhood of 15 percent to 20 percent. In the United States and Canada, there has been a more or less steady decline in unit cost of labor. However, in Mexico,

Table 6.9

Productivity in NAFTA Countries

Year	Mexico	United States	Canada
1993	100.0	100.0	100.0
1994	109.9	103.4	104.7
1995	115.3	108.6	109.1
1996	125.7	114.5	108.2
1997	130.9	120.9	108.6
1998	136.4	127.8	112.7
1999	139.0	135.2	118.4
2000	145.7	142.7	118.8
2001	146.3	145.5	114.4
2002	151.9	150.7	117.7

Source: Instituto Nacional de Estadística, Geografía e Informática (INEGI) website, www.inegi.gob.mx, 2002.

Note: Productivity is an index, normalized here to one hundred for 1993 for comparability across NAFTA countries.

the reduction is anything but steady. There was a tremendous drop between 1994 and 1995 (lingering even in 1996). But, from 1996, unit labor cost shows a rising trend. Since all of this is measured in U.S. dollars, the reason for this abrupt fall is obvious: the devaluation of the Mexican peso in 1995.

Different location advantages in the three countries partly explain the phenomenon of cross-border integration of business in the region. In this regard, the three countries compete with each other to attract business investment. However, as a region, North America competes in the international stage with other economic regions in the world. The attractiveness of the region is influenced not only by the business climate in all three NAFTA countries, but also by their ability to effectively manage the borders within the region.

The Insecurity Complex: Security and Border Management

All three NAFTA members have good reasons to create a security perimeter to lower border transaction costs. With almost 90 percent of Canada and Mexico's exports destined for the U.S. market, they are hardest hit by border costs as a percentage of economic activity. Moreover, border costs influence the destination of foreign direct investment from outside the NAFTA region and thus may put Canada and Mexico at a relative disadvantage vis-à-vis the United States. However, in terms of security, the United States stands to gain the most from a common perimeter.

Including Mexico in a North American security perimeter lowers costs and enhances security. It will be a challenge to overcome institutional, legal,

Table 6.10

Unit Labor Cost in NAFTA Countries

Year	Mexico	United States	Canada
1993	100.0	100.0	100.0
1994	93.4	99.3	94.0
1995	56.0	96.8	91.5
1996	52.1	95.0	95.3
1997	57.1	92.7	93.9
1998	56.8	89.9	86.2
1999	62.7	87.5	83.5
2000	70.2	85.7	85.1
2001	80.1	86.7	86.0
2002	79.7	85.8	83.6

Source: Instituto Nacional de Estadística, Geografía e Informática (INEGI) website, www.inegi.gob.mx, 2002.

Note: Unit Labor Cost is an index, normalized here to one hundred for 1993 for comparability across NAFTA countries.

and political barriers in Mexico. But Mexico is a necessary element in any security strategy (Leiken 2002). For the first time, the U.S. government has signaled that it will do its utmost to make sure the southern border is not excluded from security considerations (Chen 2002).

The movement of illegal goods and illegal migrants points to the importance of Mexico. Ignoring Mexico leaves a large hole in the U.S. security perimeter. If it is so easy for goods (including elephants), people (including illegal aliens not just from Mexico), and capital (such as drug-related money) to move across the border, how does the United States plan to improve security without Mexican cooperation? Since the United States cannot set up an impenetrable fence along its southern border, it needs Mexico to be a part of its security strategy. If Mexico is not brought on board, the United States might regret leaving Mexico outside its security perimeter in the future. Of course, given the level of corruption, apathy, and downright hostility toward the "gringos" on the Mexican side, making Mexico an integral part of U.S. security strategy will not be an easy task. But it is absolutely essential. After all, the biggest foreign "invasion" before the attack on September 11, 2001 was launched by the famous Mexican General Pancho Villa on March 6, 1916, in the tiny village of Columbus, New Mexico (Woolley 2001).

The Right Stuff: Striking a Balance

Balancing trade and security issues in the cross-border transportation of goods is not that difficult to manage because most trade involves a relatively small number of companies and flows through a relatively small number of ports. The real risk is that the issue of security might be hijacked by special interests to serve their particular agendas rather than the public good. The case of the Mexican trucking industry's access to the U.S. market serves as a cautionary tale in this regard.

Striking the right balance between economic integration and security needs means resolving problems where they do exist—for example, with respect to illegal migration from Mexico and corruption of Mexican government officials by foreign business interests.

Striking the right balance also means avoiding overreactions, as has occurred in the United States with respect to the freezing of assets allegedly associated with Al Qaeda and to the racial profiling of Canadian citizens born in Middle Eastern and Muslim countries. The importance of the rule of law over the long term outweighs the need to undermine it in the short term. As our chapter on corruption illustrates, undermining the rule of law may have long-term security implications

Balancing economic integration with security not only means examining issues on their own, but also entails an analysis of how various issues relate to each nother. Laws and policies must be designed to support each other. For example, U.S. policy regarding immigration not only fails to resolve the problem of illegal immigration, but undermines U.S. labor laws as well. The issuing of visas to dead hijackers six months after September 11 illustrates the need to coordinate the activities and policies of different government agencies within the United States. The same degree of policy coordination must be achieved among the agencies of the NAFTA countries as well.

Mexico has asked the United States to help to defray the cost of additional security. Given the size of the Mexico's northern neighbor and its economic strength, such a petition makes sense. However, Mexico needs to take a hard look at its own internal resources as a source of revenue. The Mexican economy has an extremely large informal sector. Depending on the measure used, the size of Mexico's informal economy varies, but it is often estimated to encompass about 50 percent of all economic activities. In contrast, the size of the informal economy in the United States or Canada is 5 percent to 8 percent.

This informality affects the government's command over the economy. One measure of government command is government tax revenue as a percentage of GDP. In Mexico, the tax revenue of the government as a percentage of GDP is around 13 percent. In contrast, in Canada and the United States (counting all levels of government including state/provincial and local), this figure is over 20 percent. Even in Brazil, Latin America's other large economy, the figure is over 20 percent. The informal economy breeds illegal activities and corruption. Thus, in more ways than one, informality affects the ability of Mexico to contribute to North American security and its own security environment.

Along Came a Spider: Weaving a Seamless Web

The themes explored in this book are all interconnected. The management of cross-border flows of goods, people, and capital affect the competitiveness of business, the economic prosperity of the region, and regional security. Institutional problems, such as internal and cross-border business barriers, interagency coordination, and government corruption, affect the ability of governments to provide a secure and prosperous business environment, both within each country and across the region as a whole. In addition to these linkages, there are numerous interlocking connections between all of these issues.

Capital flows in the form of foreign direct investment have a major impact on merchandise trade by stimulating intrafirm trade. In the NAFTA region, foreign direct investment in Mexican assembly plants has stimulated considerable growth in cross-border flows of goods across the Mexico–United States border. Similarly, the regional integration of the automotive sector has sparked considerable foreign direct investment and merchandise trade between all three NAFTA countries. In turn, flows of goods and capital require more cross-border flows of people to conduct trade and investment activities and to provide services (such as transportation and financial transactions) that accompany international trade and investment.

International trade and investment also affect people movement less directly. Foreign direct investment creates jobs that attract workers. With greater foreign direct investment in Mexico's manufacturing sector, there are more jobs to keep Mexican workers at home. Export-led growth has the potential to reduce the wage gap between Mexico and the United States, further reducing incentives for undocumented Mexican workers to seek work in the United States. Corruption, however, has the opposite effect. Corruption and other barriers to business make it more difficult to achieve the economic growth needed to close wage gaps and to enhance Mexico's attractiveness for foreign direct investment. Corruption also increases the need to scrutinize cross-border capital movements.

Security is an issue that weaves itself into every aspect of North American integration and the central topics analyzed in this book. The migration of undocumented workers from Mexico to the United States—and the wrongheaded policies on both sides of the border that perpetuate the problem—divert resources that could otherwise be used to deal with the movement of individuals who pose a real security threat. The lack of personal security in Mexico—an issue closely linked to corruption in the police force—

makes Mexico a less attractive destination for foreign direct investment by transferring security costs from the government to the private sector. Personal security risks also complicate the recruitment of the expatriate managers that forms an integral part of international investment strategies. The need to stem the international capital flows associated with terrorist financing can increase the transaction costs for legitimate capital flows. Finally, security requires investments in the systems used to move and monitor the cross-border flow of goods—though such investments may increase the efficiency of cross-border goods transportation at the end of the day.

To manage North American integration and security in an intelligent fashion, government policies need to be coordinated across disciplines and international borders. This is no small challenge, as illustrated by the apparent inability of the United States government to effectively coordinate policies and laws relating to people movement in order to achieve the stated goal of resolving the problem of illegal immigration from Mexico. Overcoming political obstacles to sensible policies, for example with respect to agricultural subsidies in the United States, requires leadership. These challenges need to be met to get to where we want to go—a secure, prosperous, and economically integrated North America.

Winds of Change: Drawing Lines in Sand and Snow

Our central message is that Canada, Mexico, and the United States may be separated by borders, but these lines in the southern sands and the northern snows are shifting and blurring with every change in the wind. And the winds of change have been blowing indeed. The terrorist attacks and border closures of September 11 have vividly demonstrated that NAFTA is not enough.

The terrorist threat has both united and divided the three countries. On the Canada–United States border, this threat to security and commerce prompted even more cooperation on border and security issues. It also demonstrated that the ties that bind Canadians to their American cousins are far stronger than any differences that divide them. However, the ill-conceived policy of singling out Canadians born in Middle Eastern and Muslim countries—a policy developed with inadequate consultation—produced a predictable reaction of anger on the part of Canadian parliamentarians. Alienating allies and neighbors makes for poor security strategy.

On the Mexico–United States border, a democratic change of regime opened the door to a new era for Mexico–United States relations. The friendship between President Fox and President Bush looked full of promise. But the relationship soon soured. President Fox went out on a political limb in an effort to get the United States to look seriously at migration reforms. But

President Bush's obsession with far-flung regimes left this important issue sitting on the back burner to stew. Ignoring the neighbor and the opportunity to resolve an issue of importance to both economic development and security enhancement is likewise a poor strategy.

Booming cross-border business has also been both a blessing and a curse for the two regional relationships. That we continue to speak of the region in terms of two bilateral relationships ten years after the signing of a trilateral trade agreement is a reflection of geographic, political, and economic realities. At the end of the day, however, the citizens, businesses, and governments of the three countries recognize that their destinies are intertwined.

Huge growth in trade and investment flows in the 1990s has set Mexico apart from the rest of Latin America and most other developing countries in the world. There are two sets of factors driving this phenomenon. First, Mexico is setting itself up with a wide range of free trade agreements with many countries and regions around the globe. Mexico began negotiating a free trade agreement with Japan in 2002. It already has free trade agreements with the other powerhouses of the world—NAFTA and the European Union. In fact, the European Union is by far the largest source of the foreign direct investment in the world. In 2000, the European Union invested $773 billion abroad, whereas the United States invested a mere $135 billion. Even in Latin America, the so-called backyard of the United States, the European Union investment was more than double that of the United States (Vodusek 2001). A detailed analysis of the data shows that 70 percent of European Union investments in Latin America were concentrated in two countries only—Argentina and Brazil. Two seismic changes took place in 2002 in these countries. First, Argentina faced a financial meltdown. Second, the Brazilian government took a sharp left turn with the election of Lula da Silva as president. Both events could give future European Union investors second thoughts about investing in these countries. If they decide to invest in Latin America in the future, recent political and financial upheavals in South America and the Mexico–European Union Free Trade Agreement will make Mexico look extremely attractive.

Mexico's economic integration with the United States has proved to be a vaccination against contagion from the south, shielding the peso from the turbulence of Argentina and Brazil. At the same time, increasing economic dependence on the United States has made Mexico vulnerable to shocks from the north, such as the U.S. recession and the economic fallout from the terrorist attacks. Moreover, disagreements over trucking and agricultural policies tend to stand out in the public mind more than the majority of trade that flows smoothly. Above all else, the failure to make progress on the issue of migration stands out as a sore point in the relationship.

Likewise, Canada's economic ties to the United States bring both good and bad. In recent years, Canada's economic performance has put it at the top of the G-7 countries. At the same time, the ongoing dispute over exports of lumber to the United States has harmed Canadian communities that rely on this commodity and left many Canadians wondering why such barriers continue long after the signing of the Canada–United States Free Trade Agreement. Nevertheless, Canadians have come to embrace the opportunities presented by their close relationship with the neighbor to the south and to assert themselves in the face of a sometimes overzealous United States government. Indeed, polls have demonstrated not only a desire for closer ties, but also a newfound confidence among Canadians that they can deal with Americans on a more equal footing than in the past.

The United States is a superpower that dwarfs its NAFTA partners by comparison. This makes it easy to forget that Canada and Mexico are major players in their own right, both economically and politically (if not militarily). Both countries rank in the top ten in terms of global trade and foreign direct investment flows. Both are members of the Organization for Economic Cooperation and Development, an organization whose members drive the global economy and formulate important policies relating to economic growth, corporate governance and security. Canada, as a member of the World Trade Organization (WTO) "quad" (the top four traders in the organization), has a great deal of influence in setting the agenda for global trade liberalization. Similarly, Mexico has begun to exert increasing influence on the world stage, as host of the 2002 Monterrey Summit, the 2002 Asia Pacific Economic Cooperation meeting, and the 2003 WTO ministerial conference, as well as in the United Nations Security Council. Both countries are thus in a position to help or hinder the U.S. agenda in the global arena. Canadian support for U.S. military interventions, in the Gulf War, Afghanistan, and elsewhere, lends legitimacy to U.S. actions, even if Canada's contribution is sometimes forgotten by Washington. And Mexico's Security Council vote was not insignificant to U.S. efforts to marshal support for war with Iraq.

Conclusion

Compared with the United States and Mexico, Canada emerges from our study smelling like a rose. This reflects the reality that Canada has to do better than its neighbors in order to compete with them, given its relatively small market compared to the United States and its small population compared to both of its NAFTA partners. Canada also gets favorable reviews simply because its policies and actions have been well managed in all the areas we have discussed.

The Canadian government moved quickly to increase funding for border infrastructure and to further enhance already high levels of cooperation with the United States to facilitate cross-border movement of goods. With respect to people movement, Canada introduced legislation on terrorism, tightened up its refugee system, signed a new refugee accord with the United States, introduced new visa requirements for risky countries, and beefed up staff to process visa applications at its overseas posts. With respect to NAFTA visas, Canada—like Mexico—does not discriminate between its NAFTA partners. And, unlike the United States, illegal immigration from Mexico is not a serious problem for Canada. Thus, Canada does not impose a nonimmigrant visa requirement on Mexicans. Canada even has a history of accepting political refugees from the United States. With respect to capital movements, Canada's participation in, and implementation of, international agreements on money laundering and terrorist financing also earn good reviews, as does its attractiveness for foreign direct investment. With respect to corruption and business barriers, Canada ranks better than either the United States or Mexico.

Mexico still has a lot of work to do, but its star is rising. General lack of security remains a problem and affects the movement of goods, people, and capital. With respect to goods, truck hijacking represents both a security risk and a transportation problem. With respect to capital movements, security problems could decrease Mexico's attractiveness for foreign direct investment, though it does not appear to have had a major impact so far. Other factors act as a counterweight and bode well for Mexico's attractiveness over the long term: Mexico's growing network of free trade agreements, its large and growing internal market, its land advantage over other developing countries in the wake of the U.S. port lockout, and its political and economic stability compared to other major Latin American countries.

With respect to money laundering and terrorist financing controls, Mexico has implemented international agreements but needs to do more to enforce these laws. With respect to people movements, personal security problems decreased Mexico's attractiveness for expatriate managers. On the migration issue, Mexico needs to continue to push for reforms in the United States. However, Mexico also has its own responsibilities regarding this issue. The more attractive Mexico is for Mexican workers, the more they will stay home rather than risk an illegal journey to the United States. This requires addressing the barriers that complicate setting up businesses in Mexico, improving education levels, and continuing to attract foreign direct investment that creates better job opportunities. In addition, Mexico needs to continue to reduce the cost of transferring migrant remittances from the United States to Mexican communities, in order to expand the pool of development capital that this money represents. Mexico also needs to improve its fiscal situation. Seeking handouts from U.S. and Canadian taxpayers does not sit well as long as Mexican taxpayers continue to avoid paying their fair share of taxes.

Above all, Mexico needs to continue to work on the issue of corruption, which affects its ability to advance in all of the areas addressed in our study. Resolving the corruption problem will entail cooperation on the part of Mexico's NAFTA partners in enforcing antibribery laws against their own companies, but most of the responsibility falls on Mexico's shoulders. The government must work hard to solidify the democratic functioning of its institutions, continue efforts to alter public attitudes, and continue to enhance transparency in order to make progress against corruption and firmly entrench the rule of law to ensure that laws are applied in practice.

The United States earns good grades for moving quickly to ensure that increased border security would not unduly impede the cross-border movement of goods in the region. The public-private cooperation promoted by the U.S. Customs Trade Partnerships against Terrorism (CTPAT) program provides an ideal way to ensure that the majority of merchandise trade moves smoothly and securely across borders. In addition, the United States moved quickly to enhance and expand border and security cooperation with Canada through the "Smart Border" plan and other agreements and endeavored to do the same with Mexico. However, a one-size-fits-all approach may not work on the two borders, so the United States should not view its arrangements on the Canadian border as a generic precedent that can be applied to Mexico without modifications that take into account the differences that exist on the two borders.

Regarding money laundering and terrorist financing, the United States has shown leadership in getting OECD countries to follow the precedent set by its Foreign Corrupt Practices Act and in prosecuting offences. However, it must guard against the overzealous application of its laws in freezing assets and prosecuting suspected terrorists, particularly when it comes to citizens of its allies. Moreover, the large number of financial institutions and the proliferation of regulatory agencies at different levels of government complicate efforts to monitor financial transactions effectively.

The United States gets a failing grade for its policies that affect illegal migration from Mexico. Agricultural subsidies, a lack of enforcement of immigration laws in the workplace, the discriminatory application of labor laws and visa regulations, and protectionist visa requirements for temporary workers all defeat the stated goal of resolving the problem of illegal immigration and divert resources away from people who represent genuine security threats.

The private sector has a big role to play in balancing economic and security needs in North America. With respect to goods, the cross-border integration of the private sector facilitates voluntary compliance with programs such as CTPAT, reducing the need for trilateral cooperation or new trilateral institutions. Firms can use technology, such as satellite tracking of goods, while governments invest in border infrastructure and technologies such as electronic scanners. However, more intergovernmental cooperation is needed to harmonize highway standards and to remove barriers to the integration of the transportation industry.

With respect to capital, the three governments have already harmonized their laws by participating in the Financial Action Task Force on Money Laundering (FATF) and by implementing international agreements on money laundering and terrorist financing. Here, too, the private sector plays an important role through vigilance and compliance with reporting requirements. The cross-border integration of the financial services sector—particularly in Mexico—facilitates monitoring of suspicious transactions. However, people movement does require greater trilateral cooperation. While firms still play a role, for example with respect to intracompany transferees (the human equivalent of cross-border production chains), governments have a larger role to play. Governments need to share information on people movement and cooperate on visa requirements. Even here, however, there is much each government can do on its own to improve internal policies that affect people flows.

Growing business and economic links will ensure that relationships among the NAFTA countries endure and grow more intense as time goes by. In this book, we have analyzed the central issues that will drive the NAFTA relationship into the future. While there is much that each country can do on its own to secure a prosperous future for the region as a whole, growing interdependence makes it essential that they move forward together. Only a combination of domestic reforms and cross-border cooperation on a complex web of issues can ensure that national security and economic integration advance hand in hand.

References

Chapter 1: Bordering on the USA

CIA Factbook, Internet edition. 2002. (available at www.cia.gov/cia/publications/factbook/index.html, accessed February 23, 2003).

"Defying U.S Could Chill Relations: Envoy." 2003. www.globeandmail.com, February 28.

Fife, Robert. 2002. "66 Percent Favour Stronger Ties to U.S." *National Post*, October 21.

Fulford, Robert. 1998. "Review of Paul Johnson's book *A History of the American People*." *Ottawa Citizen*, March 22, visited on the web on August 25, 2002, www.robertfulford.com/Johnson.html.

Lipset, Seymour Martin. 1991. *Continental Divide: The Values and Institutions of the United States and Canada*. New York: Routledge.

Merolla, Jennifer, Laura B. Stephenson, Carole J. Wilson, and Elizabeth J. Zechmeister. 2001. "Public Opinion and NAFTA," paper presented at the Annual Meeting of the American Political Science Association, San Francisco, California, August 2002.

Maddison, Angus. 2001. *The World Economy: A Millennial Perspective*. Paris: OECD.

Chapter 2: Get Me to the Plant on Time

"Automakers Forecast." 2002. *Mexico City News*, October 11.

Bradsher, Keith. 2002. "Asian Companies Relieved Over Reopening of U.S. Ports." *New York Times*, October 10.

Brieger, Peter. 2002. "U.S. Port Dispute Halts Honda." *National Post*, October 21, FP4.

"Bush to Seek Court Order Opening West Coast Ports." 2002. *New York Times*, October 8.

Davis, Donald R., David E. Weinstein, Scott C. Bradford, and Kazushige Shimpo. 1997. "Using International and Japanese Regional Data to Determine When the Factor Abundance Theory of Trade Works." *American Economic Review* 87 (2), 441–46.

Greenhouse, Steven. 2002a. "With Few Port Jobs at Issue, Economic Stakes Are Vast." *New York Times*, October 2.

Greenhouse, Steven. 2002b. "The $100,000 Longshoreman: A Union Wins the Global Game." *New York Times*, October 6.

Greenhouse, Steven. 2002c. "White House Moves to Intervene as Port Talks Break Off." *New York Times*, October 7.

Heckscher, Eli F. 1919. "Utrikeshandelns verkan pa inkomstfordelningen" (The effect of foreign trade on the distribution of income) *Ekonomisk Tidskrift* 21: 497–512.

"Honda's Ontario Plant Stays Shut After U.S. Ports Lock-out." 2002. *National Post*, October 15.

ICF Consulting. 2002. "Economic Effects of Transportation." Department of Transportation, Washington, DC, January.

Leonard, James. 2001. "Impact of the September 11, 2001 Terrorist Attacks on North American Trade Flows." *Manufacturers Alliance e-alert*, Arlington, VA.

Murphy, Dean. E. 2002. "Dispute Lingers as Longshoremen Return to Work." *New York Times*, October 10.

Organization for Economic Cooperation and Development (OECD). 2002. "The Impact of the Terrorist Attacks of September 11 on International Trading and Transport Activities." Unclassified document, TD/TC/WP(2002)9/final, Paris, France.

Ohlin, Bertil. 1928. "The Reparations Problem." *Index* (Svenska Handelsbanken, Stockholm) 28 (April): 2–23.

Prentice, Barry E., and Mark Ojah. 2001. "NAFTA in the Next Ten Years: Issues and Challenges in Transportation." Paper presented at the NAFTA in the New Millennium Symposium, University of Alberta, May 24–25.

Sanger, David E. and Steven Greenhouse. 2002. "Bush Invokes Taft-Hartley Act to Open West Coast Ports." *New York Times*, October 9.

Statistical Abstracts of the United States. 2001. Internet edition.

"The Trojan Box: The Biggest Threat May Now Come from Containers, Not Aircraft." 2002. www.economist.com, February 7.

Walkenhorst, Peter and Nora Dihel. 2002. "Trade Impacts of the Terrorist Attacks of 11 September 2001: A Quantitative Assessment." Paper presented at the Workshop on The Economic Consequences of Global Terrorism, DIW, Berlin, Germany, June 14–15.

"When Trade and Security Clash." 2002. *The Economist*, April 6.

World Customs Organization. 2002. *Resolution of the Customs Co-operation Council on Security and Facilitation of the International Trade Supply Chain*. June.

Chapter 3: Do You Know the Way to San Jose?

Alvarez, Lizette. 2000. "Congress Backs Big Increase in Visas for Skilled Workers." *New York Times*, October 4.

Barboza, David. 2001a. "Tyson Foods Indicted in Plan to Smuggle Illegal Workers." *New York Times*, December 20.

Barboza, David. 2001b. "Meatpackers' Profits Hinge on Pool of Immigrant Labor." *New York Times*, December 21.

Becerra, Hector. 2002. "The 371,000 [U.S.$203,000] Fell Off Back of a Truck, Says Honest Franco." *Sydney Morning Herald*, August 17.

Canadian Broadcasting Corporation (CBC). 2002. "Waves of U.S. Immigration to Canada." Text to accompany *The National Magazine*'s "Our American Cousins," aired Friday, September 27, www.tv.cbc.ca/national/pgminfo/border/waves.html.

Cleeland, Nancy. 2002. "Employers Test Ruling on Immigrants." *Los Angeles Times*, April 22.

Commission for Labor Cooperation. 2000. *Protection of Migrant Agricultural Workers in Canada, Mexico and the United States*. Legal Background Paper, NAALC Secretariat, Dallas, Texas.

CONAPO. 2000. *Crecimiento económico, libre comercio y migración*. Mexico, January.

Cornelius, Wayne. 2003. Seminar on the Mexico–United States Border, Instituto Tecnológico Autónomo de Mexico, February 21.

Drucker, Peter. 1999. *Management Challenges for the 21st Century*. New York: HarperBusiness.

Dunfield, Allison. 2002. "U.S. Backing Away from Border Brouhaha." *Globe and Mail*, October 31.

Ethier, Wilfred J. 1986. "Illegal Immigration: The Host Country Problem." *American Economic Review* 76: 56–71.

European Union. 2002. "Free Movement of Persons within the European Union." www.Europa.Eu.int/en/agenda/schengen.html.

Eye on Washington. 2001. No. 18, November 9, www.ieeEusa.org/forum/EYEONWASHINGTON/01eow18.html.

Fuentes, Víctor, and Benito Jiménez. 2002. "Pelean mexicanos los salarios en EU." *Reforma*, September 16.

Gal-Or, Noemi. 1998. "Labor Mobility Under NAFTA: Regulatory Policy Spearheading the Social Supplement to the International Trade Regime." *Arizona Journal of International and Comparative Law* 15: 365.

Gerber, Jim. 2002. "Are Incomes in Baja California 'Catching Up' to San Diego?" *Cross-Border Economic Bulletin*, April–May, University of California, San Diego.

Gruber, Bill. 2002. "Address to Free Trade in the Western Hemisphere: The Challenges and the Future," paper presented at Center for the Study of Western Hemispheric Trade, Texas A&M International University, Laredo, Texas, April 10–12.

Hagan, John. 2001. *Northern Passage: American Vietnam War Resisters in Canada*. Cambridge, Massachusetts: Harvard University Press.

Hanson, Gordon and Antonio Spilimbergo. 1999. "Illegal Immigration, Border Enforcement, and Relative Wages: Evidence from Apprehensions at the U.S.–Mexico Border." *American Economic Review*, 89 (5), 1337–57.

Hanson, Gordon, Raymond Robertson and Antonio Spilimbergo. 2002. "Does Border Enforcement Protect U.S. Workers from Illegal Immigration?" *Review of Economics and Statistics* 84 (1): 73–92.

Hémery, David. 1997. *European Citizenship*. www.chez.com/bibelec/publications/international/p1.html.

Human Resources Development Canada and Industry Canada. 1999. *International Migration of Skilled Workers: Facts and Figures*. Ottawa, Industry Canada, December, www.strategis.ic.gc.ca/SSI/ra/hand_e.pdf, citing Survey of 1995 Graduates Who Moved to the U.S., Statistics Canada and Human Resources Development Canada.

Immigration and Naturalization Service (INS). 2001. Table 38, Nonimmigrants Admitted as Temporary Workers, Exchange Visitors, and Intracompany Transferees by Region and Country of Citizenship, Fiscal Year 1999, www.ins.usdoj.gov/graphics/aboutins/statistics/TempExcel99/Table_38.xls.

INS *Statistical Yearbook*, Internet edition, 2002.
"International Recruitment." 2000. *Healthcare Matters* 36, December, www.hrplaza.com/hcrc/pdfs/hcmatters_00_12.pdf.
Ko, Marnie. 2002. *Report Newsmagazine*, Alberta Edition, June 24.
Lin, Irene. 2001. "Peel an Orange, Contemplate History." www.ustrek.org/odyssey/semester2/031001/031001irenebraceros.html.
Ljunggren, David. 2002a. "Upset Canada Issues Rare Caution on Travel to U.S." *Globe and Mail*, October 31.
Ljunggren, David. 2002b. "Ottawa Says U.S. Relents on New Security Rules." *Globe and Mail*, November 1.
Martin, Philip. 2002. "Trade and Migration: The Mexico–U.S. Experience, Research on Immigration and Integration in the Metropolis." Prepared for the United Nations University World Institute for Development Economics Research (WIDER) conference in Helsinki, September 27–28, on Poverty, International Migration and Asylum.
McIlroy, James. 1996. "NAFTA Cross-Border Provision of Services." *Canada–United States Law Journal* 22: 203.
"Medical Marijuana Users Take Refuge in Canada." 2002. www.cannabisnews.com/news/thread12972.shtml.
Mickelburgh, Rod. 2002. "U.S. Holds Canadian as al-Qaeda Conspirator." *Globe and Mail*, July 27.
Moore, Oliver. 2002. "Visa Rules Won't Affect 'Snowbirds,' Ridge Promises." *Globe and Mail*, May 16.
Nadeau, Serge, Lori Whewell, and Shane Williamson. 2000. *Beyond the Headlines on the "Brain Drain."* www.isuma.net/v01n01/nadeau1/nadeau1_e.pdf.
North American Free-Trade Agreement Implementation Act (supersedes the United States–Canada Free-Trade Agreement Act of September 28, 1988) of December 8, 1993 (107 Statutes at Large 2057), www.ins.usdoj.gov/graphics/aboutins/statistics/LegisHist/573.htm.
Obdeijn, H.L.M. 2002. *Economic Growth: From Open Labor Market to Fortress Europe*. History of International Migration Site, www.let.leidenuniv.nl/history/migration/chapter9.html.
OECD, *Maintaining Prosperity in an Aging Society*, Paris, 1998.
O'Neil, Peter. 2002. "Canadian Visa Scandal Disclosed in Hong Kong." *Vancouver Sun*, September 6.
Organization for Economic Cooperation and Development (OECD). 2002. GDP per Capita, 2000, at Current Prices in U.S. Dollars, Updated February. www.oecd.org/pdf/M00018000/M00018518.pdf.
Orrenius, Pia M. 2001. "Illegal Immigration and Enforcement Along the Southwest Border." *The Border Economy*, 30–34. Dallas: Federal Reserve Bank of Dallas.
"Please Come, We Need You—Canada's Latest Census." 2002. *The Economist*, April 13.
Safe Third Country Agreement between the Government of Canada and the Government of the United States. 2002. www.cic.gc.ca/english/policy/safe percent2Dthird.html.
Summers, Edward, and William Treacy. 2002. "The North American CPA Profession and International Trade." Paper presented at Free Trade in the Western Hemisphere: The Challenges and the Future, Centre for the Study of Western Hemispheric Trade, Texas A&M International University, Laredo, Texas, April 10–12.

Tu Than Ha and Colin Freeze. 2002. "Canadian Soil a Long-time Staging Ground for al-Qaeda." *Globe and Mail*, September 7.
United States Embassy in Mexico. 2002. "The U.S. and Mexico at a Glance." www. usembassy-mexico.gov/eataglance1.htm.
United States, State Department Notice. 2002. "Enhanced Border Security and Visa Entry Reform Act of 2002," May 2.
Warren, Robert. 1995. "Estimates of Undocumented Immigrant Population Living in the United States." Department of Justice, Working Paper.
Woods, Allan. 2002. "Border Deal Targets Refugees." *Globe and Mail*, June 28.

Chapter 4: Doing the Laundry

A.T. Kearney, FDI Confidence Index, Global Business Policy Council, 2002, www.atkearney.com/pdf/eng/FDI_Confidence_Sept2002_S.pdf.
Birkinshaw, Julian and Neil Hood. 1998. "Multinational Subsidiary Evolution: Capability and Charter Change in Foreign-owned Subsidiary Companies." *Academy of Management Review*, 23: 773–95.
"Canadian Judge Thwarts IRS Probe." 2002. *Globe and Mail*, July 11.
Courchene, Thomas J. and Richard G. Harris. 1999. *From Fixing to Monetary Union: Options for North American Currency Integration*. C.D. Howe Institute Commentary 127, June.
DePalma, Anthony. 2001. "Canada Altering Its System of Vigilance Against Terror." *New York Times*, December 3.
Dunning, John H. 1995. "Reappraising the Eclectic Paradigm in an Age of Alliance Capitalism." *Journal of International Business Studies*, 26, 461–92.
Eiteman, David K., Arthur I. Stonehill and Michael H. Moffett. 1995. *Multinational Business Finance*. Addison-Wesley Publishing Company.
Ethyl Corporation v. *Government of Canada*, documents available at www.dfait-maeci.gc.ca/tna-nac/dispute-e.asp#chapter11.
"Eye on Investors, Mexico Pays US Company." 2001. *New York Times*, October 29.
Financial Action Task Force on Money Laundering (FATF), various documents, www1.oecd.org/fatf/.
Green, Eric. 2000. "De Facto Monetary Union Predicted Between U.S. and Mexico." *Washington File*, December 7, www.mac.doc.gov/nafta/ar-dec7percent231.htm.
Greenwood, John, and Deborah Allen. 2002. "Did the Currency Board Fail Argentina, or Did Their Government Fail the Currency Board?" Cardiff Business School Working Paper, United Kingdom.
International Bureau of Fiscal Documentation. 1999. *Taxation and Investment in Canada*, June 21.
Iritani, Evelyn. 2001. "Ruling in Canada Strikes at Companies' NAFTA Trade Suits Courts: Decision Could Blunt Legal Challenges to Governments' Power to Enforce Health and Safety Regulations." *Los Angeles Times*, June 5, C1.
Krugman, Paul, and Maurice Obstfeld. 1994. *International Economics*. Third Edition, Harper Collins, New York.
Laidler, David, and Finn Poschmann. 2000. *Leaving Well Enough Alone: Canada's Monetary Order in a Changing International Environment*. C.D. Howe Institute Commentary 142, May.
Leopold, Evelyn. 2002. "U.S. Sanctions List Shrinks Due to Lack of Evidence." *Reuters*, August 23 (news.yahoo.com).

Lozano-Ascencio, Fernando. 1998. "Las remesas de los migrantes mexicanos en Estados Unidos." In Mexican Ministry of Foreign Affairs and U.S. Commission on Immigration.

Reform Migration Between Mexico and United States. Binational Study, Volume 3, 1189–1214.

Metalclad Corporation v. *The United Mexican States*, 40 *International Legal Materials* 36 (2001).

Molander, Roger C., David A. Mussington, and Peter A. Wilson. 1998. *Cyberpayments and Money Laundering: Problems and Promise.* MR-965–OSTP/FinCEN, published by RAND Corporation.

Organization for Economic Co-operation and Development (OECD). 1998. *Survey of OECD Work on International Investment,* 6. Paris: OECD.

Orozco, Manuel. 2002. *Attracting Remittances: Market, Money and Reduced Costs.* Report commissioned by the Multilateral Investment Fund of the Inter-American Development Bank. Washington, DC, January 28.

"Ottawa Freezes Assets of Hamas–related Groups." 2001. *Globe and Mail,* December 4.

"Metalclad Reaches Preliminary Agreement with Mexico; $15,626,260 to be Paid in Settlement of NAFTA Case." 2001. *PR Newswire,* June 13 (news.yahoo.com).

Pope & Talbot Inc. v. *Government of Canada* (April 10, 2001).

Robert Azinian, Kenneth Davitian, & Ellen Baca v. *The United Mexican States* (1999) 39 *International Legal Materials* 537 (2000).

Rugman, Alan M. 1981. *Inside the Multinationals: The Economics of Internal Markets.* New York: Columbia University Press.

Rugman, Alan M. 2001. *The End of Globalization: Why Global Strategy is a Myth and How to Profit from the Realities of Regional Markets.* New York: Amacom.

S.D. Myers Inc. v. *Government of Canada* (November 13, 2000).

Thompson, Ginger. 2002. "Migrants to U.S. Are a Major Resource for Mexico." *New York Times,* March 25.

United Mexican States v. *Metalclad Corporation* (British Columbia Supreme Court), 2001 BCSC 664.

"U.S. Moves Widely Against Al Qaeda Finances." *Globe and Mail,* November 7, 2001.

WTO. 1995. *Guide to GATT Law and Practice.* 6th ed., vol. 1. Geneva: Bernan Press.

Chapter 5: Invisible Elephants

Anti-corrupcion informes, available at www.respondanet.com/spanish/anti_corrupcion/informes/TM30oct01.pdf.

Appleson, Gail. 2002. "Porn Star Gannon Sent to Jail." *Toronto Star,* October 24.

Brunetti, Aymo Gregory Kisunko and Beatrice Weder. 1997. *Institutional Obstacles for Doing Business: Data Description and Methodology of a Worldwide Private Sector Survey by World Bank.* Working Paper.

Craddock, Catherine. 2001. "But Crime Does Pay." *Business México,* September.

DeBaise, Colleen. 2002. "Ex-Lehman Broker Charged With Laundering Drug Money." Dow Jones News Service, June 27.

Dollar, David Raymond Fisman, and Roberta Gatti. 1999. "Are Women Really the 'Fairer' Sex? Corruption and Women in Government." Development Research Group, World Bank, May.

Dunfee, Thomas W. and David Hess. 2000. "Fighting Corruption: A Principled Approach: The C2 Principles (Combating Corruption)." *Cornell International Law Journal*, 33 (3), 595–628.

Ferriss, Susan. 2002. "Kidnappers Target Mexico's Rich and Famous" *Atlanta Journal-Constitution*, October 3.

Jacoby, Mary. 2002. "House Votes 420–1 to Expel Traficant." *St. Petersburg Times*, July 25.

Kielmans, Martin. 1998. "Expropriation by 2 countries is alleged—Pakistan, Indonesia criticized." *Business Insurance*, November 2.

Lagos, Marta. 2000. "Assessing Perceptions of Corruption in Latin America," Latinobarómetro Research Group.

Lizarraga, Daniel. 2001. "Dan mexicanos 'mordidas' por $23 mil millones al año." *El Norte*, October 31.

Notimex General. 2001. "Opera Coordinacion Binacional De Seguridad En Frontera Mexico-EU." October 19.

OECD. 2000. *No Longer Business As Usual*. Paris, June.

Policía Federal Preventiva, Annual Report 2000.

Sistema Nacional de Seguridad Pública, Annual Report 2000.

Sjaifudian, Shetifah. 1997. "Graft and the Small Business." *Far Eastern Economic Review*, October 16: 32.

Sullivan, Kevin. 2001. "3–Ton Elephant Tiptoes Into Mexico." *Washington Post*, January 30.

Tanzi, Vito. 1998. "Corruption Around the World." *IMF Staff Paper,* 559–94.

U.S. Department of State. 2001. "Fighting Global Corruption: Business Risk Management." Washington, DC.

Zagaris, Bruce and Scott Ehlers. 2001. "Drug Trafficking and Money Laundering." *Foreign Policy in Focus*, 6:18, May.

Chapter 6: Three's Company

Chen, Edwin. 2002. "Bush Touts 'Smart' Border for the U.S. and Mexico." *Los Angeles Times*, March 22.

Johnson, Kevin. 2002. "Mail from INS Stuns Flight School." *U.S.A Today*, March 13.

Leiken, Robert S. 2002. "Immigration Accord Would Help Mexico Lock Our 'Back Door.'" *Arizona Republic*, March 18.

Mitchell, Alison. 2002. "Bush Orders Inquiry Into Visas Granted to Terrorists After Attack." *Associated Press*, March 14.

Schmitt, Eric. 2002. "I.N.S. Reassigns Employees Involved in Visa Extensions." *Associated Press*, March 15.

Ziga Vodusek, Ed. 2001. *Foreign Direct Investment in Latin America: The Role of European Investors*. Washington, Inter-American Development Bank.

Woolley, Bryan. 2001. "Another Time, Another Place, Another Attack." *Dallas Morning Herald*, October 14.

Index

Aaran Money Wire Service, 142
ABA, 93
A.T. Kearney, 135, 136
abuse of undocumented workers, 73, 97
accountants, 90, 93
Afghanistan, 21, 102, 190
AFL-CIO, 62
age for illegal migration, 76
aging, 75, 76, 77
agricultural, 54, 189
  subsidies, 79, 86, 188
  workers, 79, 82, 86
AIA, 55
airlines, 6, 25, 63, 175
airport(s), 18, 48, 49, 64, 71, 102, 103
Akers, Fred, 65
Al-Aqsa Islamic Bank, 142
Al-Barakaat, 141, 142
Al Qaeda, 48, 102, 118, 141, 142, 143, 186
Al-Taqua, 141
ambassador, 5, 18, 20, 23, 30, 103
Ambassador Bridge, 40, 42
American Civil War, 4, 172
American Revolution, 4, 100
anthrax attacks, 127
antibribery laws, 150, 192
antiterror action plan, 26
antiterrorism law, 26
Argentina, 68, 110, 119, 136, 162, 189
Asia, 48, 73, 96, 110, 138, 144, 190
asylum, 72
Atta, Mohammad, 175
attack(s), 3, 18, 20, 21–24, 26, 37, 39, 40,
    45, 47, 50, 59, 61, 64, 65, 71, 73, 101,
    102, 108, 109, 116, 118, 140, 143

attack(s) *(continued)*
  September 11. *See* September 11
attorney general, 85, 111, 154, 169
Attwood, Margaret, 141
audit requirements, 113
Austin, Moses, 5
Austria, 72, 80, 110, 135, 147, 153
automobile production, 7
Autopact, 144

baby boom(er), 76, 96
back pay award(s), 84, 85
Banamex, 132, 139
Banca Serfin, 139
Banco Agricola, 139
Banco de Mexico, 88, 138
bank, 6, 7, 16, 30, 88, 89, 111–17, 126,
    132, 133, 138, 140, 142, 143, 151,
    158, 159–64, 170, 171
  secrecy law, 88, 116
bank fees, 138, 139
Bank of Montreal, 126
Bank Secrecy Act, 116
banking capital in Mexico, 132
banking regulation and supervision,
    113
Banrural, 88
Barakaat Enterprise, 141
Barakat Wire Transfer Co., 141
Batiz, Bernardo, 170
Becker, Gary, 152
Beetle, 144
Beit El-Mal Holding Company, 142
Belgium, 110, 135, 153
Bhutto, Benazir, 164

About the Authors

Bradly J. Condon B.A., 1985; LL.B., 1988; LL.M., 1993 is professor of international law and business at the Instituto Tecnológico Autónomo de Mexico and is senior fellow at the Tim Fischer Centre for Global Trade and Finance, Australia. He has written three books and over fifty articles on various business and legal topics. He has served as director of the Center for North American Business Studies, expert witness before the Canadian Parliament, adviser for the Commonwealth Law Association, and guest of the United States Congress on international trade issues. In 2001, Condon won the Lumina Award for Outstanding Research in law and regulation.

Tapen Sinha is the ING Comercial America Chair professor in the Department of Actuarial Studies at the Instituto Tecnológico Autónomo de Mexico. He has a concurrent appointment as professor of risk management at the University of Nottingham. He is also a research associate at the Centre for Risk and Insurance, at the School of Business of the University of Nottingham. Sinha obtained his bachelor's (1977) and master's (1978) degrees from the Indian Statistical Institute. He received his Ph.D. in economics from the University of Minnesota in 1986. He was a visiting professor at Ripon College in Wisconsin. Later, he joined the University of Wisconsin-Parkside and then the National University of Singapore. Prior to joining ITAM, he was an associate professor at Bond University in Australia. He has authored or coauthored more than ninety research papers along with four books. He has made over one hundred presentations at conferences on all continents. He has won a number of awards including the Lumina award in 2001 with Bradly J. Condon and the best paper award in 2002 at the annual conference of the Society of Actuaries.